Witness and Existence

Photograph by Jill Stephenson

WITNESS AND EXISTENCE

ESSAYS IN HONOR OF
Schubert M. Ogden

Edited by
Philip E. Devenish and
George L. Goodwin

The University of Chicago Press
Chicago and London

PHILIP E. DEVENISH is assistant professor of practical theology and coordinator of ministry studies at the Divinity School of the University of Chicago. George L. Goodwin is dean of faculty at the College of St. Scholastica.

The University of Chicago Press, Chicago 60637
The University of Chicago Press, Ltd., London
© 1989 by The University of Chicago
All rights reserved. Published 1989
Printed in the United States of America

98 97 96 95 94 93 92 91 90 89 54321

Library of Congress Cataloging-in-Publication Data

Witness and existence : essays in honor of Schubert M. Ogden / edited
  by Philip E. Devenish and George L. Goodwin.
    p.   cm.
    "The published writings of Schubert M. Ogden": p.
    ISBN 0-226-14357-0.—ISBN 0-226-14358-9 (pbk.)
    1. Philosophical theology. 2. Bible. N.T.—Criticism,
interpretation, etc. 3. Faith. 4. Ogden, Schubert Miles, 1928–
  I. Ogden, Schubert Miles, 1928–   II. Devenish, Philip E.
  III. Goodwin, George L.
BT40.W58   1989
230—dc19   89-30283
                                                            CIP

⊗ The paper used in this publication meets the minimum requirements of the American National Standard for Information Sciences—Permanence of Paper for Printed Library Materials, ANSI Z39.48-1984.

Contents

Preface

We present these essays to Schubert Ogden in token of our respect and admiration for his work and as expressions of our friendship.

Ogden has both argued for and also exemplified an understanding of Christian theology as a single movement of reflection, the structure of which mirrors the correlation involved in the claim of the Christian witness of faith to be decisive for human existence by explicitly re-presenting its truth. Witness and existence constitute, therefore, the two poles of theological inquiry. Because theology has this correlative structure, its statements are to be understood as assessable by dual criteria of adequacy: appropriateness to the understanding of faith expressed by the primary symbols of normative Christian witness and credibility in meeting the relevant conditions of truth universally established with human existence, yet dependent for their formulation upon the resources of particular historical situations. The essays in this volume confirm Ogden's analysis of the basic structure of Christian theology, as they either emphasize one or the other of these criteria of adequacy or focus on the effort to achieve an understanding that is adequate to both.

The Introduction is to our knowledge the first attempt to provide an interpretation of the integrity in both method and content of Ogden's work as a Christian theologian. It focuses on his effort to argue for both the appropriateness and the credibility of a radically monotheistic and theocentric interpretation of a constitutively christocentric witness of faith.

The first group of essays illustrates the concern to understand the primary symbols of normative Christian witness. Willi Marxsen's essay takes up the logic and the historical vicissitudes of christological discourse in the New Testament. The essays of Hans Dieter Betz and Victor Furnish address issues in the attempts of Paul and of those who claimed to be his followers to reinterpret the Christian witness of faith in their own situations. Betz sketches the way in which Paul, having severed the ties of Christianity with the Jewish

Torah and having later recognized the difficulties of grounding Christian ethics in the work of God's spirit, finally seeks its foundation in the justice of God and its expression in obligation to God. Furnish argues that, while Paul maintains a fundamental connection between the content and the character of his own suffering as itself bearing witness to the cross, deutero-Pauline literature and Acts present his suffering as evidence for the personal faith of Paul the exemplar.

The second group of essays embodies Ogden's claim that, for theological assertions to be adequate, they must be not only appropriate but also credible, in that they confirm and are confirmed by a fully reflective philosophical understanding of human experience. David Tracy's essay sets the context for all the essays in Part II by calling attention to a central component of Ogden's theological method—the use of metaphysical argument to determine the truth-status of theological claims. Through a discussion of dialectic and myth in Plato, Tracy not only commends Ogden on the power of his theological inquiry but also suggests an alternative which he regards as ultimately more nearly adequate to the task of crediting the validity of such claims.

If Tracy draws attention to Ogden's method for determining theological credibility, the other authors in Part II illustrate their commitment to that method in addressing theological issues that are central to Ogden's project. As our own introductory essay points out, the essential features of Ogden's philosophical theology are his contentions that all humans unavoidably live by an act of existential faith, that the concept of God provides the most adequate account of the objective grounding of such faith, and that this theistic interpretation of ultimate reality both authorizes and demands authentic human existence. All three topics—existential faith, God, and authentic existence—are discussed in Part II.

Both Brian Gerrish, in his essay on F. H. Jacobi, and Van Harvey, in his essay on Nietzsche, provide historical and constructive insights on the topic of existential faith. Gerrish carefully analyzes Jacobi's notion of faith, compares it to Ogden's notion of "basic confidence," and concludes that Ogden avoids difficulties attending Jacobi's position. Harvey, in his analysis of Nietzsche's attack on the Kantian paradigm of faith, shows that it is correct to argue that belief in God itself rests upon a deeper belief in reason and that Nietzsche's nihilism is the major challenge to theistic belief and to its underlying existential faith.

The theistic grounding of existential faith is the subject of the essays by John Cobb, Charles Hartshorne, and Maurice Wiles. How shall we best conceive the ground of faith? John Cobb surveys diverse definitions of "God," together with the various strategies underlying the choices of definition; he concludes that a phenomenology of receptive experience which is suspicious about modernity's commitment to suspicion regarding external reality provides the starting point for a reconstruction of the meaning of "God." Charles Hartshorne's review of his own theistic conceptuality stands as a convenient summary of the neoclassical theism which Ogden shares. The essay has the additional merit of engaging Ogden on the issue of Ogden's critique of Hartshorne's use of analogy. Maurice Wiles employs the notion of "vocation" to provide a careful discussion of what it means to speak about God's activity in history. By addressing some of Ogden's own thoughts on this topic, Wiles advances the conversation between the two and illustrates Ogden's determination to bring serious theological reflection to bear on the most practical religious issues.

The concluding essay by Chris Gamwell argues that the considerable efforts of Karl-Otto Apel to provide a transcendental justification of ethical norms which, like Kant's, is independent of metaphysics, proves in spite of itself to require for this purpose a transcendental metaphysics such as one finds in Ogden's work. In this sense, Gamwell's essay brings the volume full circle. For the burden of the argument of the Introduction is that it is precisely this moral life which is the chief expression of authentic existence that Ogden's entire project as a Christian theologian is intended to serve.

A complete bibliography of the published writings of Schubert M. Ogden is given as an Appendix.

We wish to thank Mrs. Dolores Odland for secretarial assistance in preparing the manuscript.

Philip E. Devenish
George L. Goodwin

Introduction
Christian Faith and the First Commandment:
The Theology of Schubert Ogden

PHILIP E. DEVENISH AND GEORGE L. GOODWIN

Our purpose in this introductory essay is twofold. We seek to orient the reader to Schubert Ogden's thought as a whole and to indicate as clearly as possible its significance for Christian faith and theology. This may not only seem like, but may also in fact be, a heavy burden to bear in a single essay. And yet, we are convinced that it is precisely the simplicity of Ogden's theological project and the coherence of its presentation that make it possible to fulfill this purpose.

Our thesis is that one can equally well understand Ogden's thought as christocentric, as radically monotheistic, or as theocentric. Indeed, in our view, to have shown not only that these three features must characterize any adequate Christian theology, but also how they imply each other, is the main achievement of his work. In Part I we show that, according to Ogden, the material content of an appropriately understood christocentrism is strictly radically monotheistic. In Part II, we show how Ogden's analysis of human experience implies this same radical monotheism. Part III concludes the argument of the essay by identifying the theocentric character of the ethics such radical monotheism necessarily implies. Thus, all three approaches lead to the same conclusion, namely, that Christian thought and action find their center in God alone.

In short, we shall argue that Ogden's expressly christocentric theology is strictly at the service of the "first commandment" as found both in the Hebrew Bible and in the New Testament. That is to say, his theology is consistently and radically monotheistic in content and so fulfills the command of the Decalogue to "have no other gods before me" (Ex. 20:3 Deut. 5:7). Therefore, it is likewise theocentric in its ethical implications and so can show that to "love your neigh-

bor as yourself" is precisely to fulfill the New Testament commandment to "love the Lord your God with all your heart, and with all
your soul, and with all your mind, and with all your strength" (Lev.
19:18, cf. Mark 12:31 par.; Mark 12:30 par.).

I. Christocentrism as Radical Monotheism

Schubert Ogden's work as a whole and in all its parts is that of a
Christian theologian. Its constitutive object is the Christian witness
of faith it exists to serve through fully critical reflection upon this
witness.[1] Theology, therefore, properly attempts to ground its
method and content in the witness it exists to interpret and seeks
to validate.

According to Ogden, the distinctively Christian form of the explicit witness of faith of the Christian religion, "present only in the
form of all the various witnesses and kinds of witness," is the christological claim that Jesus is decisive for human beings in their quest
for authentic existence (1986a: 4). Thus, for Ogden, theology is necessarily christocentric; indeed, in this sense, theology simply is
christology.[2] Furthermore, since, on Ogden's view, the christocentric claim of the distinctively Christian explicit witness turns out
to be radically monotheistic in both content and logic, theology
proves to be radically monotheistic in character. As Ogden puts it,
"Faith in God is not merely an element in Christian faith along with
several other elements; it simply *is* Christian faith, the heart of the
matter itself" (1967b: 6).

From the constructive point of view of its doctrinal content, the
key to Ogden's entire theology is his *Sachkritik* or critical interpretation of christology. Thus, he focuses on "the point of christology,"
that is, "its meaning . . . , the matter with which it has to do, the
way in which it deals with it, and the reason or purpose it has in
doing so" (1975g: 375). What then, on Ogden's view, is christology
about?

An exegetical investigation into the character and emergence of
what Ogden calls the "christology of witness" of early Christianity,
"that relatively more spontaneous, less deliberate thought and
speech about Jesus which are christology in the primary sense," will
permit us to answer this question (1986a: 1). Indeed, it is only to the
extent that, following Ogden's advice, we come to understand what
the Christian witness of faith has already been that we shall ever be
able properly to grasp what it is, precisely for the sake of determining what it should now become as decisive for human existence.[3]

As is now well known, Ogden has "changed his mind" in relocating the "primary test of appropriateness of theological statements" from "the witness of Scripture" (1973a: 6) to "the witness of the apostles that is contained in the New Testament" (1986a: 10), more specifically (and more materially) to "the meaning to be discerned in the earliest layer of Christian witness, and this means the Jesus-kerygma of the apostolic community" (ibid.: 65). How are we to understand the emergence of christology in the earliest layer of Christian witness, if "it is the meaning to be discerned precisely in the Jesus-kerygma by which the appropriateness of all explicit christology and, consequently, all other theological assertions is to be judged" (ibid.)?

It would be premature to suppose that we have more than initial insights into the process of the emergence and development of christology which finds expression in the history of tradition of which the writings of the New Testament are the primary documentation. Indeed, one can only hope that, just to the extent that Ogden's argument (here following that of Willi Marxsen) for the earliest Jesus traditions as the *norma normans non normata* of the appropriateness of theological assertions finds acceptance, historical theologians will turn their attention to this crucial process.

We will attempt here to build on Ogden's critical appropriation of Willi Marxsen's insight that the New Testament contains two basic forms of christology of witness, the "implicit" christology of the "Jesus-kerygma" reconstructed as the earliest layer of apostolic testimony and the "explicit" christology of both the "Christ-kerygma" and the "Jesus Christ-kerygma" of the New Testament writings in their present form (1982a: 129).[4]

Implicit Christology

The Jesus-kerygma is both linguistically and logically the simpler of the two basic forms. Even here, however, distinct manners of presentation can be discerned. On the one hand, words and deeds that have already been experienced as decisive for understanding the ultimate meaning of one's life as life before God, words and deeds either experienced as or taken to be those of Jesus, can simply be presented again, precisely as decisive in their new context and now expressly *as his*. Thus, for example, the Beatitudes (Matt. 5:3–12 [par. Luke 6:20–23]) are presented not only as decisive but also as the words *of Jesus*. This is significant. Spoken simply as such and without regard for (or, possibly, even without knowledge of) its

3

source, such prophetic-apocalyptic preaching of salvation would remain fully within its Jewish context. When, however, such preaching is presented *as preaching of Jesus,* that first stage of what we may call "transfer" or "assimilation" has occurred, whereby the decisive or salvific function of the preaching is now ascribed to the preacher. "Jesus" (the preacher) has now become a kind of "shorthand" for his preaching.[5]

More nearly explicit presentations of as yet implicit christology occur when, for example, Jesus' preaching and acts of healing are already cast in language taken from authoritative tradition. Thus, for instance, Jesus is presented as saying, "The blind receive their sight and the lame walk, lepers are cleansed and the deaf hear, and the dead are raised up, and the poor have good news preached to them" (Matt. 11:5 [incorporating Isa. 35:5f.; 29:28f.; 61:1]; cf. Luke 4:16–30). Such a summary of Jesus' activity already presents a claim to its decisiveness. This claim to decisiveness is now expressly transferred to the person who has performed the activity, though no explicit identification of him is as yet made, when the conclusion is drawn, "and blessed is the person who takes no offense at me!" (Matt. 11:6).

In both of these examples there occurs a transfer of an implicit claim to decisiveness, an assimilation from the "work" to the "worker," from the "proclaimed" to the "proclaimer." Jesus' works and words are presented again not only as the decisive gift and demand of authentic existence before God, which they have already been experienced to be, but also expressly as the works and words *of Jesus.* Naturally, they are not decisive because they come from Jesus; on the contrary, Jesus is decisive precisely because and in the sense that their decisiveness is assimilated or transferred to him.

It is evident that implicit christology in its variety of expression is intrinsically soteriological in character. It is, as Ogden puts it, a "christology of *witness,*" that is, kerygmatic transmission of words and deeds already taken as decisive for the speaker's existence and shared in expectation that these may now become similarly decisive for the hearer. Naturally, this witness makes its soteriological point in the terms of the theistic tradition of which it is a part. Indeed, not only such christology, but also the theism it employs, is constitutively soteriological in its meaning. Furthermore, implicit christology is theocentric, in the sense that what is proclaimed as said or done by Jesus is proclaimed precisely as saving activity, the source of which is God.

For all this, the salvific activity of God to which witness is borne in implicit christological form not only is, but is expressly witnessed to as, the activity *of Jesus.* What is involved in the process of retelling these words and deeds, words and deeds taken as disclosing the saving activity of God, as the words and deeds of Jesus?

By means of the form of shorthand enshrined in ordinary language both then and now, the name "Jesus" is used to identify and to connect relevantly similar features of a series of moments over time. The enduring individual or person, Jesus, is abstracted from the concrete events of word and deed which are encountered. The salvific meaning experienced in and through such events is now taken by a process of "transfer" or "assimilation" to apply to the person, Jesus. The person, Jesus, is now spoken of as that proximate source of events of word and deed through which one has discovered the ultimate meaning of one's life. One then retells these words and deeds in such a way as to make Jesus the immediate and God the ultimate source of their saving power. The witness of implicit christology has a soteriological and a theocentric point.

Explicit Christology

The New Testament also contains a second and intrinsically more complex form of christological witness, namely, that "explicit" christology of which the "Christ-kerygma" of most of the early tradition and the "Jesus Christ–kerygma" of the synoptic gospels are characteristic. This form of witness reflects that logically further step in the process of the emergence of christology of making fully explicit what had remained more or less implicit in the Jesus-kerygma.[6] Here the transfer from discrete words and deeds experienced as soteriologically decisive ("Jesus' acts") to the personal life identified through them ("Jesus") is now made explicit. This occurs most directly by ascribing various *titles* to the agent whose actions have been taken to be decisive. Naturally, in a culturally and linguistically diverse environment, there is a wide range of candidate expressions already to hand from which to make the point that it is the activity of this person, Jesus, which has been and remains decisive.[7] Nonetheless, the titles fall into two logically distinct categories, depending on whether they focus directly on the decisive *activity* of the person, Jesus, or on the *person*, Jesus, as an indirect form of shorthand for such decisive activity. It should be emphasized that this categorization is a logical, not a cultural or linguistic, one. (Here, at least, issues regarding various "Judaisms" or "Judaism and

5

Hellenism" are secondary; the logical structure of the titles applies across the board in any case.)

A first group of titles has its logical "home" primarily in the sphere of the decisive activity of Jesus. These we may call "functional" titles. Thus, for instance, Jesus is called "savior" because his activity has been understood as salvific, "prophet" because it is taken to disclose the word of God, "teacher" because his words and deeds are definitively instructive, "door" because through his activity the hearer enters a new life-space. All such titles express in a direct way what Jesus is taken to have done, in the hope that pointing to its doer will enable it to occur again.

Another group of titles has its logical "home" primarily in the identity of Jesus as the person to whom such decisive doing has been assimilated. This group of titles we may call primarily "personal." Thus, for example, Jesus is called "Messiah" or "Christ" because his activity is understood as that which was to have been (or which is still to be) performed by God's anointed one; "Son of God," because he is taken to have done what is expected of such a one (in whatever religious and cultural context);[8] "Son of Man," in that his words and deeds are understood to have the decisive, "eschatological" character anticipated only from this figure; "Son of David," because his achievement can be seen as what was expected of him who was to be the great ruler's true heir. Such titles as these express *who the person is that does what Jesus does.* Naturally, this is a process of interpretation which moves in both directions. Who Jesus can be taken and said to be is conditioned by the complex of ideas a title is capable of eliciting; what the title can now be taken to mean when applied to Jesus is conditioned by the activity of the one to whom it is now applied.

To summarize what we have said to this point concerning explicit christological witness by means of honorific titles, Jesus is said to be who he is either directly, in reference to what he does, by means of functional titles, or indirectly, as the one who does what he does, by means of personal titles. In each case, since explicit christological titles emerge from a soteriological interest and serve a soteriological purpose, and since in the tradition in which they arise such a soteriological point is expressed in theistic terms, these explicit christological titles are as intrinsically theocentric as is implicit christology.

A second group of explicitly christological formulations concerns Jesus' origin, destiny, and the course of his life (1982a: 21). This group, which can be argued to be logically of a piece, reflects a yet more complex process of interpretation. For such formulations presuppose and build upon the crucial transfer from activity to person made explicit by means of titular ascription.

Thus, for instance, one reasons that, as the decisive "Son of God," Jesus' origin must be that which is taken to befit and to account for such a figure as he. This may be, and in fact is, understood in a variety of ways, depending on the religious-cultural context. In Mark, the origin of Jesus' sonship is explained in terms of adoption by God (1:11). In Matthew and Luke it is accounted for by means of notions of virginal conception (Matt. 1:18, 20; Luke 1:35). In John, Jesus' origin is presented through an idea of pre-existence with God (1:1f.).[9] The important point for the present purpose is not the variety of formulations but the common inference and shared presupposition that, in order for Jesus to be the "Son of God," whose activity is decisive for human existence, his origin must be of the sort that accords with his special function and status.[10] Such reasoning is somewhat complex. It reflects a further stage of accounting not only for who Jesus *is* as the one who does what he does, but now also for *how he must have come to be* who he is as such a one. What is at issue no longer concerns the level of christological assertion but that of a presupposition of such assertion. People have begun to account for what they take to be the "conditions of the possibility" of his decisiveness.

A similar process of reasoning seems to be involved in efforts to account for Jesus' destiny as the decisive one and also for certain qualifications regarding the course of his life. Thus, for example, it can be inferred that the destiny of the decisive one must be to be raised (Mark 16:6; Paul, passim), or exalted (pre-Pauline tradition in Phil. 2:9), to ascend (Heb. 4:14), or to be raised and also to ascend (Luke-Acts [Luke 24:7, 46; Acts 1:9]).[11] As is the case in interpretations of Jesus' origin so, too, what is significant here is not the variety of functionally interchangeable formulations of his destiny but the logical point that such a unique destiny is (and in a sense, must be) inferred as the implication of his decisive role. He who through his activity has been disclosed as *of* God must, it is now reasoned, not only come *from* God but also go *to* God—in whatever way befits the conceptual context of the interpretation at issue.

It should not be surprising now to discover that this same logical process can be argued to be at work when assertions are made regarding the course of Jesus' life. So, for example, as the one taken to be soteriologically decisive on the basis of what he does, Jesus is said variously to have resisted temptation (Matt. 4:1–11 par.; Mark

14:32–42), exhibited godly fear and obedience (Heb. 5:7ff.), endured suffering in an exemplary way (1 Pet. 2:21ff.) or to have been sinless (Heb. 4:15, 7:26ff.).[12] Once again, such formulations follow as inferences about the character of Jesus based either directly on what he does or indirectly on who he is as the one who does what he does. They serve to state purported presuppositions or implications of his saving activity, rather than to warrant it. At least with regard to the work of the New Testament writers, according to Ogden, "there is no good reason to suppose" that such further inferences are not "christological predications, [rather than] statements of their reasons for making such" (1982a: 74). Even such perhaps doubly indirect explicit christological assertions as these regarding the origin, destiny, and life of the person, Jesus, are at the service of his decisive, soteriological activity.[13]

In following Ogden's exegetical lead in attempting to suggest the logic of a plausible reconstruction of the emergence of christology in early Christian traditions, we have discovered that the various forms of implicit and explicit christology are intrinsically, albeit sometimes derivatively, soteriological in character. What is said of Jesus derives from and witnesses to what is taken to be his decisive activity in confronting human beings with the ultimate meaning of their lives as lives before God. In its constitutive attention to the Christian witness of faith, theology is christocentric. Because that witness is intrinsically soteriological, the christology that emerges from it is theocentric.

Christocentrism as Radical Monotheism

Ogden's consistently soteriological interpretation and the theocentrism that results from it simplify profoundly the material content of Christian witness and theology. We can indicate this critical and constructive simplification with reference to what are traditionally called the doctrines of Christ and of the trinity.

As we have seen, the key to the logic of the implicit christology of the earliest apostolic witness is that moment of transfer or assimilation whereby deeds and words of Jesus, taken as soteriologically decisive encounters, are now connected and made to coalesce in the person, Jesus. "Jesus" has now become a form of shorthand for the series of discrete yet causally related events constituting the life-career of this enduring individual. The important point is that this is not so much an inference as it is a way of speaking. One does not infer something about the person of Jesus (about his inner life or ontological constitution); one rather refers to a selection of Jesus' actions as the person named "Jesus." A connectedness among soteriologically decisive events in the life of the person, Jesus, is recognized and given expression through a name. In the process, a variety of what Van Harvey calls "perspectival images" is created.[14] But no new or additional data concerning the person of Jesus are created. "Jesus" refers to that thread of decisiveness taken as common to the deeds and words, on the basis of which such images are formed, and this name is taken to identify a single individual.

While the logic of explicit christology is far too complex and various to clarify in any adequate way here, one observation may serve to indicate the significance of Ogden's work for simplifying the material content of Christian faith and theology. As explicit christology developed in its various strands, what Willi Marxsen calls a *"metabasis eis allo genos"* occurred time and again.[15] This step concerns not only, as Marxsen puts it, "assertions about the quality of Jesus" but also claims about so-called saving events related to Jesus' origin, career, and destiny.[16] In case after case, what were actually inferences based on the soteriological significance of the person, Jesus, were taken as independent data to be related to him. Thus, for instance, that Jesus "must have been raised" (an *inference* drawn to account for the condition of the possibility of experiencing his soteriological decisiveness, understood in a certain way, even after his death) now comes to be treated as the *fact* that "he was raised."[17] What originally had been inferences drawn to account for the experience *of* salvation came to be regarded as data to be accounted for as necessary *to* salvation. At issue here is a certain variety of what Rudolf Bultmann, following Martin Heidegger, calls "objectifying thinking." Inferences are objectified to become new data. What is needed, and what Ogden has contributed to in signal fashion in his own work on christology, is the refinement and extension of Bultmann's efforts (of which "demythologizing" is but one aspect) to carry out what Ogden calls "something like a Heideggerian 'dismantling' (*Destruktion*)" of the material content of the Christian witness of faith and, thus, of theology as well (1982a: 86).

With regard to the doctrine of Christ, it may help to summarize our findings in this way: While both implicit and explicit forms of christology show an interest in what we have called the person, Jesus, namely, that enduring individual identified by various words and deeds, each can be seen to show no interest whatever in the person *of* Jesus, meaning thereby "his qualities, his mode of being, his relation to God," considered "independently of any question about the identity of the person who asks [about] it or of the ultimate reality with which he or she has to do" (1982a: 16). In terms of Ogden's hermeneutical analysis of christological language, the implicit and explicit christology of the early Christian tradition alike witness to "the meaning of Jesus for us" rather than to "the being of Jesus in himself" (1982a: passim). The "person of Jesus," conceived in whatever way as "the being of Jesus in himself," simply does not belong to early christology, with its intrinsically soteriological character.

If the point of christology does not concern the person of Jesus at all, then the very distinction of "person" and "work" whereby traditional doctrines of Christ are structured is itself misconstrued. Contrary to the widely shared view expressed by Paul Tillich that "the doctrine of the two natures in the Christ raises the right question but uses the wrong conceptual tools" to answer it (1982a: 7), Ogden's analysis makes clear that "the far more serious difficulty with traditional christology, as well as with the usual efforts to revise it, is not its conceptual tools but . . . the wrong question it asks and tries to answer by means of its conceptuality" (1975g: 390). Whether, as with classical or modern ontological forms of christology, one seeks to account for the person of Jesus in one or another set of metaphysical conceptualities or, as with revisionary forms of psychological christology, one seeks to account for the person of Jesus in one or another set of concepts taken from philosophical anthropology, one's nonsoteriological interest in the person of Jesus leads one to ask the wrong question. In each case, and for the same reason, one fails to provide an appropriately Christian christology. For the very distinction of "person" and "work" that structures traditional christology in all its forms is out of touch with the witness it is meant to interpret.

The truly revisionary christology for which Ogden calls and on which he has labored throughout his entire theological career is a christology meant to *reform* traditional christology on the basis of its appropriateness to its expression in the earliest apostolic witness. This is the structurally and materially simpler enterprise of expressing the theocentric, indeed, the radically monotheistic meaning of this witness to the words and deeds of Jesus (or in shorthand form, the person, Jesus) for us. We can now see why, on Ogden's view, it is precisely because and insofar as theology is christocentric that "this theme [of the reality of God] is, in the last analysis, the *sole* theme of all valid Christian theology, even as it is the *one* essential point to all authentic Christian faith and witness" (1966a: x). The person of Jesus, the being of Jesus in himself, plays no role in christology. Any material content other than or in addition to the reality of God is simply and quite literally beside the point.[18]

Such a revolutionary reform of the doctrine of Christ as that required by Ogden's consistently soteriological "christology of reflection" has equally fundamental significance for the structure and content of the doctrine of the trinity (1986a: 12). The main point here is that a genuinely revisionary trinitarian understanding of God begins, as does christology, with the recognition of the intrinsically soteriological point of the Christian witness of faith. From a critical point of view, this means that, since "the person of Jesus" has no place in christology, neither does it play any role in any appropriately Christian trinitarianism. From a constructive standpoint, there do, indeed, prove to be "three persons in one substance." And yet, any "immanent" trinitarianism such as that for which Ogden himself argues can only ever be shown to be appropriately Christian by being derived precisely from that "economic trinity" or "trinity of revelation" which, in turn, must be shown to emerge from an analysis of the intrinsically soteriological and, as such, theocentric event of encounter with the Christian witness of faith (for Ogden's doctrine of the trinity, see 1980a).

We have seen that Ogden's christology is consistently theocentric in its approach and exhaustively or radically monotheistic in its material content. Christocentrism, with its focus on the person, Jesus, turns out ultimately to expel the person of Jesus from Christian faith and theology.

Indeed, our thesis is that just this desire to uphold the radically monotheistic and theocentric character of Christian faith has been the center and basis of Ogden's entire theological project since his dissertation. As he puts it there, "unless the *theocentric* basis and sanction of 'christocentrism' is explicitly acknowledged, emphasis on Jesus Christ can be a snare and a delusion and a mere travesty of authentic apostolic faith" (1961a: 143). There is pathos in the fact that this has rarely been adequately appreciated in the history of Christian thought. As we have seen, focus on the person of Jesus, his being in himself, in abstraction from the soteriological significance of the person, Jesus, for us, has informed the very structure of traditional christology. The primary constructive significance of Ogden's work for explicitly Christian theology is its effort to return such theology to its proper service of faith in God alone; nothing more, and nothing less. Precisely wherein he takes such radically monotheistic and theocentric faith to consist, both as gift and demand for human life, we shall now go on to show.

II. Radical Monotheism as Metaphysical Gift

We have seen how Ogden's analysis of the Christian witness of faith, "present only in the form of all the various witnesses and kinds of witness," leads to radical monotheism (1986a: 4). In what follows, we hope to show that his analysis of human existence, as this "can be fully understood only through the whole of human history and all the forms of culture," leads to the same radically monotheistic and theocentric conclusion (ibid.). This will enable us to understand and to assess Ogden's attempt to validate the claim of the Christian religion to be "*the* religion," a claim which, as he says, can be sustained "only if it is somehow expressed or implied by the whole of human life" (ibid.: 87).[19]

Our intent in this section is to analyze and to interpret Ogden's claim that for all human beings, "faith in God cannot but be real because it is in the final analysis unavoidable" (1966a: 21). The argument for this claim is in two parts: (1) all human beings live by an act of existential faith; (2) the ground of this existential faith is most adequately understood as God, properly conceived. In this sense, radical monotheism is metaphysical gift.

The Reality of Existential Faith

The key to Ogden's philosophical anthropology, from the point of view of its significance for philosophical theology, is his contention that "to exist in the characteristically human way is to exist by faith" (1986a: 70).[20] "Faith" is understood here as "our basic confidence or assurance simply as human beings that life is worth living" (1986a: 106). Basic confidence is, for Ogden, "the most primitive mode of our experience," "an awareness at once of being and of value" (1969a: 85). "It is an awareness not merely of ourselves, and of our fellow creatures, but also of the infinite whole in which we are all included as somehow one" (ibid.). The sense of the importance and the value of the self and the other is derived from the dim awareness of their transcendent worth to the encompassing whole. Basic faith, then, refers to "our inalienable trust that our own existence and existence generally are somehow justified and made meaningful by the whole to which we know ourselves to belong" (1986a: 107).

Essential to Ogden's analysis is a distinction he draws between two levels of human existence, "the *existential* understanding or faith that is constitutive of human existence as such and the *reflective* understanding or faith whereby what is presented existentially can be re-presented in an express, thematic and conceptually precise way" (1986a: 71). According to Ogden, what is constitutive of human existence is, as we have seen, existential faith (synonyms: "primal faith," "common faith," "original confidence," "basic confidence," "underlying confidence"). This is the faith which is expressed at "the level of self-understanding and life-praxis" (1986c: 12). "Reflective faith," on the other hand, refers to conceptual or symbolic re-presentations of the reality of existential faith. This is faith expressed at "the level of theoretical reflection on our self-understanding and praxis of life" (ibid.). Religious beliefs, secular humanism, Nazi or communist ideologies are examples.

This distinction between levels of faith or understanding provides the context for Ogden's discussion of the relation between faith and reason. In one sense, "faith" and "reason" coincide. Since existential faith involves accepting one's life and its setting and adjusting oneself to them in a self-conscious way, "faith itself, as already involving self-consciousness, is a mode of understanding" (1986a: 70). Thus, when "faith" and "reason" are taken in the broad sense as referring comprehensively to the distinctively human mode of being, "it is indifferent whether we say that one exists humanly solely on the basis of faith or say, rather, that one never exists humanly except as a being who understands" (ibid.). In another sense, however—and this is the essential point of Ogden's use of the metaphor "level"—we must recognize "the irreversible priority of faith in human existence" (ibid.). That is to say, existential faith always precedes any reflective attempt to re-present, to understand, or to justify it. Existential faith and reflective faith are thus logically distinguishable but really inseparable aspects of every conscious moment of adult experience: existential faith issues in reflective re-presentations, and any reflective faith is an instance of existential faith seeking understanding.

According to Ogden, not only do the two levels of human existence never occur apart from each other, neither do they ever exist simply as such. "Reflective faith" is an abstraction which finds concrete expression either as true faith or as false faith, depending on the accuracy and adequacy of its re-presentation of the underlying existential faith. Existential faith, for its part, is an abstraction which is concretely manifested either authentically or inauthentically (see discussion in III below).[21]

Finally, Ogden's use of the term "faith" is intended to be inherently positive but not eulogistic. That is to say, faith may be false as well as true, or inauthentic as well as authentic, but precisely because it always exists only as true or false, or as authentic or inauthentic, faith itself can never be merely negative in the sense of merely absent. "Unfaith is not the absence of faith, but the presence of faith in a deficient or distorted mode" (1966a: 23).

With these preliminary clarifications in mind, we are now in a position to evaluate Ogden's central claim that "given human beings such as ourselves, faith in some mode is not an option but a necessity" (1986a: 107), so that "to exist as a self at all is possible solely on the basis of faith" (ibid.: 69). This is a strong claim and, for many, a controversial one. What about despair, suicide, nihilism? The full weight of Ogden's philosophical anthropology rests upon this fundamental contention that existential faith is unavoidable in human life. How does Ogden justify this contention?

In one sense, existential faith cannot be justified, if we mean by "justification" the appeal to more fundamental levels of experience or to more fundamental truths. "The existential faith by which we live neither needs justification nor ever can be justified. Rather, it is the very ground of justification" (1986a: 72). We may say, however, that the reality of existential faith can be shown transcendentally to be the necessary condition of the possibility of other things—indeed of anything—that we do. Consider the following three variations on this theme:

Moral Thought and Action Presuppose Existential Faith

Moral struggles give rise to ethical discussion; ethical discussion, in turn, betrays a profound truth about moral struggles, namely, that our attempts to realize and to understand moral values rest upon the assumption that human life is valuable. Normative ethical discussion is concerned, in part, with the question about what moral norms are and how they are to be determined, and philosophers have provided various answers: the categorical imperative, utility, natural law, and so on.[22] Broadly speaking, all answers fall into one of two groups: moral values are seen either as intrinsic values (Kant and other deontologists) or as instrumental values which are means to intrinsic values (Aristotle, Aquinas, Mill, and other teleologists). In either case, intrinsic values are characterized as "the dignity of human life," "a full human life," or "the common good." Moral activity, then, presupposes the value of human life.

Ogden makes this point by arguing that the normative question, What is the standard of moral activity? raises the deeper question—in Stephen Toulmin's term, the "limit question"—Why be moral, anyway (whatever "moral" turns out to mean)? Serious ethical inquiry requires an answer to this question, but ethics itself cannot provide the answer. "One ought to follow the Categorical Imperative because it is the morally right thing to do" is circular; "one ought to follow the natural law because it leads to human happiness" is question-begging: why pursue human happiness?

Ogden identifies existential faith as the only adequate answer to the moral limit question: "moral thought and action are existentially possible only because their roots reach down into an underlying confidence in the abiding worth of our life" (1966a: 36). We strive to do the "right" thing because of the implicit conviction that our lives are worthwhile and so are worth living in some manner that maximizes and harmonizes our various pursuits of happiness.

Intellectual Inquiry Presupposes Existential Faith

Although Ogden does not fully develop the point, he suggests a parallel analysis with respect to inquiry, namely, that our attempts to understand reality rest upon the supposition that reality is understandable. In natural science, for instance, "we assume that the world of events of which we are a part is so ordered that our experience of phenomena in the past and the present warrants our having certain expectations for the future" (1966a: 33). The scientist cannot but presuppose that reality is knowable in the sense that predictions depend upon its orderliness.

We may also make the same point—that understanding depends upon faith—in a general epistemological context. All intellectual activity rests not only upon the conviction that there is truth but also upon the conviction that, as William James put it, "our minds and it are made for each other."[23] Even if we argue that our minds are not capable of knowing reality—or that they are capable of knowing it only in a severely restricted sense—still, we must believe that we are capable of knowing *that* truth. However we come at the epistemological question, therefore, we unavoidably illustrate, as a presupposition of our intellectual inquiry, a basic confidence in our ability to know the truth. Inquiry as such thus involves what Whitehead called "an ultimate moral intuition into the nature of intellectual action—that it should embody the adventure of hope."[24]

Existential Faith Is Presupposed Even by Its Denial

Although this is a curious and seemingly paradoxical point, it is, we believe, profoundly true. Ogden's insight is that if the most primitive level of our experience were of the worthlessness and absurdity of life, the announcement of this fact should cause no alarm and call for no particular response. "As a matter of fact, on these terms, even the hatred of life is without point and the pronouncement of life's vanity as meaningless as everything else" (1966a: 139). Basic faith, in other words, can be denied only at the price of self-contradiction. What is at issue here is the *practical* or *pragmatic* contradiction between performance and concept. The philosopher "cannot question the worth of life without presupposing the worth of questioning and therefore the worth of the life by which alone such questioning can be done" (1967b: 35). Again, "even the suicide who intentionally takes his own life implicitly affirms the ultimate meaning of his tragic choice" (1966a: 36). The point is that the practical carrying out of the denial of existential faith is, in the nature of the case, impossible, because the denial is itself intended to be positive or meaningful. This is Camus' insight in "The Riddle": "a literature of despair is a contradiction in terms."[25]

The conclusion of these arguments is that existential faith is indeed unavoidable for all human beings, because all our moral and intellectual activities, including even our attempts to deny existential faith, are manifestations of existential faith: "we have no alternative, finally, but to trust somehow that life is worth living—everything we think, say, or do necessarily implying such a trust" (1986a: 107). In other words, nihilism is not a real possibility at the existential level.[26]

It is difficult to overestimate the significance of this claim regarding existential faith; for, as we shall see, it is a short step from existential faith to theism. Consider: precisely because it is inevitable, existential faith must be evoked by and grounded in external reality; it cannot be illusory. At issue here is the question of what is meant by "illusion" and "reality." To claim to know that something is an illusion is also to claim to know what is real, since it is only by the standard of the real that the illusory can be recognized as such. If, then, all human beings inevitably and unavoidably and necessarily manifest this deepest level of experience that may be appropriately characterized as "basic confidence" or "existential faith," such experience cannot be illusory precisely because there is no other mode or deeper level of existential awareness with which to compare it.

Given the reality of existential faith, therefore, the question becomes, How shall we understand reality so as to take account of the fact that it evokes this basic confidence in the final worth of our lives? What Ogden calls "the existential question" or "the question of faith" or "the religious question"—the question that "has to do with the ultimate meaning of one's very existence as a human being" (1982a: 30)—"is never the question *whether* there is a ground of basic confidence in life's worth . . . rather, the question of faith is always *how* the ground of confidence can be so conceived and symbolized that our consent to life can be true and authentic" (1986a: 108). The question is not whether we trust but in what we trust. In the nature of the case, noetic existential faith cannot but have an ontic correlate. It remains now to understand this ontic correlate of faith in a way that is true and to respond to it in a way that is authentic.

The Grounding of Existential Faith

What understanding of reality is most congruent with our experience of existential faith? According to Ogden, to say that reality inevitably evokes from us a sense of basic confidence is to say that reality is theistic, where the word "God" functions formally to account for our basic confidence. Thus, on his view, "the primary use or function of 'God' is to refer to the objective ground in reality itself of our ineradicable confidence in the final worth of our existence. . . . The Word 'God,' then, provides the designation for whatever it is about this experienced whole that calls forth and justifies our original and inescapable trust" (1966a: 37).[27]

To be more precise, we should distinguish, as Ogden sometimes does, between the terms "god" and "God," because the question, "What accounts for existential faith?" may mean, "What do people *in fact* identify as the source of life's meaning and value?" or it may mean, "What really *is* the ground of all meaning and value which ought to be recognized as such?" The term "god," in other words, may have a variety of referents, depending upon what people take as providing the ultimate basis for their existence.

How are we to distinguish "the one true God" from "the many false gods"? We may do so according to a single criterion with two aspects. First, there is that aspect which concerns the truth or falsity, that is, the internal consistency and experiential adequacy of any particular conceptual understanding of the reality of God. Second, there is that aspect which concerns the ultimacy of any particular idea of God, that is, its ability to confront us with the promise and the demand of authentic existence. We turn to the first point now, and to the second in the next section of the essay.

Charles Hartshorne has argued persuasively that any answer to the theistic question (in Ogden's terms, any answer to the question about how we are to conceive the ground of existential faith) must be one of three types: classical theism (God is wholly infinite and wholly independent of all nondivine reality), neoclassical theism (God is, in different respects, both infinite and finite, both independent of and dependent upon nondivine reality), or atheism (there is, in no sense, an infinite God.)[28] It is well known that Ogden argues for the neoclassical or "panentheistic" option, the details of which, having been most carefully worked out by Hartshorne, we do not intend to discuss at length here. What we do want to point out is *why* Ogden has critically appropriated Hartshorne's neoclassical theism.[29]

Basically, there are three reasons: (1) Neoclassical theism provides a more adequate theoretical account of the reality of existential faith than does either classical theism or atheism. (2) Such a neoclassical theism can be given cognitive meaning in terms of experience and is coherent, avoiding the insuperable and unnecessary paradoxes and antinomies of classical theism. (3) Neoclassical theism "seems immeasurably more adequate" than classical theism as a "theological witness to the God of Jesus Christ," that is, as making the point of christology (1966a: 66). It is the first reason that particularly concerns us here.

From the standpoint of the human experience of existential faith, Ogden's basic argument for neoclassical theism is this: If our underlying awareness is of ourselves and the world as having abiding worth, then our concept of God must take account of two essential characteristics: "First, God must be conceived as a reality which is genuinely related to our life in the world and to which, therefore, both we ourselves and our various actions all make a difference as to its actual being . . . second, we can think of God only as a reality whose relatedness to our life is itself relative to nothing and to which, therefore, neither our own being and actions nor any others can ever make a difference as to its existence" (1966a: 47). Only a being understood as in this sense "dipolar" could ground existential faith.

This, then, is the basic logic of neoclassical theism: God is both supremely related to us (hence our sense of worth) and also supremely absolute and independent of us (hence our sense of enduring or abiding worth in an everlasting deity). That these twin insights are complementary rather than contradictory may be shown by distinguishing the abstract features of the divine existence (*that* God knows, loves, exists necessarily and perfectly) from the actual, concrete divine manifestations of these features (*how* God knows and loves me, how God exists now *for me*). Precisely because God concretely knows and loves every contingent creature with perfect adequacy in each moment of change, the quality of God's knowledge and love is necessary and changeless. In other words, that which is supremely related (adequately related to all that is actual and capable of being so related to whatever is even possible) is, for that very reason, supremely absolute (existentially independent of any particular state of affairs because existentially capable of adequate relation to any conceivable state of affairs).[30]

These somewhat technical points may be expressed more simply. Ogden adopts neoclassical theism as the most adequate reflective re-presentation of the ground of existential faith because a neoclassical understanding of deity is the central concept of a metaphysics in which real internal relatedness is taken as essential to all reality. To exist is to exist socially in relation to neighbors and temporally in relation to ancestors and descendants. Neoclassical theism understands by "God" the supreme instance of reality, and so the supreme form of social and temporal relatedness.

Ogden's argument against classical forms of theism at just this point is that such conceptions of God do not unequivocally assert God's real internal relatedness to the world. Thomas Aquinas, whose work Ogden discusses as the most influential and impressive example of such a type of theism, argues that "since therefore God is outside the whole order of creation, and all creatures are ordered to Him, and not conversely, it is manifest that creatures are really related to God Himself, whereas in God there is no real relation to creatures, but a relation only in idea, inasmuch as creatures are referred to Him."[31] Such an understanding of God as wholly absolute cannot do justice to our primordial awareness of our own and the world's worth, because neither we nor the world really make a difference to the encompassing whole.

Only that which is both everlasting and universally related can function adequately to account for existential faith. If classical theism in its various forms lacks the affirmation of universal relatedness which is necessary to account for this, atheism, whether humanistic or naturalistic, by definition either lacks such universal relatedness or lacks everlastingness, or both.

While these brief remarks cannot constitute a definitive argument against classical theism or atheism, neither is this appropriate or necessary here. One may refer, as does Ogden, to the extended treatment of these issues in Hartshorne's work in particular.[32] Nonetheless, these observations do serve to identify the insight expressed in Ogden's claim that neoclassical theism is the most adequate conceptual understanding of the ground of basic faith.

All human activity presupposes existential faith; existential faith presupposes a ground; such a ground is finally to be conceived as supremely related and supremely absolute: this is Ogden's argument for the existence of God. It is strictly transcendental and constitutes, in Maurice Blondel's words, "not so much an invention as an inventory . . . of the fundamental beliefs of humanity" (1966a: 43 n. 71).

The reality of God is unavoidable, because the existential faith which is unavoidable in human life can finally be adequately understood only as faith in God. At this point the fundamental insights of philosophical anthropology and the presuppositions of the understanding of revelation in the New Testament coincide. One may speak interchangeably of the "metaphysical gift" or the "original revelation" of God. Since reality is inherently theistic, any notion of "nature" as that which is unrelated to God is meaningless. Everything is related to "the supernatural" or, rather, the very basis of the distinction between "nature" and "grace" or between "natural" and "supernatural" is removed. All reality is graced. The "God of the philosophers" turns out finally to be the God not only of Abraham, Isaac, and Jacob but also of Jesus Christ.[33]

Although the reality of God is unavoidable, this is not to say that all people necessarily reflectively grasp or understand this gift, much less that they recognize it *as God*. Because there is no guarantee that people will always (or indeed, that some will ever) exist fully self-consciously, and because, even if they do, there is always the possibility that they will be confused, Ogden addresses the problem of "theoretical atheism" or "Godlessness of the mind." One may have a truncated understanding of reality which does not fully explicate existential faith; one may even have an explicitly atheistic understanding of reality which flatly contradicts existential faith. The crucial point is that in either case the problem is one of conceptual confusion: theoretical understanding is not isomorphic with lived practice; what is implicitly felt is not explicitly acknowledged. "It is always possible in a particular case that no real correlation exists between the reflective denial of God and the existential affirmations by which the person in question actually lives" (1966a: 24–25). Any reflective account of common features of our human experience that makes explicit what is always implicit will somehow bear witness to the reality of God, even if only to deny false conceptions of it.

For Ogden, the issue of true and false understandings of God, although important, is completely secondary to another issue which constitutes the deeper problem confronting human beings: the problem of "existential godlessness" or "godlessness of the heart" (1966a: 23). Because his writings are characterized by and are associated with the highest demands for conceptual clarity and logical rigor, it is important to realize that it is Ogden himself who warns that we must not succumb "to an intellectualistic misunderstanding of faith" (1966a: 24 n. 40), wherein the problem of human life is seen exclusively or even primarily in terms of how we *think* about God. While he argues that we ought to think as clearly as possible about the implications of basic faith and about the cognitive claims which are entailed by Christian faith, so as to avoid "the inhibiting effects of a theoretical atheism" (1967b: 39), Ogden contends that "the crucial question is not the question of how one expresses or conceives one's faith; it's the question of how one lives it" (ibid.: 53). True reflective belief, while important, is finally for the sake of authentic existence.

III. Gift as Moral Demand

We have seen that Ogden's analysis of existential faith leads to the conclusion that ultimate reality is most adequately understood theistically. Having examined true and false conceptual understandings of existential faith, we now examine its authentic and inauthentic lived expressions.

What does Ogden mean by authentic and inauthentic forms of existential faith (which he frequently designates simply as "authentic existence" and "inauthentic existence")? In answering this question, it is helpful to take account of Ogden's critical appropriation of Clifford Geertz's analysis of religion, according to which religion is a system of sacred symbols, a specific form of culture which involves a synthesis of world view and ethos. Religion functions to describe the structure of ultimate reality and to draw from that world view the necessary implications about how we ought to live. "The powerfully coercive 'ought' is felt to grow out of a comprehensive factual 'is' and in such a way religion grounds the most specific requirements of human action in the most general contexts of human existence" (1982a: 32, citing Geertz).

Following Geertz then, Ogden contends that the existential or religious question, which "has to do with the ultimate meaning of one's very existence as a human being" (ibid.: 30), involves both a metaphysical and a moral aspect, the latter being the question "about the authentic understanding of our existence authorized by ultimate reality" (ibid.: 35). The answer to the religious question thus involves both metaphysical claims and moral demands and so functions "to provide a metaphysical foundation for morals" and "to express the moral meaning of the metaphysical" (ibid.: 34).

The moral aspect of the religious question itself involves two questions: How ought I to understand myself in relation to ultimate reality? and How ought I, therefore, to act in relation to others? The point here is that any answer to specific moral questions (How ought I to act?) presupposes an answer to the prior question, How ought I to understand myself authentically? Likewise, authentic self-understanding entails moral obligations. Self-understanding is thus the inner and fundamental decision whereby "the self as such is constituted," and "all outer acts of word and deed are but ways of expressing and implementing" this inner decision (1966a: 177). Thus, the moral aspect of the religious question just *is* the understanding of oneself in relation to ultimate reality which always implies specific moral obligations in whatever specific context one is set.

Formally speaking, then, what Ogden means by "authentic existence" or "the authentic lived expression of existential faith" is twofold: (1) understanding oneself in the light of radical monotheism so as to trust completely in God alone as the source and center of value and meaning; (2) actualizing the necessary moral implications in the light of a theocentric ethics through utter loyalty to God in all one's relations to others.

Monotheism and the Logic of Radical Trust

How are we to understand ourselves authentically in the light of ultimate reality? We have seen that we all live according to a basic confidence that our lives have final meaning and that only the reality of God, as both supremely related and as supremely absolute, can account for this confidence. But what does it mean to say that our lives have final meaning? How are we to understand "final meaning" in the face of our inevitable death?

One usual religious response to this question is to argue that we somehow survive our death and so continue to live everlastingly— the doctrine of subjective immortality. But, as Whitehead, Hartshorne, and Ogden have convincingly contended, this answer depends upon a mistaken analysis of death as a threat to final meaning.[34] According to these thinkers, the fundamental threat of final meaninglessness is not death as termination of our lives but death as an instance of the broader problem of transience. The most basic problem is that our lives perish moment by moment, and death is a particularly graphic and dramatic example of this transience. The specter of meaninglessness has to do not with the finite duration of our lives overall but with the moment-by-moment finite impact of our actions. Our choices, our dreams, our hopes survive only imperfectly in our own lives, even less so in the lives of our children and their descendants. Memories of our lives increasingly fade, so that eventually it is as if we had never existed at all. In Whitehead's words, our lives are "passing whiffs of insignificance." To say that our lives are meaningless, in other words, is to say two things: other finite beings are at best only imperfect recipients of our actions; memories of our lives fade, so that at some point it will matter to nobody that we ever lived. Where do our lives go when everybody has forgotten them or when there is nobody to remember them?

Once the problem of meaninglessness is cast in these terms, it is obvious that subjective immortality is really no solution to it. If each moment of our lives finally perishes, then, even if we live forever more, our lives are finally meaningless, too.

According to neoclassical theism, what rescues our lives from final meaninglessness is not an infinite sequence of moments in our own lives but God's supreme relatedness to each moment; our actions literally make a difference to God and abide in God forevermore. In some small but enduring manner, our lives contribute to God and create divine experience. "For God thus to accept all of his creatures in the sense of creatively synthesizing all of them into his own everlasting life, is for him to redeem all of his creatures, in that he thereby delivers them from the meaninglessness of not making any difference to anything or anyone more enduring than themselves" (1979a: 84).

Expressed otherwise, such objective immortality means that the final significance of our lives cannot be found in ourselves or in our neighbors; it can be found only in our contribution to deity. "In this sense, all things exist, finally, not merely for themselves or for one another, but, as the Christian witness has classically affirmed, for the glory of God, as contributions to his unique and all-encompassing life" (1979a: 85). The point of our lives is God.

What Ogden means by authentic self-understanding is simply accepting our creaturely status and living the truth that the final meaning of our lives is to be found only in God. Conversely, inauthentic self-understanding is the attempt to find final meaning in anything other than God. Inauthentic faith is idolatry.

Sin and the Logic of Idolatry

The key to Ogden's understanding of idolatry is that it consists not in the absence but rather in the perversion of basic trust. Because, as we have seen above, existential faith is unavoidable in human life, being presupposed by all we do, it cannot be merely absent but must be expressed somehow. "Even a false or inauthentic faith, which we sometimes speak of as 'unfaith,' is not simply the absence of faith but faith itself in its negative mode, rather as evil is the negative mode of worth, or disvalue is the negative mode of value" (1986a: 72). Since, as we have shown, nihilism is not a genuine existential option, it is idolatry which is the real threat to authentic faith in God.

It is commonly supposed that idolatry is the diversion of faith wholly away from God to some nondivine object. However, given the meaning of God as universal and necessary, such a view cannot be literally true. As Ogden puts it as over against frequent misunderstandings of the matter, "the real issue of faith at the deepest, existential level is never *whether* we are to believe in God, or even, as is sometimes said, *what* God we are to believe in; the issue, instead, is *how* we are to believe in the only God in whom anyone can believe and in whom each of us somehow must believe" (1966a: 24). What is universal is unavoidable; to maintain otherwise is to treat God as one, even if the greatest, merely finite object.

The idolatry in which inauthentic faith consists is properly understood not as merely the diversion of existential trust, but rather as the division of such trust between the idol and God. "The idolater is always the adulterer, the one who adulterates the unqualified confidence he owes to God alone by resting it in part in something alongside of God—whether himself or one or more of his fellow creatures" (1967b: 38). Moreover, the inauthentic self-understanding of idolatry manifests itself not merely as such a division, but also as a distortion or perversion of trust. Thus, "the idolater regards [some nondivine thing] as having a unique significance as a symbol or sacrament of God's presence. His idol is for him the indispensable evidence of God's power and favor" (1966a: 24). One not only divides one's existential faith between God and some nondivine object, one also perverts it, with the result that this object becomes the condition for reflective faith in God as well. In this way one comes to misunderstand oneself not only "in the bottom of the heart," but also "in the top of the mind" (ibid.: 23).

Such idolatrous perversion of trust can come in many forms, for any finite object of human interest is capable of becoming an idol.[35] Indeed, the more importance an object comes to assume, the greater the temptation there is that it will seduce one from unqualified confidence in God alone. That very "christocentrism" which, precisely in an effort to honor Jesus, so asks about his being in himself as not only to divide trust between this and God but also to pervert the trust that belongs to God alone, thereby makes him an idol. Thus, interest in the person of Christ exemplifies both the logic of idolatry among those who would be authentically human as Christians and the pathos of idolatry for all who would be authentically human in any way at all.

We are now in a position to understand why Ogden interprets the Christian doctrine of sin in the language of idolatry; for, as he puts it, "what is properly meant by 'sin' is precisely a distorted existential knowledge of God and of one's neighbor and self in God" (1966a: 216). Whether seen as a division of existential trust between some nondivine object and God or as a perversion of that trust, sin simply is idolatry. As such, sin is likewise eccentricity, the inauthentic centering of one's life in something *alongside* God.

Like idolatry, sin is a distinctively religious category. Whereas the former describes the universally tragic human situation in terms of an eccentric and disproportionate relation involving the self, others, and God, the latter describes it in terms of an inauthentic mode of distinctively human existence. As idolatry is primarily a matter of that inner human activity whereby the self as such is constituted and derivatively a matter of those outer acts of word and deed whereby such inner decisions are expressed and implemented, so, too, is sin. Thus, any merely moral misunderstanding of sin, according to which this refers either solely or even primarily to such outer acts, is excluded. By the same token, it is precisely this radically monotheistic and theocentric interpretation of idolatry and sin which leads to what we shall see is a correspondingly radical interpretation of moral obligation.

If Ogden interprets inauthentic existence as idolatry or sin in the manner we have described, he naturally interprets authentic existence, faith or salvation, as their contrary. If what characterizes inauthentic existence is idolatrous eccentricity, the centering of the self in something alongside God, authentic existence is rather a theocentric and also radically monotheistic centering of oneself and others in God alone. The distinguishing mark of sin is bondage to anxiety in futilely attempting to secure final meaning for our existence through trust in and loyalty to nondivine objects, which are inherently incapable of providing such meaning. Ogden can describe the distinctive character of faith in an extended summary passage as:

> existence in freedom—and that in two distinct, albeit closely related senses of the word.
>
> Faith is existence in freedom, in the first place, in the negative sense of *freedom from*—freedom *from* all things, ourselves and the world, as in any way essential to determining the ultimate meaning of our lives. . . . Because the mystery encompassing our existence is the limitless acceptance of God's love, faith as the acceptance of that acceptance, and, in that sense, as trust in God's love, is existence in freedom *from* literally everything else.
>
> For the very same reason, faith is existence in freedom, in the second place, in the positive sense of *freedom for*—freedom *for* literally everything else, ourselves and the world, as all worthy of our own love and devoted service. . . . Just because the mystery encompassing our lives is God's boundless acceptance, faith as the trusting acceptance of that acceptance is also the freedom to accept all those whom God accepts and, therefore, is existence in freedom *for* all things, our fellow creatures as well as ourselves (1979a: 55–57).

It will not be amiss to remind ourselves that Ogden is speaking throughout of that radically monotheistic and theocentric form of authentic existence which he argues is precisely Christian faith. Such Christian faith in God alone, precisely as existence *"in* freedom is, by its very nature, also existence *for* freedom—for the freedom of all the others, for whom the Christian is freed to live through utterly trusting in God's love" (ibid.: 59). Thus, Christian faith is also moral demand.

Theocentrism and the Logic of Loyalty

Although Ogden is not known primarily as a moral theologian, we want to indicate in this concluding section the significance for ethics of his commitment to monotheism. On Ogden's view, authentic existence involves "not only trust in God's love but also loyalty to God and, therefore, to all those to whom he himself is loyal—which means, of course, literally everyone" (1979a: 56). Faith must find expression in good works. In fact, as we shall argue, monotheistic faith is less than radical if it does not issue in a theocentric ethics.

We referred earlier to Ogden's appropriation of Clifford Geertz's description of religion as providing a metaphysical foundation for morals and as expressing the moral meaning of the metaphysical. The basis for a theoretical account of the relation between ontology and axiology is contained in the neoclassical thought which Ogden critically appropriates.[36] Because moral value is a species of value in general, it is important in formulating a theocentric ethic to make explicit the general relation between what is and what is valuable.

Neoclassical thought involves both a relational theory of being and a relational theory of value. As the meaning of "being" is irreducibly relational, so, too, is the meaning of "value." In the most fundamental sense, "to be" means "to be in relation"; nothing exists except as subject for some object or as object for some subject. All reality is social. Who we are in any moment, for example, is a result of the integration of our relations to our past and future selves, and to our neighbors, including God.

Consider, as an example, Aquinas's relation to Aristotle: Aquinas is subject, Aristotle is object. (Aquinas, of course, may be the object in other relations and Aristotle may be a subject in other relations, for example, his own relation to Plato.) We say that Aquinas is internally related to Aristotle, meaning thereby that the being of Aquinas is constituted, in part, by the relation to Aristotle; Aristotle influences Aquinas. Aristotle, on the other hand, is externally related to Aquinas in the sense that, as subject, Aristotle is unaffected by

Aquinas. The being of Aquinas makes no difference to Aristotle. Thus, subjects are internally related to objects, and objects are externally related to subjects.

This relational theory of being is reflected in a relational theory of value. "To be valuable" means "to be good or bad for some thing including oneself." To say that all value is a function of being in relation does not mean, however, that all value is simply instrumental or contributory.[37] We may still distinguish intrinsic and instrumental value as follows: As objects, beings have instrumental value in their merely logical, external relations to subjects (Aristotle is instrumentally valuable to Aquinas in the sense that Aristotle contributes to Aquinas's own value); such beings as are concrete subjects have intrinsic value in their real, internal relations to objects (Aquinas has intrinsic value in his relation to Aristotle). Both intrinsic and instrumental value are a function of being in relation.

Whitehead has written, "It is as true to say that God creates the World, as that the World creates God."[38] Stated more technically, neoclassical metaphysics holds that "God creates the World" in the sense that the being of anything that is so much as even possible is dependent for its being upon the necessary existence of God. In this regard, God is unsurpassable as the object of all actual and possible subjects and, therefore, is the greatest conceivable instrumental value. "The World creates God" in the sense that all nondivine reality contributes to and so constitutes the actual experience of deity. In this regard, God is unsurpassable as the subject for all actual and possible objects and, therefore, is the greatest conceivable intrinsic value. As both the necessary ground of our existence and the perfect recipient of our lives, and thus as the supreme instance of both instrumental and intrinsic value, God is both the creator and the redeemer of world process.

We may go further: because everything that is depends upon God for its very existence, God's being the supreme instance of instrumental value means that whatever intrinsic value anything else has is to be understood, finally, in relation to God's instrumental value. In this sense, *God as creator is the primal source of all nondivine intrinsic value.* (Indirectly, therefore, God as creator is also the ultimate source of all nondivine instrumental value, because whatever intrinsic value is required to explain a particular instrumental value is itself to be understood, finally, in relation to God.) Likewise, because God is the one all-inclusive and enduring individual, whatever abiding instrumental value anything else has is to be understood only in relation to God's abiding intrinsic value. In this sense, *God as redeemer is the final center of all enduring nondivine instrumental value.*

What we mean by a theocentric theory of value, then, is the appropriation of these two insights that God is both the supreme instance of instrumental value and so the source of all nondivine intrinsic value and the supreme instance of intrinsic value and so the center of all nondivine abiding instrumental value. What we mean by a "theocentric ethics" is the specification of these insights with regard to how we ought to act in relation to one another and to God. We may distinguish three aspects of such an ethics.

In the first place, a theocentric ethics will regard all nondivine intrinsic value as dependent upon divine instrumental value. This recognition should engender, as James Gustafson has pointed out, "reasons of the mind and heart for being moral."[39] For example, our moral obligations toward other persons derive not only from the rational motives of the pursuit of the common good or from the universalizability of our maxims, but also—and more profoundly—from the religious recognition that others are recipients of God's efficacious love.

In the second place, a theocentric ethics will see not only that God, as the supreme instance of intrinsic value, is the center of all nondivine instrumental value, but also that, precisely as divine, such a center is both all-inclusive and everlasting. This insight has direct moral implications.

God's all-inclusiveness means that to actualize what is good for God is thereby to actualize what is good for the whole and all its parts. Only in the divine case can self-interest and the common good coincide, because only that which is the subject of all conceivable objects can provide an inclusive center for the instrumental value of all beings. If the center of instrumental value is located in any nondivine reality—as in egoistic or sexist or racist or nationalistic or homocentric value-theories—then the ethics expressive of such a center will be necessarily partial and so exclusive of some others. Slavery may be judged advantageous if the slave-owner is taken as the center of value. Only theocentrism can provide a truly inclusive ethics. In the words of H. Richard Niebuhr, "the good" is:

> Not only what is good for me (though my confidence accepts that as included), nor what is good for man (though that is also included), nor what is good for the development of life (though that also belongs in the picture), but what is good for being, for universal being, or for God, center and source of all existence.[40]

Soli Deo gloria.

God's everlastingness means that the moral significance of our actions consists not only in their effects on other finite beings, great as that may be, but also in their impact on an all-good and abiding deity. The positive value of a Mother Teresa and the negative value of a Holocaust endure, literally, forever.

In the third place, a theocentric ethics implies that our action in relation to others should be expressive of our commitment to God. As Gustafson puts it: we are "to relate to all things in a manner appropriate to their relations to God."[41] To say that God alone is the source and center of all intrinsic and instrumental value is not to say that no nondivine thing has value. To the contrary, it is only to point out that whatever has intrinsic or instrumental value ultimately derives that value from its relation to God.

Theocentric ethics, therefore, does not mean that we are to be loyal to God alone; obviously, we are to be loyal to others as well. Rather, we must be loyal both to God *and to others precisely in their relations to God.* As Ogden expresses it, "to be loyal to God's demand is to be loyal to God and to all the others to whom God is also loyal" (1982a: 158). What theocentrism forbids is anything other than utter loyalty to God alone or (what is the same thing) disproportionate loyalty to anything other than God. To be utterly loyal to God is to be appropriately loyal to others, and to be appropriately loyal to others is to express utter loyalty to God. "In this sense, the freedom for which Christ has set us free is the freedom of love, both of God and, in God, of all whom God also loves (ibid.: 158). Just this is the point made when Jesus is presented as saying that the greatest commandment is to "love the Lord your God with all your heart, and with all your soul, and with all your mind and with all your strength" and that the second commandment is to "love your neighbor as yourself" (Mark 12:29–31; par.). As Ogden points out, the second commandment in no way compromises the first, because "it is precisely by withholding nothing of ourselves from our love for our neighbors as well as for all of our fellow creatures that we can alone obey the first commandment" (1982a: 159). Loving the neighbor appropriately is loving God; loving God utterly is loving the neighbor appropriately. The two commandments entail each other. Just because nothing other than God is ultimate, everything alongside of God finds its proper importance.

What works of love does a theocentric ethics require? Important for answering this question is a distinction Ogden draws between God's redemptive activity, to which we are called to witness, and

God's emancipatory activity, in which we are called to participate (1979a: 82–95).

As the one subject for all objects, God is the one enduring individual whose life is partly influenced by the lives of all others; God is the individual to whom all things finally make a difference. In this sense, as we have seen above, only God can redeem us from death and transience and meaninglessness. Because God's love is boundless—accepting into the divine life even our sinful rejections of God—God redeems us from sin as well, "reconciling the world to himself" (2 Cor. 5:19). Since such redemptive activity belongs to God alone, our participation in it consists exclusively in our witnessing to God's redemptive activity in such a way as to open up for others the same possibility of existing in faith.

Not only does God receive the world to reconcile and redeem it, God also acts upon the world to emancipate it. Such emancipatory activity is an expression of the divine creative action whereby, as the object for all subjects, God influences the lives of all others.

According to neoclassical thought, God's activity in relation to the world is best understood on a social rather than a deterministic model. Because all concrete reality, including nondivine reality, is partly determinative of its own being—because, as Jules Lequier has expressed it, "Thou hast created me creator of myself"—it makes no sense to think of God acting on the world by making all the decisions and so determining all the details. Since God's emancipatory activity is the intrinsically social activity of love, the power of God to emancipate is the power that belongs to love.[42]

The activity of God upon the world may be understood in two senses. In the first place, God sets the limits, for example, the natural laws, within which creaturely decisions are made. Such limits are the optimal ones for nurturing freedom in that they maximize the opportunities for success while minimizing the risks of failure. Thus, while God determines the cosmic order, the details of the local orders are determined by other free agents. In Hartshorne's words, "God is needed not to put everything precisely in its place, for things must put themselves in their places; but he is needed to see to it that there are appropriate places for things to put themselves into."[43]

In the second place, God influences the world just by being the one unavoidable object for all possible subjects in their own processes of self-creation. On the panentheistic understanding of deity, God includes our choices in the divine life; we, in turn, include God's inclusion of our choices in our own subsequent decisions. We feel God's feeling of us. The world is God's body, "the living garment of deity" (Plato). This awareness of God's awareness is the meaning of the existential faith we discussed above, as well as the fundamental meaning of conscience and divine judgment. Whatever we are explicitly aware of, we are at least implicitly aware of as included in the divine life, and, in this sense, "God constitutes the essential and inclusive object of our awareness."[44] Thus, God acts on the world by reacting to it:

> To alter us he has only to alter himself. God's unique power over us is his partly self-determined being as our inclusive object of awareness. . . . it is by molding himself that God molds us, by presenting at each moment a partly new ideal or order of preference which our unself-conscious awareness takes as object, and thus renders influential upon our entire activity.[45]

To understand clearly the nature of divine activity in the world is to see clearly not only what God alone can do but also what we alone can—and must—do. If, as Ogden argues, only God can determine the optimal cosmic order and provide the optimal reaction to our activities within that order, only we can make the local decisions and, by allowing God's judgments to be efficacious in our decisions, make it possible for others, also, to create themselves freely (1979a: 88–90). God "will not emancipate us without ourselves—nor will he emancipate others without our participation in his emancipating work of establishing the optimal conditions of their freedom" (ibid.: 92). In the nature of the case, the running of the universe is a cooperative enterprise. If we cannot, by ourselves, emancipate either ourselves or others, we can, by ourselves, see to it that we and others are not emancipated.

If it is to be faithful to the commandment to love God with our *whole* being, our participation in God's emancipatory activity must cover the full range of creaturely need and the full scope of human responsibility. "This means that our returning love for God and for all our fellow creatures in God is in its own way boundless, even as is the prevenient love of God for all of us" (1982a: 158). In our own historical situation, where ideological understandings of human existence function "to justify the interests of a particular group or individual by representing these interests as the claims of disinterested justice" (1986a: 146) and where, therefore, many human beings are denied full freedom by being excluded from active participation in the existing social and cultural order, "our moral respon-

sibility as Christians has to include a specifically political responsibility," namely, the responsibility to change the social order so as
to eliminate injustice (1982a: 163). In this sense, then, "once given
modern historical consciousness . . . the praxis of love and justice
that scripture undoubtedly does attest faith to be can be rightly interpreted only as being or essentially including the praxis of liberation . . . whereby the existing order itself is so transformed as to
include all the others who must still suffer the oppression of being
excluded from it" (1986a: 148–49). "Christian theology today *must*
be conceived as a theology of liberation" (ibid.: 150).

Toward the end of each of his two books on christology, *Christ
without Myth* (1961) and *The Point of Christology* (1982), Ogden
refers to the Last Judgment scene in Matthew (25:31–46). The point
of the reference is the same in each case, namely, that "the only final
condition for sharing in authentic life that the New Testament lays
down" is not christological or even theological (1961a: 143). "Not a
word is said about believing in Christ, or even in God, but only
about acting to meet the most ordinary of human needs" (1982a:
167). For all the complexity it exhibits as fully critical systematic
theology today, Ogden's work is ultimately at the service of an emi-
nently simple and practical point: that we are to feed the hungry,
clothe the naked, visit the sick and the imprisoned, and act to
change the structures of society which contribute to injustice. Precisely because his theological analysis is so rigorous, Ogden is able
to show why such mundane moral obligations are not a matter of
the mere preference of personal sentiment or political liberalism but
are grounded in the way things are. Theological theory exists finally
for the sake of moral praxis. "Ought" is derived from "is."

Metaphysical gift demands monotheistic faith; monotheistic
faith entails theocentric loyalty; theocentric loyalty requires works
of love. We should not want to be God, nor should we expect God to
do our work.

IV. Conclusion

As we have seen, Ogden's thought as a whole is in the strictest service of a single point which is as simple as it is profound. On his
view, the christocentric point of the Christian religion is a form of
life which consists in that ultimate confidence in and utter loyalty
to God alone which, precisely as such, permits appropriate trust in
and demands proportionate service to all others. The Christian wit-

ness of faith lives from and asks for such a life of both radically monotheistic and theocentric faith and good works, a life which looks to God alone for the courage to meet any and all real creaturely needs and which finds its deepest satisfaction in the contribution it thereby makes to the glory of God.

Notes

1. On Ogden's view, the Christian witness of faith is both the condition of the possibility of Christian theology (1986a: 118) and the object, inquiry about which constitutes Christian theology a field of study distinct from religious studies (ibid.) and philosophy (ibid.: 88). The service of Christian theology (henceforth, simply "theology") to the Christian witness of faith is always both necessary and indirect (1986b: 93–97). References to Ogden's work are taken from the bibliography at the end of this volume.

2. In Ogden's words, "indeed *all* the assertions of a properly Christian theology—are the elaboration [of] the assertion 'Jesus is the Christ'" (1975g: 376).

3. Ogden uses these distinctions of what the Christian witness of faith "has been," what it "is," and what it "should now become" to define and to relate the respective disciplines of "historical," "systematic," and "practical theology" (1986a: 7–15). In proceeding in such exegetical fashion, we are trying to credit Harnack's dictum, cited by Ogden, that "if history never has the last word in theology, it always has the first"(ibid.: 10).

4. As Marxsen observes in his contribution to this volume, the term "implicit christology" "is problematic insofar as it first emerges in retrospect from the standpoint of an already explicit christology" (p. 48). While the *term* is problematic in this respect, this need not be so of the point that it is meant to make. For Marxsen's most comprehensive exegetical discussion of the christology of the "Jesus-," "Christ-," and "Jesus Christ-kerygma," see idem, "Christology in the New Testament," in *Interpreter's Dictionary of the Bible,* supplementary volume (Nashville: Abingdon Press, 1976), pp. 146–56.

5. In the case of the Matthean Beatitudes, the words are offered as coming from the mouth of one presented as having gone "up on the mountain" to speak with them (Matt. 5:1). The role of the speaker is thus qualified as that of one who has come "not to abolish, but rather to fulfill" the law and the prophets (5:17). Jesus has come to matter, and precisely as he whose activity is experienced as soteriologically decisive.

6. It should be stressed that there is nothing necessary about this development. In fact, it seems not to have happened (or perhaps to have happened only in the most modest way) in the Gospel of Thomas. For a recent discussion of christology in Thomas, see Stevan L. Davies, *The Gospel of Thomas and Christian Wisdom* (New York: Seabury Press, 1983), especially chap. 5.

7. See especially Willi Marxsen, *Der Exeget als Theologe* (Gütersloh:

Gütersloher Verlagshaus Gerd Mohn, 1968), "Jesus hat viele Namen" (pp. 214–25).

8. See, for instance, Willi Marxsen, *The New Testament as the Church's Book* (Philadelphia: Fortress Press, 1972), pp. 116–21.

9. Ogden, 1975g: 393f., citing ibid., pp. 118f.

10. For the distinction of function and status, see Nelson Pike, *God and Timelessness* (New York: Schocken Books, 1970), pp. 31 ff., and Philip E. Devenish, "Divinity and Dipolarity: Thomas Erskine and Charles Hartshorne on What Makes God 'God'," *Journal of Religion* 62 (October 1982): 348–54.

11. See Willi Marxsen, *Die Sache Jesu geht weiter* (Gütersloh: Gütersloher Verlagshaus Gerd Mohn, 1976), pp. 74–78.

12. These are Ogden's examples (1982a: 74).

13. This is an important point—or rather, contains several important points. While Ogden holds, with Bultmann, that "neither do the gospels speak of Jesus' own faith nor does the kerygma make any reference to Jesus' faith," he fully realizes that this is an exegetical judgment open to qualification by further exegetical study (1982a: 73). In any case, Ogden argues, statements in the New Testament concerning the course of Jesus' life are not what he calls the "empirical-historical assumptions about who Jesus actually was" that they may at first appear to be but rather "existential-historical assertions about Jesus as he truly is, which is to say, as he is believed to be by those who bear witness to him" (ibid.: 73f.). Moreover, exegesis confirms that such statements about the character or faith of Jesus are made "not by way of grounding this assertion but simply [as] one of the ways of formulating it" (ibid.: 74). Further, these two points are distinct from the question whether the "faith of Jesus," in the sense of "the subjective faith *by which* he believed" or, more precisely, Jesus' "self-understanding," can be either identified or shown to be true and authentic (ibid.: 68f.). This Ogden has consistently answered in the negative. As he puts it, "The conclusion is inescapable that one cannot possibly answer the question whether the conditions necessary for making this assertion are in fact satisfied" (ibid.: 70,; see also 1962c and 1964b; 1985d). Finally, whether such conditions are satisfied (or even satisfiable) or not historically, such empirical-historical claims as they may underlie are, in any case, as Ogden has argued throughout his career, theologically irrelevant (1961a: 85–88, 181; 1962c; 1962d: 214; 1975g: 392; 1982a: 50–61; 1985d: 54–58).

14. Van A. Harvey, *The Historian and the Believer: The Morality of Historical Knowledge and Christian Belief* (New York: Macmillan, 1966), pp. 267–75.

15. Willi Marxsen, "The Limit to the Possibility of Christological Assertions," in this volume p. 51.

16. Ibid.; see also idem, "Die sogenannten Heilsereignisse zwischen Karfreitag und Pfingsten," in *Die Sache Jesu geht weiter* (Gütersloh: Gütersloher Verlagshaus Gerd Mohn, 1976), pp. 72–81.

17. For an extended argument in support of this point, see Philip E. Devenish, "The So-called Resurrection of Jesus and Explicit Christian Faith: Wittgenstein's Philosophy and Marxsen's Exegesis as Linguistic Therapy," *Journal of the American Academy of Religion* 51 (June 1983): 171–90.

18. What is not beside the point, however, is that while, on Ogden's view, christology does not *contain* any "more" than "God's own gift and demand to my existence," precisely as the event of witness whereby it is constituted, christology *is* more, namely, this gift and demand "actually represented to me as a historical event and hence . . . not merely [as] an idea or general truth" (1975g: 385). As he can also express it, "*what* Christian revelation reveals to us is nothing new, since such truths as it makes explicit must already be known to us implicitly in every moment of our existence. But *that* this revelation occurs does reveal something new to us in that, as itself event, it is the occurrence in our history of the transcendent event of God's love" (1986a: 43f.). Indeed, that this event takes place simply *is* the point of christology.

19. On Ogden's view, Christianity makes this claim for itself in a very specific sense. According to him, what is "*immediately* and *proximately* necessary to our authenticity" is that "original self-presentation of God that is the constitutive event of all human existence" and which he calls "original revelation" (1986a: 39). However, human beings also have need for "the *objectification* of existence, in the sense of its full and adequate understanding at the level of explicit thought and speech" (ibid.: 41). It is just the event of such "decisive revelation" as this that Christian revelation claims to be. Insofar as it is, it is in being thus "mediately and remotely necessary" to human authenticity that the event of Christian revelation constitutes Christianity "the religion."

20. See also "Faith and Existence in the Philosophy of F. H. Jacobi" in this volume, where Brian Gerrish discusses Jacobi's notion of existential faith and compares it to Ogden's.

21. As Ogden explains, "What I mean by 'basic confidence' is, in Heideggerian terms, [an] 'existential' (*Existenzial*)" (1966a: 128 n. 32), that is, in Heidegger's own language not an "ontic" term identifying "a property which Dasein sometimes has and sometimes does not have, and *without* which it could *be* just as well as it could with it," but rather "an ontological-structural concept" which designates "the Being of a possible way of Being-in-the-world." Martin Heidegger, *Being and Time*, trans. John Macquarrie and Edward Robinson (New York: Harper and Row, 1962), pp. 83–84.

22. Significantly, normative disputes are always about *what* the standards of morality are, rather than *whether* there are standards. Even ethical relativism adheres to group standards, and Jean-Paul Sartre's attempt to demonstrate that "everything is permitted" actually concludes, as Ogden demonstrates, that it is not permitted to act in such a way as to diminish human freedom. See Ogden's essay, "The Strange Witness of Unbelief," in *The Reality of God* (New York: Harper and Row, 1966), pp. 120–43.

23. William James, "The Will to Believe," in George I. Mavrodes, ed., *The*

Rationality of Belief in God (Englewood Cliffs, N.J.: Prentice-Hall, 1970), p. 167.

24. Alfred North Whitehead, *Process and Reality: An Essay in Cosmology,* corrected edition, ed. David Ray Griffin and Donald W. Sherburne (New York: The Free Press, 1978), p. 42.

25. Albert Camus, "The Riddle," *Atlantic Monthly,* June 1986, p. 85.

26. For discussion of this point, see our reviews of Hans Küng's *Does God Exist?:* Philip E. Devenish, "Christianity Confronts Modernity," *The Journal of Religion* 60, no. 1 (January 1980): 72–81, and George L. Goodwin, "Nihilism Overcome?" *Religious Studies Review* 8, no. 2 (April 1982): 143–46.

27. In the Preface to the paperback edition of *The Reality of God,* Ogden acknowledges a distinction between "the completely general sense" of the word "God" "to mean the objective ground of our basic confidence in reality itself" and "the distinctively theistic sense" of the word "God" (1977a: x–xi). "The burden of theistic argument is to show that theism's constitutive concept of 'God' is not only *a* way of conceptualizing the ground of our faith in the worth of life but also the *only* way, in the sense of being the most appropriate way in which this can be done. For this reason, to establish 'the reality of God' in the distinctively theistic sense of that phrase logically requires that one establish more than 'the reality of faith' and its objective ground" (ibid., xi). In what follows, we will attempt to show that Ogden's appropriation of a neoclassical theistic conceptuality is an argument not only that existential faith is grounded in "the God who transcends the God of the religions" but also that "the God of theism" is the most appropriate conceptual representation of the objective ground of our basic confidence (ibid.)

28. Charles Hartshorne, "The Formally Possible Doctrines," in *Man's Vision of God and the Logic of Theism* (Hamden, Conn.: Archon Books, 1964), pp. 1–56.

29. The appropriation is not wholesale. Recently Ogden has argued that assertions about God can be either literal or symbolic but not analogical. Because Hartshorne's neoclassical metaphysics is a categorial metaphysics which employs both analogical and literal assertions, Ogden concludes that it must be replaced by a transcendental neoclassical metaphysics which employs literal assertions only. See *The Point of Christology* (San Francisco: Harper and Row, 1982), pp. 135–45, and "The Experience of God: Critical Reflections on Hartshorne's Theory of Analogy," in *Existence and Actuality: Conversations with Charles Hartshorne,* ed. John B. Cobb, Jr., and Franklin I. Gamwell (Chicago: University of Chicago Press, 1984), pp. 16–37. Hartshorne replies to Ogden's criticism in his contribution below; see pp. 186–88.

30. Hartshorne contends that metaphysical categories—such as being-becoming, necessity-contingency, immutability-change, absolute-relative—always come in pairs of ultimate contraries, so that the meaning of one term requires its polar contrary. For example, immutability is an ab-

straction from changing actualities, and what is concretely changing contains an abstract aspect of immutability. See "A Logic of Ultimate Contrasts" in Charles Hartshorne, *Creative Synthesis and Philosophic Method* (LaSalle, Ill.: Open Court, 1970), pp. 99–130.

31. *Summa Theologica*, vol. I, trans. Fathers of the English Dominican Province (New York: Benziger Brothers, 1947), p. 66 (Ia, 13, 7 in corpore); cited by Ogden in 1966a: 48.

32. See especially the following books by Charles Hartshorne: *Beyond Humanism* (Lincoln, Neb.: University of Nebraska Press, 1968); *Man's Vision of God and the Logic of Theism* (Chicago: Willett, Clark, 1941), reprinted by Archon Books, 1964; and, with William L. Reese, *Philosophers Speak of God* (Chicago: University of Chicago Press, 1953).

33. This is the logic of Ogden's argument in "On Revelation" (1986a: 22–44). "The special revelation affirmed to be decisive by the Christian witness of faith is simply the full and adequate explication of God's original revelation to human existence" (ibid., 42). What is presented to me originally in each moment as grace is now re-presented to me decisively in Christian terms as the grace of God.

34. See especially: Alfred North Whitehead, "Immortality," in *The Philosophy of Alfred North Whitehead*, ed. Paul A. Schilpp (Evanston: Northwestern University Press, 1984), pp. 682–700; Charles Hartshorne, "Time, Death, and Everlasting Life," in *The Logic of Perfection* (LaSalle, Ill.: Open Court, 1962), pp. 245–62; Schubert Ogden, "The Promise of Faith" (1966a: 206–30) and "The Meaning of Christian Hope" (1975e).

35. As John Calvin puts it, "man's nature, so to speak, is a perpetual factory of idols" (*Institutes of the Christian Religion*, ed. John T. McNeill, trans. Ford Lewis Battles, 2 vols. [Philadelphia: Westminster Press, 1960], 1:108). As we have suggested, not only one's own but even the doctrine of subjective immortality have proven to be favorite idols.

36. Franklin I. Gamwell's extended argument that "a comprehensive moral principle must be a specification of a comprehensive evaluative variable that is metaphysical" may be regarded as the most important contribution to date on this issue (*Beyond Preference: Liberal Theories of Independent Associations* [Chicago: University of Chicago Press, 1984], p. 150). See also Gamwell's "Religion and the Justification of Moral Claims," *Journal of Religious Ethics* 2 (Spring 1983): 35–61, his contribution to this volume, and his "The Divine Good: An Essay in Modern Moral Theory" (unpublished) for considerations which lead to a neoclassically theistic interpretation of such a variable.

37. The following remarks are based on Ogden's unpublished 1979 notes, "On Intrinsic and Instrumental Value."

38. Whitehead, *Process and Reality*, p. 348.

39. James M. Gustafson, *Can Ethics Be Christian?* (Chicago: University of Chicago Press, 1975), pp. 82–116.

40. H. Richard Niebuhr, *The Responsible Self* (New York: Harper and Row, 1963), p. 125.

41. James M. Gustafson, *Ethics from a Theocentric Perspective*, vol. 1: *Theology and Ethics* (Chicago: University of Chicago Press, 1981), p. 184.

42. The significance of this line of argument for the definition of omnipotence is worked out in Philip E. Devenish, "Omnipotence, Creation, Perfection: Kenny and Aquinas on the Power and Action of God," *Modern Theology* 1, no. 2 (January 1985): 105–17.

43. Charles Hartshorne, "A New Look at the Problem of Evil," in *Current Philosophical Issues: Essays in Honor of Curt John Ducasse*, ed. Frederick C. Dommeyer (Springfield, Ill.: Charles C. Thomas, 1966), p. 210.

44. Charles Hartshorne, *The Divine Relativity: A Social Conception of God* (New Haven: Yale University Press, 1948), p. 140.

45. Ibid., pp. 139, 142.

Part I

The Appropriateness of
Christian Theology:
Essays in Biblical Studies

Chapter One

The Limit to the Possibility of Christological Assertions

WILLI MARXSEN

These days traditional christology is often characterized as christology from above, which is contrasted with a christology from below.

The basic form of christology from above is the statement about the incarnation of God. To focus as sharply as possible on what it is about, we should formulate it more precisely: it is about *God's* incarnation. God is the starting point. It is here that the doctrine of the trinity has its place, along with talk of the preexistence of Jesus (Christ), of his kenosis, which finds expression in the obedience of the Son and issues in the understanding of the life and work of Jesus, of his suffering and death, his resurrection and exaltation. This yields a complete picture, into which one can and does insert individual assertions from the New Testament writings. The danger in this christology from above is that the *vere homo* of the human being, Jesus, cannot really be taken seriously and usually, in fact, is not taken seriously.

But it is here that christology from below begins, precisely with the human being, Jesus, and, thus, with something self-evident. Only here the opposite difficulty surfaces, namely, that we remain with the human being, Jesus, do not reach the *vere deus*, and thus no longer attain to a christology.

In this essay I would like to try to show that we must begin "from below," and that we go beyond the limit to possible assertions the moment we reverse the direction of the assertions.

I

It might be well to remember that this problem goes back to Hermann Samuel Reimarus (1694–1768). With him began the quest for the historical Jesus, that is, for Jesus "as he actually was," prior to all human interpretation. This Jesus has to be reconstructed, since what we have in the New Testament writings is a picture of Jesus that has already been painted over. The painting-over was occasioned by "Easter" and was absolutely necessary for the disciples if they were to pursue their "purpose" and carry it through. The historical Jesus, as Reimarus saw it, had failed in his own "purpose." He wanted to be the political Messiah of his people, expected a popular uprising in Jerusalem, and died on the cross with the admission of his defeat, "My God, my God, why have you forsaken me?" The disciples, who had hoped to become ministers in the Messiah's realm, had their dreams dashed. Nevertheless, having no desire to return to life as usual, they stole his corpse and, fifty days later, asserted his resurrection. They took up ideas from the book of Daniel, made out of the Messiah (a human being) the Son of Man (a divine being from heaven), and proclaimed his return in the near future. Now they could continue their comfortable life. But they were able to achieve their "purpose" only by painting over the presentation of the historical Jesus on the basis of their new picture of him. They wanted to be able to appeal to the "historical Jesus," but, naturally, they could not present him historically. Moreover, as his return was delayed, they had to postpone its date.

Even if Reimarus's conclusion is not worth discussing, we ought all the same to realize that his way of posing the question has remained operative down to the present and, with it, some of the structures of his proposals for answering it. Thus, it is still widely taken as settled that christology began with Easter. To be sure, Reimarus thought he knew wherein "Easter" consisted, while today there is no consensus about this. Nevertheless, this is when christology is supposed to have begun. After all, the view is still advocated that the presentation of the life and work of Jesus is determined by the "Easter faith." Finally, we still concern ourselves with the question of the relation of the earthly one to the exalted one ("continuity") or else of the exalted one to the earthly one ("identity"). That the proclamation of Jesus implies a christology, which then became explicit in the community (according to Rudolf Bultmann), Reimarus would certainly have disputed, but he would not have disputed the identity of the exalted one with the earthly one. This was certainly (to express it in Bultmann's terms) shrunk down by Reimarus into the mere "that" of his having existed. It was limited to his name only. The "what" and "how" could not have played any role, since, if the disciples had presented these historically, they would have undermined the foundation of their "purpose."

Thus, Reimarus has had a lasting effect through his way of posing the question. Whoever accepts this way thereby invariably prejudges the structure of the answer, even if its content appears completely different. For our problem, Reimarus's conclusion may be formulated in this way: from the very beginning christology is always christology from above. But this has no value whatever, because it rests on a deception. From below, that is, from the historical Jesus, christology is impossible.

II

What has been worked out thus far suggests that we examine Reimarus's way of posing the question. Actually, this could already have happened with the introduction of form criticism in the 1920s. Yet form criticism achieved only the sense that an answer to the question of the historical Jesus had once again been made difficult. The quest itself was not generally given up. Obviously, the terminology that had developed in the so-called liberal theology had had too great an influence, notably, in the distinction between "historically genuine" and "construction of the community." When form criticism now emphasized that all Jesus-traditions emerged in the community, so that one always had to do with the constructions of the community (which in principle is certainly correct), taking over the term "community" proved to be fateful. For it was immediately taken to mean the "post-Easter community." But if one moved in this community, there resulted a clear separation between the time before and the time after Easter. This in turn induced one to inquire from the time after Easter (that is, on the basis of the constructions of the community) back to the time before Easter, unless one were willing completely to renounce the quest for the earthly Jesus. Thus began the so-called "new quest" of Jesus (James M. Robinson), in the course of which it was supposed to be made clear whether Christian faith (and with it, christology) had any "support in the historical Jesus" (Gerhard Ebeling). Could this succeed?

This route would not have been taken (or not taken so easily) if the term "community" had been renounced by form criticsm and if the issue had been formulated by saying instead that we owe all existing and reconstructable Jesus-traditions to people, because not a line has been passed on to us by Jesus himself. If, instead of "community," we say in a more general way "people," prejudgments that are bound to the term "community" immediately go by the board. Whether the community has existed only since Easter can remain open, since this depends on how one defines the term. But it is not clear that there had to be an Easter at all in order for people to tell about Jesus. That the news of him resounded throughout Galilee was, indeed, first formulated only later, and yet it could have been the case (even historically). This immediately suggests the conjecture that the bearers of the oldest traditions are to be sought in Galilee, not in the circle of those who came to Jerusalem with Jesus and then evidently stayed there. Whether we can reconstruct these pre-Easter traditions with the requisite certitude may remain open. Yet nothing speaks against the supposition that the material of the synoptic tradition (formulated later) has its roots there: people told about Jesus. And then it is striking that even much later people still told about him in ways in which they could have told and did tell about him during his lifetime. That faith in the risen one influenced the formation of these stories cannot be concluded from the texts themselves (apart from a few late exceptions). One can indeed establish further development but not any painting-over. (This is first to be found, and then in a thoroughgoing way, in the Gospel of John.) Whoever alleges "the influence of Easter" on the individual units of the synoptic tradition must present the evidence for this. But one may not argue on the basis of the date of their emergence, but must rather verify the alleged influence from the texts themselves. Whether the authors and those who passed on these texts knew anything about Easter we cannot decide. In their texts, they do not permit this to be recognized. Here we are evidently dealing with a completely independent line of tradition in which the Easter motif has been introduced only very late; the understanding of the death of Jesus as a saving death, however, not at all (except for Mark 10:45; 14:24).

Even if we were to succeed in reconstructing Jesus-traditions from the time of Jesus' activity, we would still not thereby have reached the historical Jesus, in the sense of "Jesus prior to every interpretation by people." Thus we ought, on the basis of Reimarus, always precisely to define this term. There is no method with the help of which we can simply leap over the people who told about Jesus. Two considerations may make this clear.

First, there is no doubt that Jesus said and did more than was later told about him. The selection of what was told goes back to the people who told it. They told only what was important to them. Whether Jesus would have made just this selection, whether the same or perhaps quite different things were important to him, cannot be ascertained by any method. The second consideration is more important still. When people told about Jesus, they always did so as they had understood his proclamation and action—and also as they had understood him. However, whether Jesus understood what he said and did in the same way as these people understood it, and whether he understood himself in the same way as they understood him and then said that he understood himself cannot be ascertained by any method. Of course, the contrary cannot be ascertained, either!

From this it follows that Jesus is never to be reached except together with the people who told about him. But this is no longer "the historical Jesus," to the quest for whom we have devoted ourselves since Reimarus. The quest cannot bypass the people doing the telling. But if we must recognize that the historical Jesus is not to be reached, must we also give up the quest for him? Even the formulation of this question suggests that a goal might be reachable which, for reasons of method, we know is not reachable. For this reason, as has already occasionally been proposed, the quest must be reformulated more precisely as "the historical quest for Jesus." Here it is not the goal but simply the direction that is indicated. Thus it remains open how far we will get when we inquire in this direction. But if we ask for Jesus historically, we never get further than the people who told about him.

With this, however, we are already in the midst of the christological problem. For, however we qualify Jesus, or would like to, it must be recognized that this is indeed only possible "from below," because it is precisely to people that we owe the oldest qualifications of Jesus. This is what is now to be elaborated.

III

There are three groups of people who could have told and, indeed, did tell about Jesus: neutral observers, opponents, and followers. They all encountered the same historical Jesus. But the pictures they draw in their telling about him are nevertheless different. Even so, the only pictures of Jesus that were preserved and included in the material of the synoptic tradition are those that arose within the last-mentioned group, the followers.

Here we have to do with people who were impressed by Jesus and upon whom he in some way left his stamp. What these people wanted to achieve by means of their pictures of Jesus one can formulate rather generally in this way: they wanted either to awaken interest in Jesus or to sustain an interest in him that had already been awakened. To this extent, the things they told were always tendentious. In the terminology we have become accustomed to using, they were "kerygmata," not "historical reports."

If now (following Bultmann) it is repeatedly stated that through Easter the proclaimer became the proclaimed, then this is in part a misleading, in part an incorrect, statement. It is quite correct (historically) that the proclaimer became the proclaimed. But this does not really help us, because the proclamation of the proclaimer (the proclamation of the historical Jesus) is not to be reached. We cannot get behind the pictures of Jesus, and by means of these pictures Jesus is always already proclaimed (occasionally he is also a proclaimer). But since this was true from the very beginning, even in his own lifetime, that Jesus was proclaimed has nothing whatever to do with Easter.

We should note, however, that Jesus (even from the beginning) was not proclaimed *only* as the proclaimer (that is, as a preacher or teacher). This inadmissible shortcut has not infrequently proven fateful in its implications. Jesus was proclaimed much more as one who did things, and his proclamation was only a part of what he did. If we direct our interest strictly to this part, we tear asunder what belongs inseparably together. (This is one of the reasons why the contemporary discussion of the Sermon on the Mount almost always miscarries.) The pictures of Jesus we can reconstruct by means of literary criticism show clearly that it was the Jesus who did things who impressed people by means of his activity, his conduct, and his preaching. And those who were impressed by what he did represent it in manifold ways and with much color in their pictures of Jesus. If we look at the individual pictures of Jesus and compare them, the impression that first emerges is apt to be rather bewildering.

As we then set about collecting and arranging this many-sided impression of Jesus' activity, so as to give it some kind of order, there emerges what we can call "implicit christology." The term is problematic insofar as it first emerges in retrospect from the standpoint of an already explicit christology. However, it is once again a shortcut if we say that Jesus' proclamation implies a christology (Bultmann). It is rather the experienced activity of Jesus that is to be characterized as an implicit christology. It is an *implicit* christology, because it is one at first qualified only by the activity of Jesus, not yet by the one who was acting. But it is an implicit *christology*, because any activity qualified in this way was asserted to be exclusively that of Jesus.

If we summarize the experiences people had in response to Jesus' activity and then asserted as qualifying it, we may speak of this activity as "eschatological." This means, more precisely, that people interpreted Jesus' activity as so many occurrences of God's reign already breaking through into this old aeon in the present; as so many anticipations of God's future recurring again and again (hence the individual traditions!).

This could be expressed very differently in each individual case. The instances of table fellowship which Jesus offered (and which one could easily misunderstand, in modern parlance, as "social action") were asserted to be anticipations of the "marriage feast" of the last days. Healings (which one could always misunderstand as miracles or as caused by the devil) were asserted to be accomplished by the "finger of God." We could also interpret the activity of Jesus as an eschatological occurrence by expressing it with the help of the terminology of expectation (Matt. 11:5), etc. In so doing, it was always clear that this qualification of Jesus' action was not unambiguous, that it could not simply be read off of the action itself. One realized throughout that there were people who interpreted Jesus' activity differently.

This ambiguity (which was, of course, responded to unambiguously by those who were impressed by Jesus' activity) then brought it about that out of "implicit christology" (explicit) christology emerged. Even if the transitions in the history of the material of the synoptic tradition are fluid, the movement in which the transitions take place is always the same: from the activity of Jesus one draws a conclusion about the one who performed it. Somewhat more precisely, whoever saw something special in the activity of Jesus qualified its agent on the basis of what was special about the activity, with the help of concepts that were available to be used. He who enacted the "eschatological activity" was qualified as the "eschatological messenger," generally by titles that were applied to him.

Here one usually points to "traditional" titles: Son of David, Messiah, Holy One of Israel, and so forth. But caution is called for. Not all of the titles grew out of the individual traditions themselves. Many were imported from the outside. This is different in different cases and also happened at different times in the history of the material of the synoptic tradition. Moreover, precisely in the case of these traditional titles it needs to be borne in mind that they have a long history behind them through which they have taken on a great breadth of meaning and that others also could and did make use of them. On the basis of the activity of Jesus, only a single sector of this breadth of meaning was meant to be taken over. But since the whole title was taken over, this led (and still leads) to overinterpretations.

We can recognize the peculiar nature of such christologizing much more clearly in the case of the title "bridegroom," for the very reason that it did not become a proper title. It occurs in the controversy about fasting (Mark 2:18–20). In contrast to the disciples of John and to the Pharisees, the disciples of Jesus do not fast. They do not need to do so, for, due to the activity of Jesus, they are now already guests at the wedding feast. (Without the metaphor: if through Jesus they have truly become disciples, they are already now living the saved life that is actually expected only after the turn of the age.) Thus the disciples do not need to gain entry to the feast of the last days by means of prior fasting (that is, by their own achievement). They already live as guests at the wedding feast now. If, then, they understand what the activity of Jesus has accomplished for them, they can qualify the one who has enacted it as "bridegroom."

The situation is similar in taking over the designation "Son of Man." The Son of Man is a figure who participates in the judgment, by granting or refusing entrance to the reign of God. But since Jesus has already lived the reign of God for people time and again through his activity, what matters is how they respond to this invitation: Do they accept it or not? Precisely on this basis, the Son of Man will one day make his judgment. What is to be noted is that, in the oldest texts concerning the Son of Man (Luke 12:8; Mark 8:38), Jesus and the Son of Man are still expressly differentiated. The activity of Jesus anticipates the activity of the Son of Man. But since the activity of Jesus now is to be understood as the Son of Man's activity (and, in fact, is so understood), it is natural for us to apply the title to him. To be sure, this happens only indirectly (and insofar, this title is different from the other christological titles). Moreover, the development within the material of the synoptic tradition is disputed in its particulars. Yet there is no doubt that at the end of the development the result is an identification of Jesus with the Son of Man. Now we can say, "The (once only expected) Son of Man was already here." The starting point for this development was that people interpreted the activity of Jesus as an anticipation of eschatological occurrence. From this standpoint, they then qualified Jesus himself.

So long as we see this connection between implicit and explicit christology, christology is relatively unproblematic. It always starts out with the experience that people have had with the activity of Jesus. At the time, various conceptions, with their correspondingly distinct terminologies, were available to qualify his activity. These, then, determined how Jesus was qualified, precisely with the help of different concepts and, correspondingly, in distinct terminologies.

This all became problematic, however, when the connection between implicit and explicit christology was severed.

IV

Explicit christology now became a new and independent starting point for further development. With this, a *metabasis eis allo genos* occurred. The *qualifications* of Jesus that had arisen out of an understanding of his activity were transformed into assertions about his *quality*. One now took these assertions for granted. That at first one could hardly have noticed the difficulties that then arose is clear enough. Nevertheless, one crossed over onto a track that led in the wrong direction, took this development as a given, and thereby wound up in difficulties. For one now made completely different assertions about the quality of Jesus that could not be harmonized with each other but that one nevertheless tried somehow to harmonize. But how are we to explain the divine sonship of Jesus if he was the Messiah? How are we to explain that Jesus was the Son of David if he was the Son of Man? Christology from below was changed into a christology from above, thereby preprogramming, as it were, the later christological controversies. Since one now started out with the assertions about the quality of Jesus, one overlooked that one would sometime have to justify them. But can one justify them at all?

It is dangerous, moreover, to work with the motif of faith here. The word "faith" now receives a completely different content. Earlier, faith was entrusting oneself to the acting Jesus, and when he was qualified on this basis such a qualification always had the character of a homology. Here, if I may express it so, explicit christology could really only be sung. But if we start out from explicit christology, what has previously been sung becomes knowledge about the quality of Jesus. And this is a completely different thing! But, then, can we still use the word "faith" in this context?

We can clarify this problem yet again by means of this consideration: even during New Testament times, individual titles of Jesus were developed further into independent stories. The narratives of the birth and of the baptism of Jesus are examples of this. The title "Son of God" is presented in the narratives in different ways. How are such stories to be dealt with at a later time?

As individual stories (which, to be sure, must first be reconstructed!), they can still always be interpreted (if we expressly reflect on the way in which they came to be) so as to show that, in them, explicit christological assertions have been led a step farther away from the activity of Jesus. In this case, they remain "songs." They do so, however, only when exegesis does not confine itself to the (reconstructed) text of the stories themselves but rather takes account of the prehistory of the text. Then, in spite of the completely different material that the authors have used in the baptism and the birth stories, there are no tensions whatever between them.

But these stories no longer encounter us as individual stories but rather stand at the beginning of the synoptic gospels. In this way, the direction is reversed: the later stage, literarily (the "song"), becomes the earlier one, temporally (a presentation of past history). Qualification has become quality (this holds true at least for Matthew and Luke), and now there emerges the irresolvable tension: From what time has Jesus been the Son of God—since his baptism or from his birth?

If, then, one reads the Gospel of John in analogy with those of Matthew and Luke (which soon happened, but which we may not do), the divine sonship which had been reflected farther back to a new and still "earlier" starting point is also reversed. With the preexistence christology that then arises, christology from above has almost reached its final form.

Now one could formulate the statement, "God became man." But this is not, as some like to say, a statement of faith. It is not so, at any rate, in the sense that one could start with it and would have to believe its content. What others have formulated as a *consequence* of their faith may not be made into the *basis* of faith for those who come later. This is how the statement came to be made: People entrusted themselves to the acting Jesus of Nazareth (a human being!). In connection with the experience of thus entrusting themselves (that is, with faith), they were able to qualify his activity and, on the basis of the activity thus qualified, also to qualify him as the one who had enacted it. But since what they experienced in faith was so overwhelming, they were not able (as a consequence of their faith) to qualify highly enough the one who had aroused this faith short of claiming, finally, that "in him God has encountered us." Thus "Jesus (subject) is God (predicate)," is a christologically possible assertion.

But if we take assertions that arose as a consequence of faith and reverse them, christology from below becomes christology from above. And with this, we go beyond the limit to the possibility of christological assertions, because we treat a statement that is only ever possible as a derivative one, as if it were primary.

V

Of the various objections one might raise against what has been proposed, two at least ought to be briefly responded to. Of course, hints must here take the place of detailed justifications.

One might object, first of all, that in a christology from below the priority of Jesus Christ (or even the priority of God) gets lost and the priority of man is put in its place. But this would be a misunderstanding.

People who have experienced the activity of Jesus always presuppose this activity (*extra nos*). The activity of Jesus remains the *proteron physai*. But it is always people who put their experiences of Jesus' activity into words. For this reason, every christology is a christology formulated by people. Whoever thinks that we must nevertheless begin christology with Jesus (for the sake of the *extra nos*) must show how we can leap over or eliminate the *proteron pros hemas* in order to reach the postulated starting point.

But we must ask further: Does not even a christology from above (in spite of the possible denial of its proponents) remain in fact a christology from below? The emergence of explicit from implicit christology (and thus from christology from below) is indeed ignored, and yet it is not thereby disposed of. For even an isolated explicit christology is formulated by people. And these people must now explain how they came to this formulation. If they justify it on the basis of their own faith in the present, we once again have christology from below.

Does not the expression *Deus dixit* also rest on a hasty inference? For whatever content follows this introductory formula has been formulated by people. They, not "God," are responsible for their formulations.

Second, one might object that I have, so to speak, gone "right past Easter" with my whole line of argument. Must not christology be christology from above, at least since and because of Easter?

Now, no consensus exists today about how the content of Easter is to be defined. (Reimarus thought he knew what it was: the deception of the disciples.) Today we ordinarily speak of the content of Easter as "Jesus' resurrection by God." But if Jesus is to be asserted as the one whom God has raised, does not a christology from above present itself straightway? I still believe that such a christology is impossible.

To begin with, we must ask again how the assertion that God raised Jesus from the dead originated. A consideration (admittedly hypothetical) can clarify the problem. A person who is keeping watch over the grave sees the dead Jesus come to life. Thus he sees Jesus rising. If this person now formulates this as "God has raised Jesus from the dead," he thereby infers from an occurrence to its author, in that he interprets a visible occurrence by qualifying it. This christological assertion would, therefore, have originated from below.

But since any such witness is a fiction, we can only refer to "visions." However these are portrayed, we have access to them only through assertions by people which (with the exception of Paul's) come to us only at second or third hand. Yet even if we ignore this, we do not get further than the claim of people that, after Jesus' death, something occurred to them which they assert to be a seeing of Jesus. On the basis of this experience, either these people themselves or others who heard of their experience make an assertion by means of which they both interpret and qualify the occurrence: "The resurrection of Jesus by God made possible the experienced occurrence."

Thus talk about the resurrection of Jesus is always a derivative assertion. Only by a reversal does christology from above emerge out of christology from below.

I would like to summarize these considerations with a statement that, in my view, has the significance of a principle for the issues dealt with here: It is a "mortal sin" of theological work to take assertions that have arisen in one direction and to argue with them in the opposite direction.

Translation by Philip E. Devenish

Chapter Two

The Foundations of Christian Ethics
According to Romans 12:1–2

HANS DIETER BETZ

The difficulties the apostle Paul experienced in conceptualizing his ethics within the overall framework of his theology forced him to rethink and revise his ideas at several points before arriving at what he apparently regarded as the final version of his thought in his last letter, that to the Romans.[1]

What were the problems that forced Paul to rethink his theology and ethics? How did he attempt to solve the problems? Why did earlier solutions prove insufficient? Why did Paul consider the final version in Romans better than the previous ones? Of what precisely does the solution in Romans consist? These are the major questions that must be raised with regard to Paul's concepts of ethics, although of course a brief essay such as the present one can hardly give more than sketchy replies at best.

I

Paul's problems were both general and specific. Specific were the actual situations he had to confront; general were the theological means he had at his disposal.

The general problem was that once he had severed the ties with the Jewish Torah, Christian ethics lacked a theological foundation. Christology and soteriology had come to fall on one side of the life of faith, and whatever constituted Christian moral life fell on the other. How were the two sides connected? Did they have to be connected at all? Why not formulate a simple symbiosis of Christian belief in God and Christ on the one side and conformity to popular Graeco-Roman morality on the other? The answer to such a proposal would certainly have to be that not only must the two sides

For a German version of this essay, see *Zeitschrift für Theologie und Kirche* 85 (1988): 199–218: "Das Problem der Grundlagen der paulinischen Ethik (Röm 12, 1–2)."

be connected but also theology must determine what is adequate and what is inadequate about morality. There was, after all, no moral consensus in antiquity about what was and what was not moral. Moreover, even things that may have been morally acceptable everywhere may not necessarily have been in conformity with Christian faith and ethics.

There were other problems as well with what passed as popular morality.[2] One problem was that popular morality already had its own religious foundations. Consisting primarily of proverbial sentences, maxims, images, metaphors, stories, and similar material, popular morality was deeply rooted in folk religion as we encounter it in all cultures of the ancient world. Religiously, therefore, this popular morality was not neutral but pagan, so that its compatibility or incompatibility with moral requirements implicit in the Christian faith had yet to be determined. In the New Testament as well as in later Christian sources, we can observe that the process of sorting things out was part and parcel of what is called paraenesis. The current widely held opinion that early Christianity simply conformed to what passed at the time as popular morality, therefore, does not correspond to what the sources tell us. Rather, the rule had to be here, too: "Test everything; hold on to the good; from every form of evil stay away" (1 Thess. 5:21–22). This rule, however, presupposes standards by which the appropriate can be distinguished from the inappropriate and further implies ethical reflection, which, in turn, requires specifically Christian foundations.

Graeco-Roman popular morality was also influenced and, to some degree, transformed by Greek philosophical ethics. Concepts such as "virtue" (ἀρετή) or "the good" (τὸ ἀγαθόν), which have their origin in Greek philosophy, had become over the centuries a part of popular ethics. Hellenistic popular ethics, which was an amalgam of folk wisdom and Greek philosophical ideas, was, of course, based on the metaphysical foundations of Greek philosophical ethics. Philosophers of the Hellenistic period interpreted these metaphysical foundations in terms of Greek philosophical religion. The prevailing popular ethics was thus religiously charged and from the very outset potentially in conflict with Christian theology.

It follows, then, that Greek philosophical ethics could not provide a suitable foundation for Christian ethics. For the Greeks, the ethics of "virtue" (ἀρετή) was inextricably bound to the concept of the immortality of the soul and the divine origin of "reason" innate in every person—the doctrines most unacceptable to Paul. What other alternatives could he have turned to? Why did he not turn to the teachings of the historical Jesus? He assuredly did not, with the exception of some instances in 1 Corinthians.[3]

The reasons for Paul's refusal to base Christian ethics on the foundations of Jesus' teaching must be sought in the letters of the apostle. He never fully explains his position, but there are sufficient indications of why for him Christian ethics could not simply continue the teaching of the historical Jesus. Paul's position on this point is analogous to the cardinal problem of christology, which Schubert Ogden, defending Rudolf Bultmann, has discussed with such clarity, namely, that the Christian faith is based on the kerygma of the crucified and resurrected Christ and not on the faith of the historical Jesus.[4] Like the other New Testament authors, Paul seems to have realized that Jesus was a Jew and that the word "faith" was religiously inappropriate as a description of Jesus' life as a Jew.[5] "Faith" (πιστεύω, πίστις) is a Christian term describing the *proprium Christianum*, just as "doing" (ποιέω) describes fully what goes on in the religious life of the Jew. Such "doing" is related to the Torah; and gentile Christians, with whom Paul was dealing and for whom as an apostle he was responsible, were by definition outside of the Torah covenant. Thus the ethical teaching of Jesus the Jew, being ipso facto based on the Torah, was inappropriate as a basis for the ethics of gentile Christians. Consequently, Christian ethics, like the Christian faith, had to be based on the kerygma of the crucifixion and resurrection of Christ. The apostle clearly indicates that he was aware of these issues and that, for the reasons given, he did not base his concept of ethics on the ethical teachings of the historical Jesus.

Analogous again to the cardinal problem of christology, this decision did not in principle invalidate everything Jesus had taught. The paraenetical sections in Paul's letters show that he could make good use of teachings going back to the historical Jesus. When he did so, however, those teachings were brought into conformity with the kerygma; they do not claim a higher authority than other paraenetical material, and they are for the most part not explicitly designated as coming from Jesus. The assumption underlying this adaptation was that the teaching of Jesus was not limited exclusively to Jewish Torah piety, an assumption also made by the gentile Christian gospel writers when they included materials from Jesus' teaching in their writings. The teachings they included were selected for their applicability beyond the borderlines of particularly Jewish Torah piety. In other words, once it was clear that the teachings of the historical Jesus could not serve as the foundation for Christian ethics, Paul could use whatever material was in conformity with the kerygma upon which his ethics was to be based.

We have thus determined that the apostle based his Christian ethics on the kerygma of the "Christ crucified" (Χριστὸς ἐσταυρωμένος), as he says, using a form of dogmatic abbreviation.[6] The actual formation of such an ethics and the ethical consequence that would follow from it were questions as controversial in antiquity as in modern times.

How does the kerygma lend itself to be the foundation for ethics? What kind of ethics follows from such an association? Paul's letters reveal that there were several clues leading toward the answers to these questions. Struggling with the problems, the apostle himself tried out several solutions in different letters before arriving at his final concept in Romans.

II

The concept of ethics in 1 Thessalonians reveals the state of Paul's thought at an earlier period of his mission. In 1 Thessalonians 4:1–2, the apostle refers to his ethical teaching as presented at the founding of the church of the Thessalonians. What kind of instruction was this? What was its religious foundation?

Assuming that the readers knew what he was speaking of, Paul simply refers to his earlier instruction in order to repeat those points pertinent to the present context: His comments are both revealing and puzzling.[7] In 4:2 he says, "You know that I gave you certain commandments through the Lord Jesus" (οἴδατε γὰρ τίνας παραγγελίας ἐδώκαμεν ὑμῖν διὰ τοῦ κυρίου Ἰησοῦ). What kind of commandments did he have in mind? Were they the teachings of the historical Jesus, or Paul's own teachings, or the church's teaching authorized by the Lord Jesus? Were they handed over in oral or written form? Unfortunately, Paul does not say. There are, however, clues, or at least possibilities for clues.

The term παραγγελίαι ("commandments"),[8] as well as the "word of the Lord" in 4:15–18, point to teachings that are at least claimed to have originated with the historical Jesus. Their content was ethical, dealing with the subject of "how you must conduct your life and please God" (πῶς δεῖ ὑμᾶς περιπατεῖν καὶ ἀρέσκειν θεῷ [1 Thess.

4:1]).[9] The article (τό)[10] prefacing the statement indicates that Paul had in mind a familiar block of material, perhaps even in written form. Moreover, the words reveal that the ethics was oriented eschatologically: "pleasing God" points to the parousia and eschatological judgment where Christians must appear "undamaged and unblemished in spirit, soul, and body" (5:23).[11] Indeed, the ethics as presented in the letter as a whole goes under the name "sanctification" (ἁγιασμός).[12] Paul assures the readers that they have been made holy by the gift of the Holy Spirit (4:8) and that their present status is one of holiness.[13] The task of Christian ethics is to preserve (τηρέω) this state of holiness up to the Last Judgment (5:23)[14] and this is to be done by the avoidance of all forms of evil and impurity.[15] As scholars have often observed, the terminology here points to baptism as the occasion when the Thessalonians received the spirit and thus indicates baptismal instruction;[16] but baptism is not mentioned in the letter, perhaps because there was no need to do so.

What is the foundation of this ethics, then? It is the cleansing power of the Holy Spirit[17] and hence the soteriology of the crucifixion and resurrection of Jesus Christ.[18] Ethical teaching, even though it may have originated with the historical Jesus, is not the foundation; it serves to preserve the status of salvation. That teaching is then succeeded by Paul's own paraenesis, which serves the same function and carries the same authority.[19]

Whereas the violation of moral rules is not an issue in 1 Thessalonians, such violation has clearly developed into a crisis in the churches of Galatia. In Galatia, not only had some Christians committed acts of grave immorality,[20] but two further matters contributed to the severity of the crisis. First, the Galatian Christians seem to have been ill-prepared for the crisis; Paul had not educated them adequately in advance to handle such a problem. Why did Paul not provide them with theological and ethical resources that would have enabled them to deal with it? Did he himself not foresee the possibility, or even the probability, of Christian sinfulness? Did he underestimate the severity of such a problem? The answers to these questions are far from clear. The fact that Paul's initial instruction must have been elementary and that we see him supplementing it in all of his letters implies that he did not foresee the problems his churches would be having and that at the beginning he did not possess a comprehensive ethical concept that could be applied to every eventuality. Thus the gradually developing nature of Paul's own theology posed problems for his churches that threatened their very existence. These developments on Paul's part also of course explain why he wrote his letters and why these letters, once he was removed from the historical scene, became indispensable doctrinal resources and even holy scripture.

Second, the Galatians, for reasons that may now have become understandable, lent their ears to Jewish-Christian competitors of Paul who offered themselves to the churches.[21] These competitors had what Paul seemingly lacked: their Christian version of the Jewish Torah provided them with a solid base and clear guidelines for ethical behavior. If the Galatians were to carry out what Paul saw them as ready to do, they would accept circumcision and Torah and thus become beneficiaries of the Sinai covenant. Paul himself, however, wrote his letter to the Galatians precisely to defend his earlier theological position and to persuade them again that reliance on the spirit, if properly and faithfully maintained, would be sufficient for the treatment of their problems.[22] Paul therefore did not offer a new concept of ethics in Galatians as compared with 1 Thessalonians; he considered it sufficient to defend and confirm the basic concept he had previously presented.

The Corinthian letters present clear evidence of further erosion of Paul's concepts of ethics. As far as we can conclude from his remarks and intimations, the apostle had to face Corinthian Christians who had not only committed outrageous acts of immorality but did so justifying them by Paul's own theology, in particular his doctrine of spirit and freedom.[23] In other words, Paul's concept of ethics itself had become the pretext for misconduct. In 1 Corinthians, we observe the apostle as he analyzes the Corinthians' understanding of Christian existence (especially in chapters 1–4) and as he establishes guidelines for ethical conduct in those areas where misconduct had occurred (especially in chapters 5–15).[24] The letter fragments assembled in 2 Corinthians show the apostle embroiled in controversy and tumult mainly because of his own apostolic performance. The church appears to be in open rebellion against him, so that Paul desperately scrambles to hang on to his church by whatever means he can (especially the "letter of tears," 2 Cor. 10:1–13:10).[25] The so-called letter of reconciliation (2 Cor. 1:1–2:13; 7:5–16; 13:11–13) is evidence that Paul finally prevailed and could turn to healing the wounds caused by the struggle. The two administrative letters of 2 Corinthians 8 and 9 inform us of the sending of a three-man delegation to Corinth to help reorganize the collection for Jerusalem and, one might suppose, a good deal of the congregational life itself.[26]

III

While Paul did not, and perhaps could not, devote much time and space to the discussion of his foundations of ethics in the Corinthian letters, the situation is different in his letter to the Romans. As a whole, this letter shows that Paul took critical objections to his theology seriously into consideration. In fact, Romans is evidence that, in dealing with these criticisms, Paul subjected his entire theology to substantial revision and expansion. Romans is more than simply a defense of previously held views; it is also the presentation of his fully developed theology in toto, notably revised at certain crucial points.[27]

One of these crucial points is Paul's concept of the foundations of Christian ethics.[28] A complete analysis of all the aspects involving change as well as continuity is impossible at this point; we must limit the present discussion to the important passage of Romans 12:1–2, where Paul sets forth the basic concepts undergirding his ethical exhortation in Romans 12:1–15:13.

Rom. 12:1–2
I exhort you, (my) brothers, by the merciful acts of God,
to present your bodies as a sacrifice living, holy and well-pleasing to God,
(which is) your reasonable religion.
And do not allow yourselves to be conformed to this age,
but let yourselves be transformed by the renewal of (your) intellect,
so that you (may be able to) test what the will of God is,
(which means to discover) the good and well-pleasing and perfect.

The exegetical problems of this passage have been discussed continuously by the scholarly commentaries; they are all too evident to anyone who attempts to translate it. Our rendering above strives to avoid the often found tendency to smooth out what appears to be a rather surprising terminology employed by Paul,[29] a terminology that apparently makes some feel doctrinally uneasy. Examination of exegetical details must here of course be limited to what is relevant to the problem under discussion.

Paul's statement consists of two sentences parallel in form and consecutive in content. They show that Paul has identified basic aspects pertaining to the ethical task: verse 1 deals with the somatic (τὰ σώματα) aspect and verse 2 with the noetic (ὁ νοῦς) aspect; or, as defined by the two concluding clauses of verses 1 and 2, the somatic aspect concerns religion or cult (λατρεία) in the narrower sense while the noetic aspect concerns the intellectual life (δοκιμάζω). Each sentence also distinguishes between what Rudolf Bultmann first called the "indicative" and the "imperative" of salvation.[30] In verse 1, the indicative is named by the phrase "by the merciful acts of God" (διὰ τῶν οἰκτιρμῶν τοῦ θεοῦ). What does Paul have in mind here?

The phrase has not been employed before in either Romans or another of Paul's letters for this particular purpose so it is not surprising that it is still the subject of controversy today.[31] Determining the precise meaning of the phrase depends, in our view, on the composition and argumentation of the letter as a whole, which of course is also still a matter of controversy. Since a full discussion of all the problems involved is impossible at this point, let it suffice to say that in our opinion Paul discusses the revelation of God's mercy in chapters 4–11 of Romans. In 1:18–3:20, he discusses the revelation of God's "wrath" (ὀργή), first in the gentile world (1:18–32), then in the Jewish world (2:1–3:8). He then turns to the revelation of "faith" (πίστις) in 3:21–31, demonstrating the manifestations of that faith in chapter 4 (Abraham); chapter 5 (Adam-Christ typology); chapters 6–8 (baptism and the *beneficia Christi:* freedom from sin [6:12–23], from law [7:1–25a],[32] from death [8:1–30],[33] and eschatological union with God [8:31–39]);[34] and chapters 9–11 (the future of Judaism and Christianity).[35]

Both the revelation of God's wrath and the revelation of faith are part of "God's justice" (δικαιοσύνη θεοῦ); this is pointed out in the programmatic statement in 1:16–17. Accordingly, God's revelation of faith is due to God's mercy, which in turn is part of God's justice.[36] This divine mercy is necessitated by the hopeless mess humanity had made for itself. Paul is in conformity with ancient notions of justice as well as with modern ideas when he conceives of mercy, and not its suspension, as part of justice.[37] As Paul explains, God reacts to human injustice with wrath and punishment because the justice which God represents requires it. That same justice, however, requires mercy because the human predicament was without hope except for mercy on the part of God.[38] As the apostle boldly declares, God even saw to it that there was no other way out, so that the enactment of mercy was justified by justice.[39] Thus the process of salvation in its entirety, culminating for Paul in the parousia of Christ and the last judgment, is due to God's mercy and, as such, is part of the revelation of God's justice. Describing this salvation by the term of "grace" (χάρις) means to designate it as a "gift" (χάρις).

Salvation in Christ, therefore, is constituted as a truly divine gift of grace to humanity.[40]

Ancient thinking, to be sure, required that the reception of the gift of salvation must take the form of a cultic ritual of thanksgiving. Given the dimensions of this gift, only the greatest thanksgiving human beings would be able to make could be considered adequate, that of self-sacrifice to God. It is for this reason that, when Paul comes to speak of the "imperative," he turns to the language of sacrifice, in this case voluntary self-sacrifice.[41] It is to be voluntary because it must be freely given, just as the divine gift was freely given.[42] Well known as this notion of self-sacrifice was in antiquity, in his previous letters Paul only rarely connected it with ethics.[43]

Use of the concept of sacrifice leads Paul to add further qualifications. What is "offered" (παρίστημι) in every form of sacrifice are "the bodies" (τὰ σώματα) of the sacrificial victims.[44] Paul concludes that this applies to the somatic side of human existence. Does he intend to make a distinction here between "body" (σῶμα) and "flesh" (σάρξ)? There is no hint that such a distinction is intended, so he seems to include the entire somatic side of human existence. The sacrifice is, of course, not bloody but "living" (ζῶσα)[45] in the sense that it encompasses the entire "new life" of the Christian.[46] It is "holy" (ἁγία), as any sacrifice must be holy, because it has been sanctified through Christ's redemption;[47] and it is "well-pleasing to God" (εὐάρεστος τῷ θεῷ), as any sacrifice must be,[48] because nothing else corresponds to "the will of God" (τὸ θέλημα τοῦ θεοῦ [v. 2]).[49]

The final statement identifies the concept of self-sacrifice as "your reasonable religion" (ἡ λογικὴ λατρεία ὑμῶν). Again, Paul's concept has been extrapolated from the religious environment; it involves a number of elements. As a sacrifice, Christian self-dedication is a ritual (λατρεία),[50] but certainly not one of mindless superstition. Rather, Paul calls it reasonable because it is endowed with reason (λογικός);[51] it can thus be reasoned theologically, as he is presently doing.

By employing such concepts of sacrifice, Paul could speak at once practically, comprehensively, and theologically. As a "religion" Christian life is practical through its sacrificial structure; by the same token, it is ethical and eschatological. It is therefore a misunderstanding to bring into the interpretation the vague terminology of "spirituality" and "spiritualization," a terminology so dear to the modern age.[52]

When Paul turns in verse 2 to the noetic side of Christian ethical existence, he has already stated in verse 1 that it involves both religious and intellectual activities. As for him Christian religion is *sensu stricto* rational, not irrational, so Christian ethics is based on that religion,[53] even though by itself it comprises different aspects. Chiastically contrary to verse 1, verse 2 considers the ethical demands and then the "indicative" upon which they are based.

There are two basic "imperatives" to be considered. The first is negative: "Do not allow yourselves to be conformed to this age" (μὴ συσχηματίζεσθε τῷ αἰῶνι τούτῳ). Nonconformism regarding the lifestyle (σχῆμα) of this "eon" is the first concern but it is merely the consequence of the second, positive, imperative: "Let yourselves be transformed" (μεταμορφοῦσθε). Both demands imply active and passive elements: they presuppose human action, but that action is qualified as allowing something to happen. Nonconformism is external, the pressure to conform coming from the outside; transformation (*metamorphōsis*) includes all of the personal life and is dependent on inner as well as outer enablement. Thus the concept of *metamorphōsis* is deeply rooted in ancient philosophical thought on human nature.[54] At any rate, in Paul's view, continuous *metamorphōsis* characterizes Christian ethical life and as well is the force that enables nonconformism.

Neither transformation nor nonconformism can simply be demanded or expected, however. First, the human being must be enabled to meet these demands, and for this reason the apostle turns to the "indicative." It is contained in the formula "by the renewal of the intellect" (τῇ ἀνακαινώσει τοῦ νοός).[55]

The formula is difficult to understand. Scholars have not investigated its undeniable background in Greek philosophy.[56] There can be scarcely any doubt, however, that the term νοῦς refers to the "intellect"[57] rather than to the more general "mind" (what would in German be *Gesinnung*).[58] The human intellect plays an important role in the ethical task, to be sure; but the question is how this intellect can function given the anthropological conditions Paul has set forth in Romans 1–11. The apostle was obviously convinced that the proper functioning of the intellect cannot be taken for granted. What, then, did he mean by "renewal"? The context of Romans allows for an answer only with regard to the basic ideas. Earlier in the letter Paul had made it clear how the human intellect was affected by sin. While originally intact (1:20), the intellect was rendered ineffective as a consequence of God's wrath, which was God's response to human failure to worship him properly (1:28).[59] Romans 7:23 shows that the intellect is frustrated by being imprisoned in the body; this is also confirmed by the existence of conscience even among the gentiles (2:14–15). "Newness of life," which is one of the benefits of baptism, is accompanied by the gift of the Holy Spirit (7:6).[60] The infusion of the Holy Spirit liberates the Christian so that he or she is no longer compelled "to think the things of the flesh" (τὰ τῆς σαρκὸς φρονεῖν [8:5]). Instead, "those who exist in accordance with the spirit [think] the things of the spirit" (οἱ κατὰ πνεῦμα [φρονοῦσιν] τὰ τοῦ πνεύματος [8:5]). "Renewal of the intellect" must therefore mean that the intellect has been liberated from its confinement through the intervention of God's spirit.[61] Consequently, we can say that the human intellect, as a benefit of the salvation in Christ, is being restored to its original function, a kind of *restitutio in integrum*.

Thus renewed, the intellect can now serve the ethically responsible person. No longer simply conforming to the conventional standards of morality and life-style, the Christian can now determine by his or her own judgment what the appropriate standards of Christian ethics are and how they should be applied. These standards are not simply given; they must be discovered through inquiry. Such inquiry involves "testing" (δοκιμάζω).[62] To be sure, the good must be identical with the will of God; it must be well-pleasing to God (12:1, 2), and this is how it can be called perfect (12:2). How such ethical reflection is to be carried out Paul demonstrates by his own paraenesis in 12:3–15:13.

Remarkably, however, Christian ethics is not based directly upon reason. First, Paul discusses the primary standards of the concepts of the church as the body of Christ (12:3–8)[63] and of love (ἀγάπη [12:9–21]),[64] and only then does he turn to concrete responsibilities (13:1–15:13). It is also noteworthy that in Romans Paul sets forth these concrete responsibilities as matters of "obligation" (ὀφειλή). Making this notion of obligation fundamental to Christian ethics marks a considerable change in comparison to previous letters of the apostle. Unfortunately, only a few scholars have investigated the concept of obligation, and the full extent with regard to Romans has yet to be pursued. At any rate, in receiving the gift of salvation, the Christian is obligated to respond to God in kind: this is the meaning of responsibility. The greater the gift, the greater the response must be,[65] which means that only complete self-sacrifice to God can be considered appropriate (12:1). This self-sacrifice applies not only to church members generally[66] but to the apostle himself in particular.[67] In practice, Christian obligations include those owed to the state (13:1–7)[68] and to law and morality in general (13:8–14).[69] In

14:1–15:13, Paul deals with the obligations owed to the "weaker" by the "stronger" members of the church.

This concept of Christian ethics as obligation is not only a somewhat new development in Paul's theology; it also has many parallels to the Roman political and ethical concept of *officium*. From these similarities one can only conclude that this new approach on the part of the apostle was intended to appeal to Roman self-understanding. It may also have had its reason, however, in Paul's own theological development. Did the Corinthian crisis cause him to shift away from grounding ethics in the spirit? Did the Galatian crisis also play a role in this respect? We can only raise these questions: Paul never feels that he should inform his readers of his reasons for not saying the same things in each letter.

IV

The changes in the foundations of Paul's ethics should now be obvious, even though only some of the relevant points have been discussed. What are the implictions of such changes? In our view, they were not made for arbitrary or trivial reasons. Paul was certainly not a "situation ethicist" in the sense that the ever-changing situations dictated his responses. Nor should one conclude that Paul was simply inconsistent, a man of contradictions. Rather, the evidence suggests that Paul was confronted by intellectual and practical problems inherent in and arising from his theology. Paul seems to have been aware of these problems as he tried to respond to misunderstandings or abuses of his views in his own churches and by his adversaries. Between the letters, there must have occurred among both his fellow workers and his opponents intense discussions of controversial points of doctrine and practice. These discussions as well as practical problems in the churches are reflected in the letters, but these reflections are indirect and presuppose a knowledge of circumstances and personalities by the readers, which we do not have. Paul's theology is not a static system that he applied to changing situations. He works on one level with formulaic statements and dogmatic presuppositions that are not subject to change; at other levels there is plenty of room for change in terminology and conceptuality. Paul can state his views in very different ways, and in his views development can be observed; but these changes do not add up to self-contradictions. There is consistency and continuity as well as change in Paul's thought. His theology is constantly in process, and what we have in his letters are something like photographic pictures taken at certain points in that process.

In conclusion, we can state that, all changes considered, in Romans Paul has not returned to grounding his ethics in the Jewish Torah (see Rom. 10:4). It is true that he speaks about the Torah much more positively here than he does in Galatians (3:19–30). In Romans, the Torah has been more fully integrated into the history of salvation. Similarly, the "indicative" of salvation has not been identified, as it could have been, with the teaching of the historical Jesus. Although Paul included some of Jesus' teachings in Romans 12 and 13, he did not expressly identify them as such. Contrary to what one would expect, Romans 12:1–2 does not even cite the kerygma of the crucifixion and resurrection of Jesus Christ. Rather, the "indicative" includes the entire history of salvation. It is within that framework that the crucifixion and resurrection of Jesus Christ plays its decisive role. In similar ways, the entire range of ethical concepts used in earlier letters is also present in Romans, but their roles and places have changed as they have become parts in a comprehensive salvation drama ranging from Adam to the Last Judgment. Neither kerygma, nor baptism, nor spirit, nor eschatology alone serves as the foundation for ethics, but a synthesis of them does provide that foundation. In the final analysis, the foundation of Christian ethics is surely the "justice of God" (δικαιοσύνη θεοῦ [1:17]). From it originates salvation itself, the merciful deeds of God (12:1), the divine will (12:2), and the "measure of faith" (13:3), the divine ἀγάπη.

Notes

1. The question can be raised whether Paul may have thought of the possibility that his letter to the Romans could be his last letter, and hence a kind of testament. He wrote the letter from Corinth, just before he left for Jerusalem to deliver the collection to the Jewish-Christian church there (15:25–29). The conclusion of the letter (15:30–33) clearly shows that he was aware of the great risks he was taking. See Günther Bornkamm, "The Letter to the Romans as Paul's Last Will and Testament," in The Romans Debate, ed. Karl P. Donfried (Minneapolis: Augsburg Press, 1977), 17–31.

2. The methodological problems in describing what popular morality was are formidable. See Lionel Pearson, Popular Ethics in Ancient Greece (Stanford: Stanford University Press, 1962); Kenneth J. Dover, Greek Popular Morality in the Time of Plato and Aristotle (Berkeley and Los Angeles: University of California Press, 1974); Willem den Boer, Private Morality in Greece and Rome (Leiden: Brill, 1979).

3. For references to sayings of Jesus having moral content or implications, see 1 Cor. 7:10 (cf. 12, 25, 40); 9:14; 11:23–33; 14:37. Two problems

remain unresolved: Why does Paul refer to Jesus' sayings only in 1 Corinthians and in 1 Thessalonians, and from what kind of source did he obtain them?

4. Schubert M. Ogden, *The Point of Christology* (San Francisco: Harper and Row, 1982); idem, "Rudolf Bultmann and the Future of Revisionary Christology," in *Bultmann: Retrospect and Prospect*, ed. Edward C. Hobbs, Harvard Theological Studies 35 (Philadelphia: Fortress Press, 1985), 37–58; also in *Rudolf Bultmanns Werk und Wirkung* (Darmstadt: Wissenschaftliche Buchgesellschaft, 1984), 155–73.

5. Contrary to what one would expect, neither the gospel writers nor Paul ever speaks of Jesus' own faith (πιστεύω, πίστις). See Dieter Lührmann, *Glaube im frühen Christentum* (Gütersloh: Mohn, 1976), 27–28; idem, "Glaube," *Reallexikon für Antike und Christentum* 11 (1981): section B, I, b (cols. 65–72); for the christological problems, see also Gerhard Ebeling, "Jesus und Glaube," in *Wort und Glaube*, vol. 1 (Tübingen: Mohr [Siebeck], 1960): 203–54; idem, "Die Frage nach dem historischen Jesus und das Problem der Christologie," ibid., 300–318. On the formula πίστις Ἰησοῦ Χριστοῦ ("faith of [= in] Jesus Christ"), see my commentary, *Galatians*, Hermeneia (Philadelphia: Fortress Press, 1979), 117–18.

6. See Betz, *Galatians*, 131–32.

7. On the problems concerning this passage, see Ernst von Dobschütz, *Die Thessalonicherbriefe*, Kritisch-exegetischer Kommentar über das Neue Testament, Abteilung 10 (Göttingen: Vandenhoeck und Ruprecht, 1909; reprinted 1974), 158–59.

8. The term occurs only here in Paul; for the verb, cf. 1 Thess. 4:11; 1 Cor. 7:10 (referring to the teaching of Jesus); furthermore 1 Tim. 1:5, 18. It refers to the teaching of Jesus also in Matt. 10:5 and 1 Clem. 49:1.

9. Cf., with a similar context, 1 Cor. 7:32.

10. See Walter Bauer, *A Greek-English Lexicon of the New Testament and Other Early Christian Literature* (Chicago: University of Chicago Press, ²1979), s.v. ὁ, section II, 8.

11. See also 1 Thess. 2:19; 3:13; 1 Cor. 1:8; 10:33; 2 Cor. 1:14; 5:10; 11:2, 15; Phil. 1:6, 10; Rom. 14:10.

12. 1 Thess. 4:3, 4, 7; cf. 3:13; 5:23.

13. 1 Thess. 1:5, 6; 3:13; 5:26, 27.

14. Cf. John 17:11–12; Jas. 1:27; 2 Pet. 3:13; Jude 1, 21, 24; 2 Cor. 6:14–7:1 (for this passage, see Betz, *Galatians*, 329–30).

15. 1 Thess. 4:3, 7; 5:22.

16. See Gal. 5:19–23, and Betz, *Galatians*, 281–89.

17. 1 Thess. 1:5, 6; 4:7–8; 5:19, 23.

18. 1 Thess. 1:10 as part of the kerygma, vv. 9–10; 4:14–17; 5:9–10.

19. 1 Thess. 4:1–5:22.

20. See Gal. 6:1; cf. 5:13, 16, 17, 19–24, and for the interpretation, Betz, *Galatians*, 8–9, 253–90, 295–98.

21. Betz, *Galatians*, 5–9.

22. Ibid., 28–33.

23. See on this point Laurence L. Welborn, "On the Discord in Corinth: 1 Corinthians 1–4 and Ancient Politics," *Journal of Biblical Literature* 106 (1987): 85–111.

24. See my article, "The Problem of Rhetoric and Theology according to the Apostle Paul," in *L'Apôtre Paul: Personnalité, Style et Conception du Ministère*, ed. A. Vanhoye, vol. 73 (Leuven: University Press; Peeters, 1986), 16–48.

25. See on this letter fragment my earlier study, *Der Apostel Paulus und die sokratische Tradition. Eine exegetische Studie zu seiner "Apologie" 2 Korinther 10–13*, Beiträge zur historischen Theologie 45 (Tübingen: Mohr [Siebeck], 1972).

26. See my Hermeneia commentary, *2 Corinthians 8 and 9: A Commentary on Two Administrative Letters of the Apostle Paul* (Philadelphia: Fortress Press, 1985).

27. James L. Houlden, *Ethics and the New Testament* (Oxford: Oxford University Press, 1979), assumes that Paul changed from an original radical asceticism to later conventional morality, but pressing Paul into such readymade clichés does not serve the interpretation of the texts.

28. Cf. Wolfgang Schrage, *Ethik des Neuen Testaments* (Göttingen: Vandenhoeck and Ruprecht, 1982), 155–76: "Der Ansatz der paulinischen Ethik." Schrage rejects all forms of development in Paul's ethical thought.

29. The translation given above follows the interpretation of John Calvin, *In Novum Testamentum Commentarii*, ed. August Tholuck, vol. 5, pt. 1 (Berolini: Apud Guilielmum Thome, 1934), 161–63, who renders λογικὴ λατρεία as *rationabilis cultus* and ἀνακαίνωσις τοῦ νοός as *renovatio mentis*. On the whole, modern translations show a peculiar tendency to eliminate the strangeness of Paul's philosophical terminology and to make it read more "churchy." In addition, the common rendering, "spiritual worship," ends up being a redundancy, since worship is spiritual anyway; or a contrast to ritual worship is imported that is not part of the Greek text. The rendering, "renewal of the mind" sounds more like repentance and does not convey the meaning of an intellectual effort. This tendency is all the more remarkable because commentaries and lexicons carry full discussions of the proper meaning of the terms.

30. Rudolf Bultmann, "Das Problem der Ethik bei Paulus," *Zeitschrift für die neutestamentliche Wissenschaft* 23 (1924): 123–40, reprinted in idem, *Exegetica* (Tübingen: Mohr [Siebeck], 1967), 36–54. Cf. also Schrage, *Ethik*, 156–61.

31. For details, see the scholarly commentaries.

32. In our view, Rom. 7:25b is to be regarded as a marginal gloss that ended up in the text. See Rudolf Bultmann, "Glossen im Römerbrief," *Theologische Literaturzeitung* 72 (1947): 197–202, reprinted in *Exegetica*, 278–84, especially 278–79; Günther Zuntz, *The Text of the Epistles: A Disquisition upon the Corpus Paulinum* (London: British Academy, 1953), 16; differently, C. E. B. Cranfield, *A Critical and Exegetical Commentary on the Epistle to the Romans. The International Critical Commentary* (Edin-

burgh: Clark, [2]1981), vol. 1, 368–70; Ulrich Wilckens, *Der Brief an die Römer*, Evangelisch-katholischer Kommentar zum Neuen Testament, vol. 6, pt. 2 (Zürich, Einsiedeln; Köln: Benziger Verlag; Neukirchen-Vluyn: Neukirchener Verlag, 1980), 96–97.

33. The three *beneficia* coincide with sections 38–40 in Bultmann's *Theology of the New Testament*, trans. Kendrick Grobel, vol. 1 (New York: Scribner's, 1951), 330–52. Notably, Bultmann omits the treatment of the eschatological union with Christ, Rom. 8:31–39.

34. See on this passage Horst R. Balz, *Heilsvertrauen und Welterfahrung. Strukturen der paulinischen Eschatologie nach Römer 8, 18–39, Beiträge zur evangelischen Theologie* 59 (München: Kaiser, 1971); Henning Paulsen, *Überlieferung und Auslegung in Römer 8*, Wissenschaftliche Monographien zum Alten und Neuen Testament 43 (Neukirchen-Vluyn: Neukirchener Verlag, 1974).

35. For the recent discussion, see Edward P. Sanders, *Paul, the Law, and the Jewish People* (Philadelphia: Fortress Press, 1983); Hans Hübner, *Gottes Ich und Israel. Zum Schriftgebrauch des Paulus in Römer 9–11*, Forschungen zur Religion und Literatur des Alten und Neuen Testaments 136 (Göttingen: Vandenhoeck and Ruprecht, 1984); Egon Brandenburger, "Paulinische Schriftauslegung in der Kontroverse um das Verheissungswort Gottes (Röm 9)," *Zeitschrift für Theologie und Kirche* 82 (1985): 1–47.

36. The concept of "grace" (χάρις, χαρίσματα), which dominates in Rom. 1–8 (see especially 3:24–26), is finally conjoined with "mercy" (ἔλεος, Rom. 9:15, 16, 18, 23; 11:30, 31, 32) in Rom. 11:28–31, summing up salvation by stating that it is all due to God's mercy (15:9).

37. See Rudolf Bultmann, ἔλεος κτλ., *Theological Dictionary of the New Testament* 2, 474–83; Albrecht Dihle, "Gerechtigkeit," *Reallexikon für Antike und Christentum* 11 (1981): section A, I, cols. 313–33.

38. See Rom. 11:32; cf. 1:20; 2:1; 3:9–20; Gal. 3:22.

39. See Rom. 3:5–8; 5:20–21; 7:7–13; 11:32.

40. See especially Rom. 3:24–26; 4:25; 5:2, 15, 17, 20–21; 6:14–15; 12:6.

41. For bibliography on this concept, see the commentaries, especially Wilckens, *Der Brief an die Römer*, pt. 3, p. 1; Ernst Käsemann, *Commentary on Romans* (Grand Rapids, Mich.: Eerdmans, 1980), 325–26.

42. See Rom. 3:24; 5:15, 17; also 2 Cor. 9:15, and on this passage, Betz, *2 Corinthians 8 and 9*, 126–28.

43. Cf. 2 Cor. 8:5; 1 Thess. 2:8; Rom. 16:4. See Betz, *2 Corinthians 8 and 9*, 47–48.

44. On votive offerings representing parts of human bodies, see F. T. van Straaten, "Gifts for the Gods," in *Faith, Hope and Worship: Aspects of Religious Mentality in the Ancient World*, ed. H. S. Versnell (Leiden: Brill, 1981), 105–51.

45. For "living" as synonymous with "bloodless" (ἀναίμακτος) see *Test. XII, Levi* 3.6; Athenagoras, *Leg.* 13.2.

46. See Rom. 1:17 (ζήσεται); 6:2, 4, 10–11, 13, 22–23; 8:2, 6, 10, 12–13, 38.

47. Because of their sanctification, Christians are called "the holy ones"

(οἱ ἅγιοι). Cf. Rom. 1:4, 7; 3:24–26; 4:25; 5:5; 7:12, 8:27; 9:1; 11:16; 12:13; 14:17; 15:13, 16, 25, 26, 31; 16:2, 15, 16.

48. See also Rom. 14:18, and Bauer, *Lexicon, s.v.* εὐάρεστος.

49. Cf. Rom. 1:10; 2:18; 15:32, and Betz, *2 Corinthians 8 and 9*, 48.

50. So, correctly, Horst Balz, "λατρεύω, λατρεία," *Exegetisches Wörter-buch zum Neuen Testament* 2, 848–52, especially 851. See also H. W. Pleket in Versnell, ed., *Faith, Hope and Worship*, 163–66.

51. See Hans-Werner Bartsch, "λογικός," *Exegetisches Wörterbuch zum Neuen Testament* 2, 876–78, who judges correctly (877): "Die Vokabel be-deutet darum keine Spiritualisierung." Differently, Bauer, *Lexicon, s.v.* λογικός. See also P. A. Meijer, "Philosophers, Intellectuals and Religion in Hellas," in Versnell, ed., *Faith, Hope and Worship*, 245–59.

52. The article by Everett Ferguson, "Spiritual Sacrifice in Early Chris-tianity and Its Environment," *Aufstieg und Niedergang der römischen Welt* II, 23/2 (Berlin: de Gruyter, 1980): 1151–89, is misleading because it as-sembles all kinds of sacrifice under the label "spiritual sacrifice" without ever clarifying what the term means.

53. Indicated by the connecting καί in v. 2.

54. This concept is most difficult to interpret, and no satisfactory inves-tigation seems to exist; the article by Johannes Behm, "μεταμορφόω κτλ.," *Theological Dictionary of the New Testament* 4 (1942; English translation 1967), 755–59, is outdated.

55. The concept is found only here; cf. 2 Cor. 4:16; Col. 3:10; Tit. 3:5; Hermas, *Vis.* 3.8.9.

56. Against Behm, "νοέω, νοῦς," *Theological Dictionary of the New Tes-tament* 4 (1942; English translation 1967), 95: "There is no connection with the philosophical or mystico-religious use."

57. The scholarly literature often shows a tendency to dilute the intellec-tual connotations in favor of those referring to moral habits. For correct interpretation, see Ferdinand Christian Baur, *Vorlesungen über neutesta-mentliche Theologie* (Leipzig: Fues, 1864), 145–49; Bultmann, *Theology*, 211–14.

58. Cf. Bauer, *Lexicon s.v.* νοῦς, 3, who renders as "mind, attitude, way of thinking as the sum total of the whole and moral state of being." This cor-responds to Bauer's German "Sinn, Gesinnung." In reference to Rom. 12:2, Bauer translates: "*be transformed by the renewing of the mind,* which comes about when the Christian has his natural νοῦς penetrated and trans-formed by the Spirit which he received at baptism. . . ."

59. Cf. Eph. 4:17ff.; Col. 2:18; 1 Tim. 6:5; 2 Tim. 3:8; Tit. 1:15.

60. Cf. Rom. 5:5; 8:9, 11, 14–16, 23, 26–27.

61. According to Rom. 8:16, the divine spirit informed the human spirit "that we are children of God." To be sure, this message conveys nothing new, but implies the liberation from ignorance.

62. For this term, see also Rom. 1:28; 2:18; 14:22; 1 Cor. 11:28, 2 Cor. 13:5; Gal. 6:4; Phil. 1:10; 1 Thess. 2:4; 5:21. For the interpretation, see Bultmann, *Theology*, 214–15.

63. See also 1 Cor. 12:12–27; Gal. 3:26–28.

64. The passage consists of a series of maxims on the theme of ἀγάπη (ring-composition).

65. Cf. Cicero, *De officiis* 1. 15. 49: "the greater the favor, the greater is the obligation" (*maximo cuique plurimum debeatur*).

66. See especially Rom. 13:8; 15:1, 27; cf. also 4:4; 8:12.

67. See on the definition of apostleship Rom. 1:14.

68. The literature on this passage is enormous. See the commentaries by Cranfield, Käsemann, and Wilckens.

69. Cicero's *De officiis* is a compendium on Roman views concerning obligation. Based on Stoic sources, it presents a more general work on private and public duties. See also Adolf Bonhöffer, *Die Ethik des Stoikers Epictet* (Stuttgart: Enke, 1894), 58–121, 193–233.

Chapter Three

Paul the ΜΑΡΤΥΣ

VICTOR PAUL FURNISH

As Schubert Ogden has observed, the apostle Paul's references to "the ministry of reconciliation" and "the word of reconciliation" (2 Cor. 5:18, 19) correspond to two different ways in which one may employ the term *witness:* for "the act of witnessing" or for the content of one's witness. In discussing the Christian kerygma and the tasks of Christian theology, Ogden himself has used the word in both senses,[1] and it so happens that Paul does, too. When writing in 1 Corinthians 1:6 of "the witness of Christ" that had been confirmed among his readers, the apostle employs the noun (τὸ μαρτύριον) as a virtual synonym for "gospel";[2] and the act of witnessing is in view when, in 1 Corinthians 15:15, he refers to having "borne witness of God that he raised Christ."

One must acknowledge, however, that the Pauline letters yield only these two certain instances of witness language used in the ways to which Ogden has referred.[3] Moreover, Paul never uses the noun "witness" (μάρτυς) as a title for himself, he does not list "witnesses" as a group distinguishable from apostles, prophets, and the like (1 Cor. 12:28), and he does not specify "witnessing" as an activity somehow distinct from such activities as prophesying, teaching, and serving (Rom. 12:6–8). It is apparently not until the end of the first century that his own role comes to be described, specifically, as that of a witness (see especially Acts 22:15; 26:16; *1 Clement* 5:7; and section IV below). Nevertheless, because for Paul the content of the gospel and its presentation are absolutely and inseparably related, and because "witness" can decribe the one as well as the other, this concept may be usefully employed with reference to his understanding of the apostolic task.

The aim of the present essay is to establish just two main points.

The thesis of this essay was first developed for the Annual Lectures at the Methodist Theological School in Ohio (January 1986), and subsequently reshaped for the Herbert G. May Memorial Lecture at Oberlin College (March 1987). I am indebted to colleagues at both schools for their hospitality on these occasions.

First, Paul's identification of the content of the Christian witness as "the word of the cross" leads him to *a kerygmatic interpretation* of his apostolic tribulations—that is, to the conviction that his sufferings are an absolutely vital part of his witnessing to the gospel (I, II, III). Second, this interpretation is no longer in evidence after Paul's death, when the church, having to adjust itself to the realities of an indefinitely extended existence in the world, seems less concerned to identify and retain the distinctive *content* of his witness than to emphasize and invoke his own role *as* a witness (IV).

I

It is clear, as regards Paul's activity on behalf of the gospel, that he understands his call to apostleship to have been a call to bear witness to Christ among the Gentiles (Rom. 1:1–5; Gal. 1:16; 2:7; cf. Rom. 15:18–21). Since he believes that he is under divine appointment for this service (1 Thess. 2:4; cf. Gal. 2:7), he regards every other apostolic task as secondary to it (see, e.g., 1 Cor. 1:17), and he can even write, "Woe to me if I do not make the gospel known!" (1 Cor. 9:16b).

The verb that he uses most frequently to characterize his apostolic service (εὐαγγελίζεσθαι) is generally rendered into English as "to preach the gospel." This translation is not inappropriate, since Paul himself sometimes uses the noun "gospel" with a verb that specifies oral communication.[4] But he believes that the gospel is made known in other ways as well, and he himself makes this point explicitly when he reminds the Thessalonians: "our gospel came to you not only in speech, but also in power and in the Holy Spirit" (1 Thess. 1:5). He can also think of the gospel as something that is "shared," and that involves the sharing of *oneself* (2:8), just as caring parents share themselves with their children (vv. 7, 11). Moreover, when in Romans 15:19 he says that he has been able to "fulfill" the gospel from Jerusalem to Illyricum, he is probably thinking of how, through his ministry, Christ has claimed the obedience of the Gentiles (see v. 18). Here, as Käsemann has suggested, one can see that for Paul the gospel "is not just proclaimed but that it fashions an earthly sphere of validity for the Lordship of Christ."[5]

It is too restrictive, therefore, to take every Pauline occurrence of the verb εὐαγγελίζεσθαι as a reference to *preaching* the gospel. Although there are a few places in Paul's letters where this is in fact required,[6] his understanding of the apostolic task suggests that ordinarily the verb should be less narrowly interpreted. One might render it "to evangelize," except for the fact that this loanword, like the noun "evangelist," has acquired connotations in English that it did not have for the apostle. Something like "to establish the gospel,"[7] or "to give presence to the gospel"—or, indeed, "to bear witness to the gospel"—would be more in keeping with the Pauline conception.

II

Three things must be emphasized about Paul's understanding of the gospel to which he bears witness.

First, *he thinks of the gospel as primarily an event, and, specifically, as the working of God's power.* It is "God's power for salvation to every one who believes, first to the Jew and then to the Greek; because God's righteousness is revealed in it, from faith for faith" (Rom. 1:16–17). For Paul, the gospel is not in the first instance a message about God, salvation, righteousness, or faith. Rather, it is God's coming in power to bestow righteousness (and thus salvation) upon those who believe (who are open to receive it). For this conception he may be indebted to the Greek text of Second Isaiah, where the verb εὐαγγελίζεσθαι is used with reference to God's return to Zion in power, bringing salvation to those who have languished in exile (see LXX Isa. 40:9–11; 52:7–10 [quoted in Rom. 10:15]; 60:6; 61:1).[8] The apostle's occasional references to the gospel as "God's *word*" are to be understood in the same way:[9] that word is a redemptive presence "at work" among those who receive it (1 Thess. 2:13). The Hebrew conception of God's word as the agent of God's power (e.g., Ps. 33:6; 148:8) surely lies behind this formulation. One thinks again of Second Isaiah, who likens the divine word to the rain and the snow that fall from heaven, making the earth "bring forth and sprout"; God's word is that through which the divine purposes are accomplished (Isa. 55:10–11). For Paul, then, the apostolic task is not just to deliver a message about salvation but to call the Gentiles to give God's power scope in their midst, and thereby to give the gospel a meaningful presence in the world.

Second, *Paul identifies the gospel event as Jesus' death on the cross.* Thus, he reminds both the Corinthians and the Galatians that "Jesus Christ and him crucified" had been the subject of his preaching to them (1 Cor. 2:2 [cf. 1:23]; Gal. 3:1b). It is, indeed, the gospel itself that is in view when he refers to "the cross of Christ" (1 Cor.

1:17; Gal. 6:12; Phil. 3:18) and to "the word of the cross" (1 Cor. 1:18). Similarly, when he says that his only boast is "in the cross of our Lord Jesus Christ," through whom the world has been "crucified" to him and he to the world (Gal. 6:14), then he is holding up Jesus' death as the decisive salvation event. Since Paul identifies the gospel with Jesus' death, and since he understands the gospel as "God's power for salvation" for those who believe, he does not hesitate to refer to "the power" of the cross (1 Cor. 1:17). But this means that he understands God's power to be demonstrated in an event which, by any worldly measure, can only be regarded as a sign of weakness (see, e.g., 1 Cor. 1:18–25).

Third, *the "power of the cross" is, for Paul, the power of God's love.* The interpretation offered in Romans 5:6–8 of the traditional creedal statement about Christ's death "for us" is characteristic of the apostle's thinking: "God demonstrates his love for us in that while we were still sinners 'Christ died for us'" (v. 8; see also Rom. 8:31–39 and Gal. 2:20). Through the power of God's love operative in the cross believers are delivered from the tyranny of their old sin-dominated selves (Rom. 6:3–11) and drawn under the rule of grace (Rom. 6:14). Thus, Paul—once more alluding to the creedal tradition—declares that "Christ's love lays claim to us, [because] one has died for all; therefore, all have died" (2 Cor. 5:14). He then proceeds (v. 15) to interpret the death that believers have experienced as their living "no longer for themselves," and to interpret the new life that they have been granted as their living for Christ (i.e., for others).[10]

Now Paul's understanding of his apostolic task may be rather more specifically formulated. Taking the gospel to the Gentiles means calling them to perceive in the apparent weakness of the cross the power of God's life-giving and life-claiming love. Where this gift is received and this claim is accepted, the gospel has won a meaningful presence in the world and God's power is at work for salvation and righteousness.

III

Several of the terms and images that Paul uses with reference to his apostolic task, including the term "apostle" itself, express his sense of responsibility to the one by whom his ministry is authorized and directed.[11] Others reflect a sense of responsibility for those to whom he has carried the gospel, and who now look to him for nurture and upbuilding.[12] But the most striking images are those that draw attention to the burdens, the risks, and the sufferings that he experiences as an apostle.[13] These are also the images that disclose what is most distinctive about Paul's understanding of both the content and the activity of Christian witness. The parade image in 2 Corinthians 2:14 probably belongs to this latter category, and it deserves special attention—not only because it has been so variously interpreted,[14] but also because it is linked with a second image which portrays the universal spread of the Christian witness.

The RSV translation of 2 Corinthians 2:14 reads: "But thanks be to God, who in Christ always leads us in triumph, and through us spreads the fragrance of the knowledge of him everywhere." This is frequently interpreted as reflecting Paul's sense of assurance that, with Christ in the lead, the apostles, like an invincible army, are marching triumphantly through the world with the gospel. It is more likely, however, that there is an allusion here to the famous triumphal processions that the Roman emperors staged for victorious generals and their troops, returned from battle. On such occasions, realistic tableaux of the decisive engagements were paraded before Rome's citizens, and so were the vanquished generals and prisoners of war. There is good evidence in first-century texts that when one spoke metaphorically of being "led in triumph," the point was not to identify oneself with the heroes of the battle, but rather with the prisoners of war who were being dragged along in shame and in defeat.[15]

If this interpretation is correct, then an appropriate paraphrase of Paul's words would be: "Thanks be to God, who in Christ always puts us on display as if we were prisoners of war paraded about in one of Rome's triumphal processions, and who manifests through us the fragrance of the knowledge of him in every place." Thus interpreted, Paul is thinking of the vulnerability of the apostolic witnesses, and of the indignities, the shame, and the humiliation to which they are subjected. Why he can, nonetheless, offer his thanks to God for such a parade of weakness, is explained by the kerygmatic interpretation of apostolic suffering that finds expression in the latter part of the sentence: it is precisely *through* these apostolic sufferings that the gospel is made known to the world.

Paul's kerygmatic interpretation of his suffering is also evident in his frequent cataloging of the kinds of hardships and adversities to which he is subjected. There are six of these lists (1 Cor. 4:9–13; 2 Cor. 4:8–9; 6:4c–5; 11:23b–29; 12:10; Rom. 8:35), and from them one learns that the apostle has been scorned, ridiculed, shamed, persecuted, beaten, stoned, imprisoned; that he has been deprived of adequate food, water, clothing, shelter, and sleep; that he has experienced extreme cold, floods, shipwreck, the dangers of city life as well as of travel in the countryside; that he has been endangered by bandits, Jews, Gentiles, and Christian opponents; that he has had to do manual labor to help support his ministry; and that beyond all of this, he has been constantly racked with anxiety about his congregations.

Two things in particular distinguish these lists from similar catalogs compiled by other ancient writers.[16] First, the apostle does not seek to dismiss his difficulties as trivial, or to minimize the suffering they cause him. Second, his purpose in reciting these many adversities is not to impress his readers with how courageously he has been able to endure them all. Clearly, he does not regard these experiences as ennobling, but as humiliating, and as demonstrating not his strength but his weakness.[17] Thus, in 2 Corinthians 11:30, looking back to the adversities catalogued in vv. 23b–29 as well as ahead to the narratives of 11:32–33; 12:2–4, 7–9, the apostle insists that, "If boasting is necessary, I will boast about my weaknesses" (see also 12:5).

How Paul can understand his boasting in weaknesses as essential to his apostolic service is made clear in 2 Corinthians 4. There he introduces the tribulations list of vv. 8–9 with the comment: "Now we have this treasure in earthen pots, in order that it may be seen that the power which is beyond any comparison belongs to God and not to us" (v. 7). The "treasure" is of course the gospel, and the earthen pots—vulnerable and expendable—are those who bear witness to it. Then, after listing several kinds of afflictions, he further describes the task of apostles as "always carrying about in the body the death of Jesus, in order that also the life of Jesus might be manifested in our bodies" (v. 10). That is, the labors, risks, and sufferings of the apostle are not to be regarded as just the unfortunate consequences of his Christian witness, or as impressive evidence of the strength of his faith. Rather, they constitute the very essence of his witness, because they disclose the life-giving death of Jesus. They are in and of themselves *kerygmatic.*

It is evident, then, that Paul's interpretation of his suffering as a vital act of Christian witness is directly related to his understanding of what constitutes the vital content of Christian witness—"Jesus Christ and him crucified." The paradox of the cross is continually re-presented in the apostle's ministry: what the world can only perceive as weakness is disclosed to the eyes of faith as God's power for salvation, as the power of God's love by which one's life is both affirmed and claimed, and through which "the word of the cross" becomes God's "word of reconciliation."[18]

IV

In the decades following Paul's death, and especially after the fall of Jerusalem in 70, the church has to face the awesome task of adjusting itself to life in a world which, contrary to the apostle's own expectation, does not seem to be on the verge of "passing away" (1 Cor. 7:31; cf. v. 29 and Rom. 13:11). The sufferings that marked Paul's career are by no means forgotten, but his own interpretation of these as manifesting the death of Jesus and, therefore, as exhibiting the essential content of his gospel, is no longer in evidence. Perhaps Paul's emphasis on "the word of the cross" is one of those things that the later church finds "hard to understand" and controversial about his letters (2 Pet. 3:16). In any event, his status comes eventually to overshadow his message, as the reference to him in 2 Peter 3:15–16 itself suggests: it is not the content of the apostle's teaching (about the Lord's forbearance) that is invoked, but rather his status as one to whom "wisdom" had been given and whose letters are part of the church's "scriptures."

An emphasis on Paul's status, although certainly not to the exclusion of his gospel, is already apparent in *Colossians*, perhaps the earliest of the deutero-Pauline letters. Here he is portrayed as the apostle par excellence, an authority in matters of faith and conduct even when, as for the readers of this letter, he remains an apostle in absentia (see, e.g., 1:25; 2:1, 5).[19] This writer not only represents Paul as having been imprisoned on account of his preaching (4:3), but attributes to him the striking declaration: "Now I rejoice in the sufferings that I endure on your behalf, and on behalf of his body—which is the church—I complete in my flesh what is lacking in Christ's afflictions" (1:24). Although the precise meaning of this statement continues to be debated,[20] there is widespread agreement about the following points.

(1) The reference to "what is lacking in Christ's afflictions" cannot mean that Christ's atoning work is in some way deficient or incomplete; indeed, elsewhere in Colossians the all-sufficiency of Christ is emphasized (see especially 1:15–20; 2:2–3, 9–10, 17). (2) The background of the phrase, "Christ's afflictions," is probably to

be found in the Jewish apocalyptic expectation that, prior to the coming of the Messiah, a period full of tribulations will have to be endured. This period is understood to occupy a fixed span on the apocalyptic calendar, and the tribulations that are to fill it are regarded as "messianic" because they will usher in the new age. Thus, (3) the author of Colossians seems to be saying that Paul's sufferings complete the quota of sufferings which must be experienced—not by Christ, but by God's people—before Christ's return. It is *for the whole church* ("on behalf of [Christ's] body"), not just for his own congregations, that Paul has suffered, because he has taken on himself the tribulations that would otherwise be the church's to bear.

In Colossians, then, the apostle's suffering is interpreted as vicarious and as benefiting the church universal. Even though the Pauline theology of the cross has not been abandoned (see 1:20; 2:14), this author's interpretation of Paul's suffering would appear to be more closely related to his view of Paul's status as a witness than to his understanding of the content of that witness. As a consequence, his interpretation diverges from the apostle's own. Although Paul, too, believes that his sufferings are for the sake of others, he does not think of them as vicarious but as kerygmatic, because "the word of the cross" is given a presence through them. And this means that, for him, the beneficiaries of his sufferings are, quite specifically, his congregations—those in such places as Corinth and Philippi to whom he has carried the gospel (e.g., 2 Cor. 4:11–12, 15; Phil. 2:17; cf. 1:12–14).

In *Ephesians*, whose author is heavily indebted to Colossians, the "holy apostles and prophets" (3:5) are said to constitute the church's "foundation" (2:20), and Paul is the prototypical apostle, the one to whom, above all others, the "stewardship of God's grace" and the revelation of the "mystery" of the gospel have been granted (3:2–3). Here Paul is not just imprisoned (as in Colossians); he is presented as "*the* prisoner" (3:1; 4:1), as one whose suffering, like his apostleship, has enduring significance for the church ecumenical.[21] Consequently, when this author thinks of Paul's ambassadorial service (2 Cor. 5:20), he thinks of it as being performed "in chains" (Eph. 6:20). One might expect that this portrayal of Paul as the church's suffering apostle would be accompanied by references to various specific tribulations that he was forced to undergo. This is not the case, however, in either Colossians or in Ephesians. Because Paul is now regarded as belonging to the whole church, the historical particularities of his suffering are no longer of much importance.

The earliest portrayal of Paul as a "witness" (μάρτυς) to the gospel is in the canonical *Acts of the Apostles*.[22] Recounting his conversion, Paul quotes Ananias as having said to him: "The God of our fathers appointed you to know his will, to see the Just One and to hear a voice from his mouth, that you may be a witness for him to all people of what you have seen and heard" (22:14–15). Before King Agrippa Paul affirms that Jesus had told him: "For this purpose I have appeared to you: to appoint you as [my] servant and as a witness to the things in which you have seen me and in which I will appear to you" (26:16). And the Lord, in an oracle, says to Paul: "Take courage, for as you have borne witness to me in Jerusalem, you must bear witness also at Rome" (23:11).

It is, moreover, specifically as a suffering witness that Paul is presented in Acts:[23] in virtually every city he must endure hostility, threats, and physical abuse, and from 21:33 (where he is arrested and ordered to be bound in chains) through the close of the narrative in chapter 28 he is continuously a prisoner of the Romans. Yet the apostle's own kerygmatic interpretation of his sufferings, according to which they are a re-presentation of "the word of the cross," is no more in evidence in Acts than it is in Colossians or Ephesians. For this writer, Jesus' resurrection, not his crucifixion, stands at the center of the church's witness (see, esp. Acts 1:22; 2:32; 3:15; 4:33; 10:39–43; 13:29–41). As a result, while Paul is portrayed as having to endure many sufferings for the sake of his witness to the gospel, his sufferings are not regarded as a constituent part of that. Nor are they regarded as vicariously beneficial for the church (Col. 1:24); indeed, in Acts one finds Paul warning the church of the afflictions that will be visited upon it after his death (20:29–30).

Although the author of Acts does not view Paul's sufferings as a constituent part of his witness, he does regard them as integral to his unique role in salvation history, which is to carry the gospel to the ends of the earth.[24] Just as his appointment to a worldwide mission is governed by a divine necessity ("you *must* bear witness" 23:11), so are his sufferings. The Lord tells Ananias in a vision that Paul is his "chosen instrument . . . to carry my name before the Gentiles and kings and the sons of Israel; for I will show him how much he *must* suffer for the sake of my name" (9:15–16, RSV). One of several important parallels between Jesus' suffering as portrayed in the Gospel of Luke and Paul's suffering as portrayed in Acts is evident at precisely this point: in each instance the suffering is to be accepted as God's will (Luke 22:42; Acts 20:14). In Paul's case, the persecutor becomes the persecuted; the one who has tacitly consented to Stephen's death (8:1) becomes a "second Stephen,"[25] another suffering witness.

In Acts, μάρτυς is not yet being used with reference to "martyrs" who give up their lives as a witness to their faith,[26] but one stage in the development toward that eventual application of the term is evident here—not only in the reference to "the blood of Stephen [the Lord's] witness" (22:20), but also in Paul's so-called "farewell address" to the Ephesian elders (20:17–38). As the last speech that he delivers before his arrest in Jerusalem, it is in fact his farewell to the whole church. Looking ahead, he says that he is about to "[go] to Jerusalem, *bound in the Spirit*, not knowing what shall befall me there; except that the Holy Spirit testifies to me in every city that imprisonment and afflictions await me" (vv. 22–23, RSV). Then he adds, "But I do not reckon my life to be of any value, nor of great worth to me, if only I may accomplish my course and the ministry which I received from the Lord Jesus, to bear witness to the gospel of God's grace" (v. 24). It is extremely important to observe that these words are spoken out of strength, not out of weakness. Here death is confidently embraced by one who knows that it is his divinely ordained role to suffer as the Lord's witness. Here, as throughout Acts, Paul's sufferings are part of a larger, heroic portrait, shadows added to the canvas in order to accentuate the bold, strong features of God's "chosen instrument."[27]

In the *Pastoral Epistles*, Paul's role as a missionary to the whole world is specifically in view only twice (1 Tim. 2:7; 4:17), but here, as in Acts, he is presented as a key figure in the history of salvation.[28] His place in the divine economy is summarized especially well in Titus 1:1–3, where it is emphasized that he is an apostle in order "to further the faith of God's elect and their knowledge of the truth which accords with godliness" (RSV), and that by divine command and at precisely the right time he was entrusted to make God's word known through his preaching. Since it is above all to provide believers with "the truth which accords with godliness"[29] that Paul has been commissioned, the author of these epistles would have his readers look to him as the church's teacher, and it is primarily as such that he is portrayed here (note the tripartite title, "preacher, apostle, *and teacher*" in 1 Tim. 2:7 and 2 Tim. 1:11). As the church's teacher he is the guarantor of what is called "sound doctrine" (1 Tim. 1:10; 2 Tim. 4:3; Titus 1:9; 2:1); yet it is especially to the model of Paul's own faith and conduct, not primarily to his precepts, that this author would have his readers look for instruction.[30]

Paul's role as the model believer is particularly stressed in 1 Timothy 1:12–17 and 2 Timothy 3:10–14. In the first of these passages he is identified as the "prototype" for (all) believers (v. 16), in that Christ's mercy has delivered even him, the "foremost of sinners"

(v. 15), from unbelief. In the second passage readers are reminded of what they have observed about Paul's conduct and faith (vv. 10–11), particularly about his endurance of "persecutions" and "sufferings." Because the church, too, can expect to be persecuted (v. 12), it is urged to adhere to what it has learned from him (v. 14). Paul's sufferings loom large through the whole of 2 Timothy, which is written as if from prison in Rome (1:15–17; 2:9; cf. 1:8, 12), and as if Paul knows that his death is imminent (4:6). Like the address to the Ephesian elders in Acts 20, it portrays Paul reviewing his ministry and reminding the church of the legacy he is leaving behind.[31]

Also as in Acts, Paul's sufferings are understood to be a necessary concomitant of his witness to the gospel: the imprisoned apostle says that it is for the gospel that he is "suffering and shackled like a criminal" (2 Tim. 2:9).[32] It is sometimes held that the next statement, 2 Timothy 2:10, presumes an understanding of the apostle's sufferings as vicarious (cf. Col. 1:24):[33] "Thus I endure everything because of the elect, in order that they also may obtain salvation in Christ Jesus with eternal glory." The language itself certainly does not suggest this, however.[34] Moreover, the context shows that it is specifically Paul's *endurance* of the sufferings to which this author is directing attention, for it is this theme that connects the affirmation of v. 10 with the (probably traditional) confessional statement employed in vv. 11–13: "if we endure we shall also reign with him; . . . if we are faithless, he remains faithful" (RSV).

It is evident, therefore, that neither a vicarious interpretation of Paul's sufferings (Colossians) nor the apostle's own kerygmatic interpretation can account for the emphasis that is placed on them in 2 Timothy. It is not the sufferings as such with which this author identifies the apostle's witness, but with his endurance of sufferings. This is one important part of the model that is provided for believers in the Pastorals;[35] doubtless all believers are in mind when "Timothy" is urged to "share in suffering for the gospel in the power of God" (2 Tim. 1:8) and to be "a good soldier of Christ Jesus" about it (2:3).

The picture with which one is left in the closing paragraphs of 2 Timothy, where military and athletic metaphors are combined, is of an apostle of heroic stature: Paul has successfully "fought the fight" and "run the race" to which he had been appointed (4:6–7), and having stood tall and strong when all his friends had deserted him (4:16–17), he now faces the certainty of execution with equanimity, confident that the Lord will see him through all adversity and deliver him at last into the heavenly kingdom (4:18).

Concluding Observations

Paul himself described the content of the Christian witness, his gospel, as "the word of reconciliation" and, more specifically, as "the word of the cross." He identified his apostolic witness to this word with "the ministry of reconciliation," and he regarded the sufferings that attended it as his "carrying about . . . the death of Jesus." One may therefore say that Paul interpeted his sufferings kerygmatically: he believed that in what he suffered no less than in what he said, "Jesus Christ was publicly portrayed as crucified" (Gal. 3:1, RSV).

This fundamental connection between the content and the character of the apostle's witness is no longer evident in the deutero-Pauline literature or in Acts. Indeed, in these writings one finds only traces of that paradox of "power in weakness" that had been the distinctive content of the Pauline witness. In these post-Pauline writings the apostle's sufferings are regarded not primarily as bearing witness to the cross but as evidence of his own faith; not as a sign of the apostle's weakness but as a demonstration of his strength. Paul is set before the church as a timeless—and timely—example of courageous endurance.

In the first half-century or so after the apostle's death the Pauline congregations had to come to terms with existence in a world that could no longer be said to be "passing away" (1 Cor. 7:31). Was it perhaps inevitable that they would find his gospel increasingly "hard to understand" (2 Pet. 3:16)? Indeed, even by the end of the first century the Christian movement as a whole faced a profound dilemma. How could it accommodate itself to an extended existence in society without surrendering the gospel that had set it apart, in radical ways, from that society? How could it bear witness to the power of the cross—to the power of self-giving, serving, suffering love—in a world that defined power in very different terms? The interpretations of the Pauline witness that one finds in the deutero-Pauline letters and in Acts must be read in the light of this dilemma. How appropriate each of these was as a response to the church's new situation in the world must of course be answered with reference, as well, to Paul's own theology of the cross.

Notes

1. For the act of witnessing see, e.g., "The Service of Theology to the Servant Task of Pastoral Ministry" ("the expression of Christian faith through words and deeds"), in *The Pastor as Servant*, ed. Earl E. Shelp and Ronald H. Sunderland (New York: Pilgrim Press, 1986) 85, and cf. *The Reality of God and Other Essays* (New York: Harper and Row, 1966), 191, 193,

200, 203, 211. For the *content* of the church's kerygma, particularly in its earliest (and for Ogden, "normative") form, see, e.g., *Faith and Freedom: Toward a Theology of Liberation* (Nashville: Abingdon, 1979), 45–46, 48, 51, 52, 55; and esp., *The Point of Christology* (San Francisco: Harper and Row, 1982), s.v. "Witness" in the Index.

2. The genitive, τοῦ Χριστοῦ, is doubtless to be understood as objective, so that Paul would be thinking of a witness *about* or *to* Christ. Cf. "the gospel of Christ" in Rom. 15:19; 1 Cor. 9:12; 2 Cor. 2:12; 9:13; Gal. 1:7; Phil. 1:27; 1 Thess. 3:2.

3. Whether, in 1 Cor. 2:1, Paul refers to the "the mystery of God" or to "the witness of God" is difficult to determine. While the majority of ancient texts have the latter, the earlier texts support the former. Just as the reading "witness" may be explained as assimilation to 1:6, so also the reading "mystery" may be explained as assimilation to 2:7. Since "mystery" accords better with the apostle's comments about wisdom in 1:18–2:13, that may be the preferable reading (see Bruce M. Metzger, *A Textual Commentary on the Greek New Testament* [London and New York: United Bible Societies, 1971] 545). If, however, one should decide the other way (thus, C. K. Barrett, *A Commentary on the First Epistle to the Corinthians*, Harper's New Testament Commentaries [New York and Evanston: Harper and Row, 1968], 62–63), then here, as in 1:6, "witness" would be essentially synonymous with "gospel," and would refer to the content of Christian witness. In either case, the genitive (as in 1:6) is probably objective, requiring that it be interpreted as *about* or *to* God. Cf. "the gospel of God" in Rom. 1:1; 15:16; 2 Cor. 11:7; 1 Thess. 2:2, 8, 9.

4. Thus: "to proclaim" (1 Cor. 9:14; cf. Phil. 1:16–18); "to preach" (Gal. 2:2; 1 Thess. 2:9; cf. 2 Cor. 4:3–5; Phil. 1:15–16); "to speak" (1 Thess. 2:2 [cf. v. 4]). Cf. Rom. 10:16–17.

5. Ernst Käsemann, *Commentary on Romans*, trans. and ed. Geoffrey W. Bromiley (Grand Rapids: Eerdmans, 1980), 394.

6. Specifically, in 1 Cor. 9:18; 15:1; 2 Cor. 11:7; and Gal. 1:11, where it is used as a synonym for "preach" or "proclaim."

7. In 1 Cor. 3, Paul himself uses the metaphors of planting (v. 6) and building (v. 10).

8. See Gerhard Friedrich's discussion in *Theological Dictionary of the New Testament*, ed. Gerhard Kittel; ed. and tr. Geoffrey W. Bromiley (Grand Rapids: Eerdmans, 1964), 2.708–10.

9. This is certainly the case in 2 Cor. 4:2 (note "our gospel" in v. 3), and also in 1 Cor. 14:36; Phil. 1:14; 1 Thess. 1:6 (note "our gospel" in v. 5); 2:13.

10. See my comments in *II Corinthians*, Translated with Introduction, Notes, and Commentary, Anchor Bible, 32A (Garden City: Doubleday, 1984), 328–29.

11. He can think of himself as a *slave* or, alternately, as a *servant* of Christ (Rom. 1:1; 1 Cor. 4:1; 2 Cor. 11:23; Gal. 1:10; Phil. 1:1; cf. Gal. 6:17), of the Lord (1 Cor. 3:5), of God (2 Cor. 6:4), of a new covenant (2 Cor. 3:6; cf. Rom. 11:23: 2 Cor. 5:18; 6:3); as a *household manager* (1 Cor. 4:1); as a person

engaged in *ambassadorial service* for Christ (2 Cor. 5:20; cf. Philem. 9); and as a *priest* "doing priestly duty for the gospel of God" (Rom. 15:16; cf. 1:9).

12. In his founding of congregations and his ministry to them he has been a *master builder* (1 Cor. 3:10), one to whom the Lord has given authority "for upbuilding, not for destruction" (2 Cor. 10:8; 13:10; cf. Rom. 15:20; 1 Cor. 3:9; 2 Cor. 12:19). But he is also like a *farmer* who plants a crop (1 Cor. 3:6; 9:11) and who harvests its fruit (Rom. 1:13); like a *father* who exhorts and encourages (1 Thess. 2:11; cf. 1 Cor. 4:14–16)—or, more specifically, like a *father of the bride*, because he has betrothed others to Christ (2 Cor. 11:2); and like a *mother*—one who tenderly nurses her infant (1 Thess. 2:7), or one whose present worries for her children are like the remembered pain of childbirth (Gal. 4:19–20).

13. E.g., he thinks of his ministry as involving *hard labor* (1 Cor. 15:10; 2 Cor. 10:15; Gal. 4:11; Phil. 2:16); as demanding the discipline and stamina of an *athlete*, especially that of a runner (1 Cor. 9:24–26; cf. Gal. 2:2; Phil. 2:16); as forcing him to do battle like a *soldier* (2 Cor. 10:3–6; cf. Phil. 2:25; Philem. 2); and as possibly requiring that he pour out his life as a sacrificial *libation* (Phil. 2:17).

14. For the range of possibilities, see my *II Corinthians*, 173–75.

15. Supporting texts, all in Latin, are assembled and discussed by Peter Marshall, "A Metaphor of Social Shame: THRIAMBEUEIN in 2 Cor. 2:14," *Novum Testamentum* 25 (1983): 302–17. It is reasonable to suppose that the metaphor was current in Greek as well as in Latin, although no first century instances of any metaphorical use of the Greek term have been identified.

16. Various parallels are noted in my *II Corinthians*, 281, and by Robert Hodgson, "Paul the Apostle and First Century Tribulation Lists," *Zeitschrift für die neutestamentliche Wissenschaft* 74 (1983), esp. 67–80.

17. This crucial point is apparently overlooked by Hodgson, who, comparing the view implicit in lists of tribulations experienced by such figures as Alexander and Heracles, suggests that Paul, too, regarded "tribulation as the path to deification" ("Paul the Apostle," 79; cf. 80).

18. Lucien Cerfaux, "Saint Paul et le *serveteur de Dieu* d'Isaïe," *Studia Anselmiana* 27–28 (1951): 351–65, followed by David M. Stanley, "Paul and the Christian Concept of the Servant of God," *The Apostolic Church in the New Testament* (Westminster, Md.: Newman, 1966): 312–51, suggests that Paul understood his apostleship as continuing Christ's role as the suffering Servant of God of Deutero-Isaiah. One must, however, take a broader view of the background of the Pauline conception, as Karl Theodor Kleinknecht has in his Tübingen dissertation, *Der leidende Gerechtfertigte: Die alttestamentlichjüdische Tradition vom 'leidenden Gerechten' und ihre Rezeption bei Paulus*, WUNT, 2. Reihe, 13 (Tübingen: Mohr [Siebeck], 1984).

19. For discussions of how Paul is portrayed in Colossians see, e.g., Martinus C. de Boer, "Images of Paul in the Post-Apostolic Period," *Catholic Biblical Quarterly* 42 (1980); Andreas Lindemann, *Paulus im ältesten Christentum: Das Bild des Apostels und die Rezeption der paulinischen*

Theologie in der frühchristlichen Literatur bis Marcion, Beiträge zur historischen Theologie, 58 (Tübingen: Mohr [Siebeck], 1979) 38–40; Helmut Merklein, "Paulinische Theologie in der Rezeption des Kolosser- und Epheserbriefes," in *Paulus in den neutestamentlichen Spätschriften*, ed. Karl Kertelge, Quaestiones Disputatae, 89 (Freiburg/Basle/Vienna: Herder, 1981), 25–69; Charles M. Nielsen, "The Status of Paul and His Letters in Colossians," *Perspectives in Religious Studies* 12 (1985): 103–22; Gottfried Schille, *Das älteste Paulus-Bild: Beobachtungen zur lukanischen und zur deuteropaulinischen Paulus-Darstellung* (Berlin: Evangelische Verlagsanstalt, 1979), 53–60.

20. In addition to the discussions in the standard commentaries, see esp., Jacob Kremer, *Was an den Leiden Christi noch mangelt—Eine interpretationsgeschichtliche und exegetische Untersuchung zu Kol. 1, 24b*, Bonner Biblische Beiträge, 12 (Cologne-Bonn: Hanstein, 1956), and, more recently, Richard J. Bauckham, "Colossians 1:24 Again: The Apocalyptic Motif," *Evangelical Quarterly* 47 (1975): 168–70; W. F. Flemington, "On the Interpretation of Col. 1:24," in *Suffering and Martyrdom in the New Testament. Studies Presented to G. M. Styler by the Cambridge New Testament Seminar*, ed. William Horbury and Brian McNeil (Cambridge: Cambridge University Press, 1981), 84–90; Nielsen, "The Status of Paul," 111–13.

21. Cf. Schille, *Das älteste Paulus-Bild*, 65–66.

22. Various persons are depicted in Acts as bearing "witness" to the gospel, including the Twelve (see, e.g., 4:33), even though only they, according to this author, can properly be called "apostles" (Luke 6:13). The concept of witnessing is prominent in both Luke and Acts. For the theme in general, see, e.g., H. Strathmann in *Theological Dictionary of the New Testament*, ed. and trans. G. W. Bromiley (Grand Rapids: Eerdmans, 1967), 4.474ff.; and, further: Norbert Brox, *Zeuge und Märtyrer*, Studien zum Alten und Neuen Testament, 5 (Munich: Kösel-Verlag, 1961); Otto Michel, "Zeuge und Zeugnis," in *Neues Testament und Geschichte: Historisches Geschehen und Deutung im Neuen Testament. Oscar Cullmann zum 70. Geburtstag*, ed. Heinrich Baltensweiler and Bo Reicke (Tübingen: Mohr [Siebeck], 1972), 15–31; Allison A. Trites, *The New Testament Concept of Witness*, Society for New Testament Studies Monograph Series, 31 (Cambridge: Cambridge University Press, 1977).

23. Correctly, Jürgen Roloff, "Die Paulus-Darstellung des Lukas: Ihre geschichtlichen Voraussetzungen und ihr theologisches Ziel," *Evangelische Theologie* 31 (1979): 510–31, esp. 529–31.

24. For discussions of Paul's place in Acts, see esp.: Christoph Burchard, "Paulus in der Apostelgeschichte," *Theologische Literaturzeitung* 100 (1975): 881–95; de Boer, "Images of Paul"; Jacob Jervell, "Paul in the Acts of the Apostles: Tradition, History, Theology," in *The Unkown Paul: Essays on Luke-Acts and Early Christian History* (Minneapolis: Augsburg, 1984), 68–76, and "Paulus in der Apostelgeschichte und die Geschichte des Urchristentums," *New Testament Studies* 32 (1986): 378–92; Lindemann, *Paulus im ältesten Christentum*, 49–67; Karl Löning, "Paulinismus in der

Apostelgeschichte," in *Paulus in den neutestamentlichen Spätschriften*, ed. Karl Kertelge, Quaestiones Disputatae, 89 (Freiburg/Basle/Vienna: Herder, 1981), 202–34; P. Boyd Mather, "Paul in Acts as 'Servant' and 'Witness,'" *Biblical Research* 30 (1985): 23–44; Roloff, "Die Paulus-Darstellung des Lukas"; Schille, *Das älteste Paulus-Bild*, 9–52; Stephen G. Wilson, *Luke and the Pastoral Epistles* (London: SPCK, 1979), 107–24. Regrettably, the present essay had been substantially completed before Mather's article came to my attention and before Jervell's 1986 article was published.

25. Schille, *Das älteste Paulus-Bild*, 21.

26. Mather correctly observes that in Acts "Paul is not presented as the martyr who dies, but [as] the martyr who is delivered again and again" ("Paul in Acts," 24).

27. Thus, while I am not persuaded by Jervell's argument that Paul is portrayed in Acts as the "super apostle" ("Paulus in der Apostelgeschichte"), the emphasis on Paul's sufferings does not in itself create a difficulty for his thesis. In developing his argument, however, Jervell himself has nothing to say about the prominence in Acts of Paul's sufferings, or even about the portrayal of him as a "witness."

28. For discussions of the portrayal of Paul in the Pastorals, see esp.: Raymond F. Collins, "The Image of Paul in the Pastorals," *Laval théologique et philosophique* 31 (1975): 147–73; de Boer, "Images of Paul"; Lindemann, *Paulus im ältesten Christentum*, 44–49; Norbert Lohfink, "Paulinische Theologie in der Rezeption der Pastoralbriefe," in *Paulus in den neutestamentlichen Spätschriften*, ed. Karl Kertelge, Quaestiones Disputatae, 89 (Freiburg/Basle/Vienna: Herder, 1981), 70–121; Schille, *Das älteste Paulus-Bild*, 69–79; Wilson, *Luke and the Pastoral Epistles*, 107–24.

29. The concern for εὐσέβεια ("godliness," which can also be translated "piety," "reverence," or "religion") is prominent in the Pastorals, esp. in 1 Tim. (2:2; 3:16; 4:7, 8; 6:3, 5, 6, 11). See also 2 Tim. 3:5.

30. Correctly, Collins, "The Image of Paul," 165–72; Lohfink, "Paulinische Theologie," 79–86; Wilson, *Luke and the Pastoral Epistles*, 111; Mather, "Paul in Acts," 38–40.

31. Cf. esp. Acts 20:24, 25 with 2 Tim. 4:6, 7.

32. Thus, also, Wilson: "in both [Acts and the Pastoral Epistles] there is an overriding sense of divine control" (*Luke and the Pastoral Epistles*, 112).

33. E.g., J. N. D. Kelly, *A Commentary on the Pastoral Epistles: I Timothy, II Timothy, Titus* (New York and Evanston: Harper and Row, 1963), 178; Collins, "The Image of Paul," 169.

34. Thus, instead of "on behalf of the elect," 2 Tim. 2:10 has "because of the elect"; contrast Col. 1:24, "on behalf of his body."

35. Endurance is also a key aspect of the portrait of Paul in *1 Clem.* 5:5–7, where the apostle is commended as "its greatest example," v. 7.

Part II

The Credibility of
Christian Theology:
Essays in Philosophical Theology

Chapter Four

Argument, Dialogue, and the Soul in Plato

DAVID TRACY

Among his many contributions to contemporary theology is Schubert Ogden's consistent emphasis on a central need for all theological work: the need to give reasons for all one's assumptions and presuppositions. The more familiar word for this activity in much of modernity is the need for argument. In one sense, this insistence on argument lies at the heart of all of Ogden's work: from his early, masterful analysis of the implicit and explicit arguments in Rudolf Bultmann's project of demythologizing, through his many contributions to process thought (his several arguments spelling out his reasons for agreement and disagreement with Charles Hartshorne, that other modern master of argument, are especially illustrative here), to his creative use of Stephen Toulmin's *The Uses of Argument* in *The Reality of God*, to his more recent use of Jürgen Habermas on "validity-claims" for theology.[1] There is, in fact, scarcely a page of Ogden where the use of finely honed arguments does not function centrally. In sum, there is no escape in Ogden's work from the demands of all authentic theology: for if theology is to be, in the most general terms, reflective inquiry on the most fundamental issues, then there can be no relaxing of the standards of such difficult but necessary inquiry.[2]

The moment in all inquiry that Ogden's work exemplifies better than that of any theologian of our time is the moment of argument. For that reason, Ogden's contributions to most of the substantive issues of Christian theology are exceptional. As Bernard Lonergan once observed of Anselm, what fascinates one about him is that he seems interested only in the really difficult and central questions: God, christology, salvation-redemption, general theological method. Consider, for example, the unrivaled clarity of Ogden's christology where what is and what is not affirmed in the central christological

An earlier version of this essay appeared in the journal of the Association of Theological Schools, *Theological Education* 24, suppl. 1 (1988).

confession is both clarified and defended while, at the same time, the confusions attendant upon the raging contemporary interest in "old" and "new" quests for the "historical Jesus" are dissolved with clarity and even brevity.[3] Any one of Ogden's substantive contributions is well worth a lengthy and critical analysis. Within all these substantive studies lies an intellectual power partly dependent, of course, on native gifts and erudition but also on Ogden's fidelity to the full demands of reflective inquiry, especially the demand for argument.

It would be very helpful for someone to analyze Ogden's many uses of argument for theological inquiry—his revisions of Bultmann and Marxsen for criteria of appropriateness; his strictly philosophical arguments on experience, on God, on process, and on general theological method itself for criteria of meaningfulness; his recent essays on "validity-claims." My aim for this paper, however, is more general and more indirect. I wish to reflect on the emergence of inquiry as dialogue and dialectic in Plato.

I undertake this task not to claim that Ogden's understandings of argument are directly influenced by Plato's notion of dialectic. There is, of course, an indirect influence—as Whitehead's justly famous and usefully exaggerated statement that all Western philosophy is a series of footnotes to Plato suggests. Ogden, as much as the rest of us, is an heir to that Platonic heritage. Indeed, it is difficult to read a single essay of Ogden's without recognizing his debt to the Greeks: the passion for the "examined life," the insistence that there is a difference between "doxic thinking" and reflective inquiry where we can and must examine our reasons for all our opinions and, in theological inquiry, our most basic beliefs and assumptions.

On the more specific sense of the nature of reflective inquiry, Ogden (here like two of this favorite conversation partners, Stephen Toulmin and Jürgen Habermas) seems more clearly an heir to the "master of argument," Aristotle, than to the dialogues of Plato. Like Toulmin and Habermas in their different ways, Ogden has continued the great Aristotelian enterprise of clarifying what argument is, both formally and substantively, and what criteria are appropriate for what kind of substantive arguments. More like Habermas than Toulmin, Ogden is less interested in rhetoric than in dialectic and remains committed to transcendental analysis of all validity-claims.

Yet Ogden's difference from both Toulmin and Habermas is equally clear: he defends the possibility, indeed intellectual necessity, of metaphysical inquiry. Like his mentors Whitehead and Hartshorne (and their and Aristotle's mentor here, Plato) he argues for the possibility and necessity of reflective inquiry on the most fundamental question, i.e. the most fundamental beliefs and pre-suppositions of all our thinking and acting.[4] This latter mode of inquiry has been named, through a curious historical accident in the transmission of Aristotle's text we know as the *Metaphysics*, metaphysical inquiry. That mode of inquiry is just as properly described (as it was by both Plato and Aristotle) as theology: i.e., that reflective inquiry demanded by reason itself on the most fundamental questions, beliefs, and presuppositions of all thinking, acting, and living. It is this "Platonic" element that has always most intrigued and most persuaded me in Ogden's work. It is the element which theologians at least cannot evade. It is indeed true that the many contemporary rediscoveries of Aristotle's *Topics* and his clarifications of dialectic and rhetoric and his notion of *phronesis* are extremely helpful for dealing with the contingent, with matters which could be other than they are. At the same time, for the theologian, there is no intellectually responsible way that the question of the one necessary individual, God, and the relationship of that reality to the most basic questions and presuppositions of all our experience, thought, and action can be adequately reflected upon except through that mode of reflective inquiry which both Plato and Aristotle insisted upon: metaphysics—or theology.

It is Plato, not Aristotle, I repeat, where the origins of this mode of fundamental inquiry we call dialectic may be found. Some further reflection on this puzzling notion in Plato may illuminate both some of the power and persuasiveness of Ogden's theological inquiry as well as the further questions which his characteristic way of doing theology could fruitfully address. This "detour" through Plato as a tribute to the clear achievements and possible limitations of Ogden's theology may prove one useful way to reflect further upon the full demands of theological inquiry itself. Such, at least, is the risk undertaken by this "indirect" reflection on the achievement of Schubert Ogden.

Dialectic in Plato

The debates on the meaning of "dialectic" in Plato continue unabated.[5] I make no claim to resolve this debate here or to provide anything like a consensus of reputable Platonic scholarly judgment on the issue. I claim only to give one plausible account of what dialectic is in Plato's texts and what that can mean for all reflective inquiry.

Indeed, I agree with David Smigelskis that rather than trying to define a specific set of characteristics that we can then name "dialectic" in Plato, it is better to begin with the general definition I have already employed, namely, dialectics is any mode of reflective inquiry on a fundamental issue.[6] Dialectics, on this reading, is not another "specialty"—it is, rather, a mode of inquiry that functions in every specialized form of inquiry.

This general description can be further specified in several ways. First, any mode of inquiry (whether in mathematics, in ethics, or in theology) that begins from some assumption and then inquires into the rational grounds for that assumption (rather than simply the consequences of that assumption) is dialectical. There is no specific subject-matter for dialectics in Plato (here the difference from Aristotle is startling); there is only the mode of inquiry which, as reflective, demands a constant examining of all our assumptions, opinions, beliefs.

There are, therefore, dialectical scientists (now named "philosophers of science") and nondialectical scientists. There are dialectical understandings of piety (*Euthrypho*), justice (*Republic*), love (*Symposium* and *Phaedrus*), courage (*Laches*) and all the other virtues, beliefs, and practices, as well as nondialectical understandings. There are dialectical understandings of the Good, the Forms, the Beautiful, and nondialectical ones. There are dialectical understandings of the traditional myths, gods, rites, and beliefs, and nondialectical ones. To repeat: any mode of inquiry that involves a sustained and rigorous reflective analysis of the basic assumptions of any given belief or practice is dialectical. Any that does not, is not.

But what "signs" can we find to indicate whether a particular mode of inquiry is or is not dialectical?[7] A modern thinker (or, for that matter, an ancient or medieval Aristotelian) would be likely to suggest "argument" (in both its formal and substantive modes) as a principal "sign" of reflective thought. Yet what is interesting in Plato is that he does not make this characteristically Aristotelian-modern move.

To be sure, the demand for argument is present in Plato throughout his work: both the formal demands for internal consistency of concepts, and, above all, the formal and substantive demands for self-consistency in the inquirer (negatively, self-contradiction). The latter demand is most prominent in Plato's use of the dialogue form itself to communicate indirectly to the reader the direct demands of face-to-face conversation; this is the *elenchus* method of inquiry characteristic of Plato's Socrates.

It is not what a particular person says that determines whether she or he is dialectical. It is only what persons mean by what they say and whether they can give reasons for that meaning that are the signs of the dialectical. And this functions best (for Plato) through that sustained and rigorous mode of question-and-answer which is the main thrust of the early and middle dialogues in which Socrates is the main dramatic figure.

In the early aporetic dialogues, the open-endedness occasioned by the aporias functions well to indicate three central Platonic presuppositions for all inquiry: the fact that the question prevails over the answer in all true inquiry; the fact that true inquiry always provokes further inquiry; the fact that true inquiry, like true education, is always directed to the horizons—the interests, experience, and character—of the actual inquirers.[8] The sophists, for Plato, give speeches—Socrates engages in conversation. Even in the great middle dialogues, especially the *Republic,* where more "constructive" results are presented, the open-endedness of the dialogue form reasserts itself to forbid dogmatism and to assure further inquiry. The loss of the dialogue in modern thought is a loss, I believe, not merely of the unexampled artistry of that form as exemplifying genuine inquiry in Plato, Cicero, Augustine, Berkeley, and Hume. It is also a loss of one crucial way to remind all genuine inquirers (i.e., all dialecticians) that the formal treatise or essay comprised of written arguments may be less faithful to the substantive and self-revelatory demands of all face-to-face encounters.

The *elenchus,* as the cross-examination of the inquirer in face-to-face conversation, is, for Plato-Socrates, the manifestation of whether one means what one says and can give reasons defending that meaning. In more explicit terms, the *elenchus* reveals whether or not *logos* is present in the inquirer's soul. It is always the "soul" of the inquirer, as we shall see below, that is ultimately at stake in all dialectical inquiry.[9] In genre terms, a dialogue can exemplify this substantive existential struggle better than a formal treatise can. In terms of inquiry, the "dramatic" character of any face-to-face dialogue allows for both a wider range of probing inquiry and a greater manifestation to all participants of the state of their character, the presence or absence of "logos" in their souls, their commitment or lack of such for the "examined life," and the relationship between the formal and substantive elements in all their arguments.

I have defended elsewhere the claim that the more encompassing term "conversation" rather than "argument" should be the principal example of inquiry demanding analysis by all contemporary inquirers—including those proponents of communication theory such as Habermas and Apel who sometimes seem to narrow too quickly the demands of "rational communication" to the sole demands of the "better argument."[10] Arguments are a necessary moment in any properly dialectical conversation. But the dialogue form is more comprehensive as a revelation of the state of the "soul" (or, alternatively, of the existential self-understanding) of the dialectical inquirer. I wish we possessed more than the fragments we presently do of Aristotle's lost dialogues. I am thankful that we do possess Plato's—for there one can find dialectical inquiry in all its complexity, ambiguity, open-endedness, and sometimes confusion. I do not regret the loss of the "unwritten doctrines" of Plato, if they ever existed, for I believe that his dialogues function better than a formal treatise as an indirect communication of a life of genuinely dialectical inquiry.

To describe the *elenchus* method as *the* sign of dialectical inquiry in Plato is not to disparage the other signs also there: including the later signs for strict argument which Aristotle, with finer logical skills and his extraordinary clarifying genius, later refined. In Plato himself, one can find the procedures of generalization, definition, and division in his early and middle dialogues and the same both used and reflected upon in his later, relatively nondialogical dialogues, such as the *Sophist,* the *Theatetus* and, above all, the *Parmenides.*

It is well known that Plato, however much he praises dialectic and the philosophic life, nowhere actually defines dialectic with the precision he brings to bear on all his other fundamental questions. In the famous section on "dialectic" in Book VII of the *Republic* the reader is made to understand the importance of dialectic—even, it can be said, to feel its import through Plato's artistically wondrous and philosophically dialectical way of relating his parable of the cave, his simile of light, and his image of the "divided line." But even here, we are not given a definition of dialectic analogous to the definition of justice.

This is, to be sure, a puzzle, but one well worth dwelling upon. For if all dialectic is reflective inquiry on fundamental issues, if dialectic shows its reflectiveness by addressing assumptions and rational grounds for any practice or belief, if dialectic functions best in person-to-person sustained cross-examination via the *elenchus* method and second-best in written dialogues which exemplify not only the arguments but the interests and characters of the inquirers (the *logos* in their souls or its absence); if attempts at definition, generalization, and division are genuine exemplifications of dialectical inquiry but not its only ones, then it follows that explicit arguments are also important for dialectical inquiry but are not its sole exemplifications. Another exemplification (and one to which such communication theorists as Habermas and Apel would do well to give further reflection via Plato) is one that no dialectical theologian can avoid: the question of myth. Is myth ever an exemplification of dialectics? If so, how? If not, why not? This central issue, which has haunted contemporary theology like a guilty romance, haunted Plato as well, especially whenever he turned dialectical inquiry to the most fundamental question of all: the nature of the whole as that whole can be understood by the dialectical thinker.

Myth and Dialectic

The dialogue form, again, seems uniquely qualified to manifest dialectic-in-action in written form. This is the case, and not merely through the artistry which is clearly Plato's. Indeed, whether Plato's model of dialogue is fashioned principally on the model of the mime or the drama is a moot point.[11] In either case, Plato's discovery of this form allows him to show the true drama he observed in Socrates: the drama of the philosophic soul in conflict with others and, often, with the other in itself.

On this reading, therefore, it is a matter of philosophical and not merely artistic import for Plato to have fashioned the dialogue form.[12] For dialogue not only nicely exemplifies the question-and-answer method of face-to-face Socratic cross-examination, it also exemplifies dialectic-at-work in the *elenchus* method and in such refinements of that mode of inquiry as arguments on definition, generalization, and division. Dialogue is also a form capable of revealing the souls of the characters in the inquiry. In more familiar contemporary terms, dialogue can reveal the existential self-understanding of the inquirers. It is this latter search that is at the heart of Plato's entire work and that makes him so clearly a contemporary of all those late twentieth-century inquirers concerned to continue the tradition of dialectical reason in Plato's sense as well as in Aristotle's clarified modes of argument. In dialogue one can show inquiry at work while also relating that inquiry directly to our primordial existential self-understanding: of the self as related to itself, to society, nature, and the whole.

Plato's principal word for such existential self-understanding is *psyche*, or soul. Amidst all the scholarly debates on Plato's understanding, in different contexts in different dialogues, of "soul," this much, I believe, is clear: besides its other functions (e.g., in movement), the term "soul" is a direct analogue of what a modern like Bultmann or Ogden means by existential self-understanding.[13] To be sure, like Ogden (or in their distinct ways, Voegelin and Lonergan), Plato's interest in this existential self-understanding is deeply informed by his belief in the differentiation of consciousness that occurs to a philosophic soul engaged in dialectical inquiry. For Plato, as his famous attack on the mimetic "poets" shows, once the philosophic drama of the soul occurs (as it did, for him, in Socrates), then even "dear Homer" and the great tragedians (including Aeschylus, to whom he otherwise seems so similar) become inadequate in their accounts of our "souls."[14]

The emergence of Socrates, the emergence of dialectical inquiry, has transformed the soul and its internal conflicts so well portrayed by the poets, especially the great tragedians Aeschylus and Sophocles. To understand "soul" properly, we must replace their mimesis of those conflicts with the new drama of the soul—the mimesis of the idea in the emergence of Socrates. But before one assumes that this is proof of the "rationalism" so often charged to the Greek Socratic enlightenment (or, for that matter, to Lonergan or Ogden!), one needs to reflect further on the drama of the soul in the Platonic dialogues.

The most convincing case for the charge of rationalism could be made if one examined only the *Phaedo*, where the rational character of the soul is sternly portrayed. But even there the figure of Socrates, the presence of myth, and the open-ended nature of the inquiry in dialogue form are far more complex than this familiar reading suggests. But the matter of the soul for Plato is complicated by several factors in other dialogues: for example, the tripartite division of the soul into rational, spirited, and appetitive "parts" in the *Republic* and the *Phaedrus* and, above all, the microcosm-macrocosm analogue that dominates Plato's dialogues in the *Republic* (soul and polis) and the *Timaeus* (soul and cosmos).

The tripartite view of the soul can be read as a challenge to any purely rationalist understanding of "soul." For it is one thing to claim (as Plato clearly does) that the rational is the spark of the divine in the human and that the rational part of the soul, once differentiated as philosophic reason employing dialectics, should justly rule the other parts which cause the inner conflicts of the soul. It is quite another matter to claim, as traditional rationalists do, that conscious reason alone is sufficient for existential self-understanding. This latter position, however familiar from many readings of Western notions of enlightenment, is not Plato's.[15]

Reason is the great hope, but only a reason that can faithfully (i.e., dialectically) acknowledge its own possibilities, complexities, and limits. However unsettled some forms of Platonism may be by the discovery of the reality of the unconscious in Freud and Jung, by the "dialectic of enlightenment" of Adorno and Horkheimer, or by the fragile character of "reason" in existentialist thought, these discoveries, on my reading, complicate but hardly devastate Plato's own account of the soul.

Reason acknowledges its own possibilities by engaging in genuinely dialectical inquiry; this surely, as the prior section urged, is at the heart of the Platonic corpus, early, middle, and late, and at the heart of all of Plato's successors—from Aristotle on argument to modern communication theorists. But reason—as dialectical reason—can and must, as rational, also acknowledge its own limits. This is the case not so much because reason, although the "ruling element" in the soul, is only one of three elements. It is the case, rather, because reason in the soul is the spark of the divine in the human: the way in which reason can recognize both its extraordinary possibilities and its own finite, limited status. Thereby the soul can be led to acknowledge all genuine manifestations of the whole and of the divine, including those not arrived at by strictly dialectical procedures. For example, before dialectical inquiry, as the use of myth in some of the early dialogues indicates, myth is a dubious aid to the soul. In the midst of dialectical inquiry, however (here the several uses of myth in the *Republic* and the *Phaedrus* are exemplary), myth is a genuine aid to the soul.[16]

The central clue here remains Plato's much disputed reading of art and myth. There can be no doubt that Plato is the great demythologizer of the traditional myths (even those of the Olympian gods) and of the poets (from Homer and Hesiod through the great tragedians).[17] For Plato, the differentiation of dialectical reason has occurred in Socrates, and the drama of the philosophic soul must dialectically challenge the anthropomorphism of the traditional myths of the gods and the heroes and the mimetic disclosure of the inner conflicts of the prephilosophic soul and the pre-Socratic polis of the great tragedians. Neither Homer, nor the traditional myths in Hesiod, nor the great characters and actions of the tragedians can "give a rational account"—a dialectical account—of themselves.

The poets can only mimetically describe the confusions of the soul in the individual and the polis while also "projecting" this confusion on their anthropomorphic portraits of the gods. To be sure, the traditional myths and the poets contain great truths worth retrieving. But, for Plato, we must demythologize the myths whenever we find ourselves in a situation of political decadence (which Plato clearly considers to be the situation of the Athens of his day or even of the earlier Periclean period) or in a situation of such intellectual decadence that the great *Peitho* or persuasion theme of Aeschylus[18] can become a travesty of true persuasion (persuasion-without-inquiry into the truth of things) as treated by the new rhetorical persuaders, the sophists.

There can be little doubt that Plato, like every dialectical theologian, does not hesitate to demythologize when either the situation (Athenian political and intellectual decadence) or the tradition (anthropomorphic portraits of the Olympian gods acting as badly as decadent humans) demands it. Plato needed to write his famous "dear Homer" passage as much as any dialectical Christian theologian today needs to write her or his "dear Paul" passage for authentic theological inquiry. But to see Plato as only the great rational demythologizer of traditional myth and art is, I believe, seriously to misunderstand him.

It is not only the case that Plato is a great *re*mythologizer—although that is indeed true, as his apparently original creation of such great myths as the myth of Er in the *Republic* and the myths of creation and Atlantis in the *Timaeus* and the *Critias* shows. It is, rather, that Plato is also the great rational-dialectical defender of the truth of both myth and art.[19]

The dialectical soul, unlike other souls, finds it necessary to give a rational account of itself. As that account proceeds, the soul, for Plato (here the descent-ascent theme throughout the *Republic* seems paradigmatic), finds itself "pulled" to a depth that both grounds it and goes beyond it which it cannot account for dialectically but can and must acknowledge through its own dialectical experience.

In modern language, authentic "existence" demands the acknowledgment of "transcendence"—and recognizes that transcendence in the "traces" or "ciphers" of transcedence of the great myths. That experience of a depth where the soul somehow "participates" in or "imitates" the whole and the divine can come in several ways: through reflection on *eros* as a divine gift (as in the *Symposium* and the *Phaedrus*); through reflection on *thanatos* as providing the clue to the truth of the philosophic life (as in the *Phaedo* or the myth of Er in the *Republic*); through the manifestations of new works of art disclosive of the soul and its kinship with the whole (as in the mimesis of the philosophic soul, which is the central drama of the dialogue form); or through new, "true" myths which disclose the soul as participating in or imitating the cosmos itself (as in the great philosophy of myth in the *Timaeus* wherein cosmos and soul can be understood only together).

True inquiry (dialectics), as true persuasion, is driven by the divine power of eros that manifests the soul's participation in the divine and the whole. Inquiry and persuasion without love are as helpless for Plato as eros without true inquiry, and true persuasion is inevitably decadent. That the philosophic life is the erotic life par excellence is, for Plato, the central clue to the eros which drives every soul in myriad forms. It is also the central clue to that mode of inquiry and persuasion which drives the philosophic soul to its own depth where it recognizes that it participates in the whole and the divine through all its eros, from physical passion to the "divine madness" which is a gift of the gods to the poets and seers (the *daimon* which drove Socrates to his calling) and the faithful, eros-driven inquiry of the dialecticians.

The dialectical soul, thus impelled by love and differentiated by true reason, eventually finds itself compelled to acknowledge the truth of myth and art. Even without the backing of Plato's controversial interpretation of *anamnesis*, this position can be warranted on Platonic grounds. The warrant is this: in the great myths and the great works of art, the soul discovers itself by discovering—acknowledging its own participation in and imitation of the whole and the divine. At the same time, the cosmos and the divine are the central clue to the psyche. Whether Plato invented or discovered the great myth of creation of the *Timaeus* remains a moot point. But that Plato accords some truth-status to that myth seems incontrovertible. One can either dismiss the myth of the creation in the *Timaeus* as the strange fantasy of an old and disillusioned philosopher or accord it the kind of truth Plato did: the truth of any great myth or any great work of art that manifests the truth of the intrinsic kinship of soul and cosmos. This truth the dialectician was already led to acknowledge in her or his inquiry upon love and persuasion. This truth the dialectician turned dialectical mythologizer and artist can now acknowledge anew by recounting the myth as a "likely story"—its likeliness is not in it details but in its central insight: the kinship of soul and cosmos.[20]

Dialectics can acknowledge even when it cannot dialectically ground this ultimate truth. Dialectics can turn to the traditional myths and poets and retrieve this truth from their confused (because anthropomorphic and not philosophically differentiated) mimetic accounts. Dialectics can lead the inquirer to find persuasive any "likely account" of what dialectical inquiry rationally acknowledges but never grounds: the reality of the divine, the reality of cosmos and soul as jointly participating in the divine. A dialectician who is also a great artist (here Plato is alone) may also risk the development of a work of art (a dialogue) that can portray the new myth in the context of genuinely dialectical inquiry: the myth of Er in the *Republic*, the myth of creation in the *Timaeus*, the myth of Atlantis in the *Critias*.

Plato, I believe, continues to persuade because there is a whole in his texts which we later "footnotes" can only glimpse: a commitment to that singular differentiation of consciousness that is Western philosophic reason; a rendering of the Socratic oral performance of cross-examination into the written texts of the dialogues; the refinement, within the encompassing genre of the dialogue, of the need for argument, for *elenchus*, for definition, generalization, division and subdivision—even, potentially, for those refinements of argument and its conditions of possibility elaborated by Aristotle in one way and by Toulmin, Habermas, and Ogden in modern terms; the insistence on the need for theological inquiry on the fundamental question of the whole and our existential relationship to that whole as a mode of inquiry demanded by dialectical reason itself; the ability to provide an artistic-philosophic rendering of existential self-consciousness in its full complexity, from rational differentiation to its acknowledgment of the eros driving all true inquiry; the defense of the truth of art and myth without romanticism and with an insistence on much necessary demythologizing.

In many ways, of course, we must each write our own "dear Plato" texts as surely as Plato wrote his "dear Homer" one.[21] But for providing us with those texts and those fuller demands of reason, all contemporary theologians can only dialectically affirm the great enterprise of theological inquiry in all its fullness in Plato. Is it not possible that Schubert Ogden—however central his contributions to the nature of theological argument as argument, however great his insistence on the role of differentiated reason in modern existential self-understanding, however strong his commitment to dialectical demythologizing—might also be led to affirm, through his own dialectical inquiry, the truth of Plato's defense of the truth-status of both myth and art?[22] One need not abandon dialectics to reach that insight. Indeed as Plato shows us, dialectics itself can guide us back to the truth of myth and art: a truth discovered by dialectics itself and always open to further dialectical challenge, a truth always demanding critical demythologizing—but truth nonetheless.

Notes

1. Schubert M. Ogden, *Christ without Myth* (New York: Harper and Row, 1961); idem, "The Experience of God: Critical Reflections on Hartshorne's Theory of Analogy," in John B. Cobb, Jr., and Franklin I. Gamwell, eds., *Existence and Actuality: Conversations with Charles Hartshorne* (Chicago: University of Chicago Press, 1984), pp. 16–37; idem, *The Reality of God* (New York: Harper and Row, 1963), pp. 27–39. Ogden's essay on Habermas and practical theology is not yet published.

2. The full demands of that task can be seen in the important recent collection, Schubert M. Ogden, *On Theology* (San Francisco: Harper and Row, 1986); see also his important notion of the "emancipation of theology" in *Faith and Freedom: Toward a Theology of Liberation* (Nashville: Abingdon, 1979), pp. 115–24.

3. Schubert M. Ogden, *The Point of Christology* (New York: Harper and Row, 1982).

4. For a characteristic argument here, see Ogden's *The Reality of God*, pp. 21–43.

5. For two good studies, see Hans-Georg Gadamer, *Dialogue and Dialectic: Eight Hermeneutical Studies in Plato* (New Haven: Yale University Press, 1980); Herman Sinaiko, *Love, Knowledge, and Discourse in Plato* (Chicago: University of Chicago Press, 1965).

6. I owe this important reflection to the comments (and paper) of Professor David Smigelskis at the seminar on "dialectic" of the Committee on the Analysis of Ideas and Methods (Autumn 1986).

7. The choice of the word "signs" is crucial: in this case one can state that the operations are important signs of dialectic but *only* signs, lest dialectic as reflective inquiry into fundamental questions be separated from its always intrinsic relationship to the subject-matter in question and thereby reduced to purely formal elements, as in all "methodologism" as distinct from "method." The well-known "conceptual analysis" approach to Plato's dialogues adds many clarifications of the logical (or illogical) character of the actual contextualized arguments of the dialogues. Nevertheless, an exclusive concern with these formal characteristics is in danger of losing both the intrinsic relationship of the inquiry to a particular question and the relationship in a particular context with particular characters. For one example of both the gains and losses of conceptual analysis, see Gerasimos Xenophon Santas, *Socrates: Philosophy in Plato's Early Dialogues* (London: Routledge and Kegan Paul). For two studies of the wider meaning of dialogue and argument in Plato, see Kenneth Seeskin, *Dialogue and Discontinuity: A Study in Socratic Method* (Albany: State University of New York

Press, 1987); Michael C. Stokes, *Plato's Socratic Conversations: Drama and Dialectic in Three Dialogues* (Baltimore: The Johns Hopkins University Press, 1986).

8. Paul Friedländer, *Plato: An Introduction*, vol. 1 (Princeton: Princeton University Press, 1969), pp. 154–71, 230–36.

9. Among the many scholars who emphasize this factor, the most striking is Eric Voegelin, *Plato and Aristotle* (Baton Rouge: Louisiana State University Press, 1957).

10. I have defended this priority in David Tracy, *Plurality and Ambiguity: Hermeneutics, Religion, Hope* (San Francisco: Harper and Row, 1987), pp. 1–28. See the representative analyses of each in: Karl-Otto Apel, *Understanding and Explanation: A Transcendental-Pragmatic Perspective* (Cambridge, Mass.: MIT Press, 1984); Jürgen Habermas, *The Theory of Communicative Action*, vol. 1 (Boston: Beacon Press, 1984).

11. Aristotle, we may recall, believed the dialogues modeled on the mime, as does David Grene in his exemplary study, *Greek Political Theory: The Image of Man in Thucydides and Plato* (Chicago: University of Chicago Press, 1967).

12. A matter nicely analyzed in the studies by Hans-Georg Gadamer in *Dialogue and Dialectic*.

13. The function of "self-movement" for soul is ontologically central in Plato—recall the famous analysis of the "world-soul" in the *Timaeus*, in *Plato*, vol. 7, Loeb edition (Cambridge, Mass.: Harvard University Press, 1952), 34A–B–40D. The struggle of the philosopher's soul for what a modern would call authentic existential self-understanding is everywhere present in Plato; above all, in the early dialogues but also in the extraordinary soul-state analogy of the *Republic* and the soul-cosmos analogy of the *Timaeus*.

14. See *Republic*, Book X. This "dear Homer" is a standard way of speaking of Plato's love and criticism of Homer.

15. The modern notion of "reason" (or, perhaps more accurately, "rationality") is considerably narrowed in scope from Plato's notion of "nous" in the "psyche," as perhaps Freud himself with his curiously Plato-like appeals to "eros" and "thanatos" recognized.

16. A helpful study here remains the classic essay, "Myth," in Friedländer, *Plato: An Introduction*, pp. 171–213.

17. For a representative study, see Hugh Lloyd-Jones, *The Justice of Zeus* (Berkeley: University of California Press, 1971), pp. 130–36.

18. For the Aeschylus-Plato analogy, see Francis Macdonald Cornford, *Plato's Cosmology: The* Timaeus *of Plato Translated with a Running Commentary* (London: Routledge and Kegan Paul, 1948), pp. 361–64.

19. It is, of course, something of a modernism to employ recent notions of myth in discussing Plato. In fact (especially in the *Timaeus*), the words *mythos* and *logos* are often used interchangeably; at other times, in the same text, they are employed as contrast words. It is nonetheless true, as both Friedländer and Voegelin argue, that the familiar modern discussion of

"myth" and "logos" is entirely appropriate (even necessary) to a fuller understanding of Plato's unusual use (and perhaps invention) of myths in the middle and later dialogues, as well as to his problems with the traditional myths. To be sure, Plato is neither a Christian nor a Romantic, much less a modern in regard to myth. Equally, contemporary debates on the truth of myth in relationship to reason are illuminating of the texts of Plato as well as illuminated by those texts.

20. The crucial words are in 29D: *ton eikota muthon* (τὸν εἰκότα μῦθον). It is more exact to state that the likeliness means both that the myth of creation is *like* the object it describes, namely, the universe as itself the image of the idea-in-becoming, as well as the fact that the story or myth is therefore *likely* or probable. Also implied by this brilliant Platonic play on the likeliness of his likely story (the myth of creation) is, I believe, the kinship of psyche and cosmos, a kinship which is finally that of image and model and helps render the likely story yet more likely.

21. In a sense, Whitehead's process philosophy may be read as his "dear Plato" letter: recall how Whitehead loved (and, in my judgment, improved upon) the myth of creation from the *Timaeus* by developing his own "likely" story of the relationship of self, cosmos, and God.

22. To do so, I believe, Ogden need not abandon his Bultmannian program of demythologizing. He might, however, reflect anew on the reflections on the possible truth of art in the "later," nonexistentialist Heidegger: see, especially, Martin Heidegger, "The Origin of the Work of Art," in *Basic Writings*, ed. David Krell (New York: Harper and Row, 1977).

Chapter Five

Faith and Existence in the Philosophy of F. H. Jacobi

B. A. GERRISH

The element of all human knowledge and activity is faith.
—JACOBI

Even to exist as a self is possible only on the basis of "faith."
—OGDEN

In philosophical accounts of religion the term "faith" or "belief" is commonly used, naturally enough, in a restricted sense: it is taken to mean the explicit acceptance of conventional religious claims, such as those embodied in the Christian creeds.[1] The question of faith and reason is then assumed to be whether religious belief, so understood, can survive rational scrutiny or can be harmonized with what is otherwise held to be true, particularly in the natural sciences. But there has been at least a minor strand in modern religious thought in which "faith" refers, or refers also, to a constant state of mind underlying every human activity, including the scientific enterprise itself. Faith, in this sense, is not peculiar to the conventionally religious; it belongs to human existence as such and is therefore common to all, whether they know it or not.

The dominant usage has credentials that are respectable enough. Thomas Aquinas (ca. 1224–74), for instance, understood faith precisely as assent to the divine truth that is summed up in the articles of the creeds. As such, faith (*fides*) occupies a position on the cognitive scale midway between knowledge (*scientia*) and opinion (*opinio*). It differs from *knowledge* because the mysteries of faith are neither self-evident nor demonstrable; the assent of the intellect to them is not brought about by the objects themselves but requires the assistance of an act of will, and that is why believing can qualify as a merit. But faith is not therefore uncertain; it differs from *opinion* exactly because opinion is accompanied by anxiety that the opposite of what is accepted might be true. Faith is founded on divine truth, and nothing is more certain than the word of God. And that it is in fact divine truth that the church proposes to the intellect for its assent can be supported by evidence, though the evidence is not coercive except to the natural intellectual acumen of demons, who consequently deserve no praise for believing.[2]

Thomas's notion of faith is, in essentials, the notion subjected to scorn by freethinkers in the age of enlightenment. Take, for instance, the placement of faith on the cognitive scale suggested by Anthony Collins (1676–1729) in his *Essay Concerning the Use of Reason* (1707). The domain of *science* is confined to propositions perceived to be true either immediately or by necessary proofs. All other propositions (that is, sentences that make truth-claims) have to be shown by proof to be probable or improbable. If they can be assessed by our own resources ("internal evidence"), they yield *opinion*. If they can be assessed only by recourse to the testimony of others ("external evidence"), they yield mere *belief*. While Collins is prepared to admit that our knowledge depends heavily on the testimony of others, he is anxious to protect us from being duped, especially by clergymen, whom he regularly perceives as making a living out of deceit and manipulation of the unwary. And no amount of testimony from others must ever be permitted to override our own experience, that is, "what we *know* to be true by the use of our Faculties." Or, as Collins also puts it: "Nothing which we judg repugnant to natural Notions ought to be assented to upon the highest Testimony whatever."[3] In a later work, his *Discourse of Freethinking* (1713), Collins points out that even those who are commended to us as authorities have only their eyes to direct them, and it is more reasonable to trust your own eyesight than to trust anyone else's. For God "can require nothing of Men . . . but that whereof he has given them an opportunity of being convinced by Evidence and Reason." In short, "faith" is the cognitive label Collins applies to propositions accepted secondhand, on the testimony of others.[4] John Locke (1632–1704) had written more restrictively, in his *Essay Concerning Human Understanding* (1690), that faith is "the Assent to any Proposition, not . . . made out by the Deductions of Reason; but upon the Credit of the Proposer, as coming from GOD, in some extraordinary way of Communication."[5] But this, clearly, is the kind of faith Collins had especially in mind.

Such a notion of faith readily lends itself to the supposition that intellectual progress in the modern world has been impeded by a continual warfare of science with religion. But it is just this pairing of science with evidence, religion with authority, that advocates of the second notion of faith place in question, arguing that a closer look requires us to acknowledge an ineradicable element of faith even in the activity of scientific inquiry. A classic case along these lines was made, for example, with characteristic rhetorical charm, by A. J. Balfour (1848–1930) in his first series of Gifford Lectures (1914). If Balfour was right, there is a commonsense creed, never summed up in formal articles, that is held by all of us in our ordinary waking moments, even by those of us who criticize it in theory. It includes belief in the existence and the regularity of an external world, a belief presupposed by every scientific experiment and every scientific generalization. Belief in God is not itself to be counted among such "inevitable beliefs," as Balfour called them, but it is more supportive of them than is the naturalism that sometimes passes for scientific; and no amount of armchair philosophical skepticism can shake us out of them.

> The philosopher admits—in theory—no ground of knowledge but reason. I recognize that, in fact, the whole human race, including the philosopher himself, lives by faith alone. The philosopher asks what creed reason requires him to accept. I ask on what terms the creed which is in fact accepted can most reasonably be held.[6]

It is faith in this second, noncompartmentalized sense that I intend to suggest by the correlation "faith and existence." Of course, the status and content of this "existential faith" (as we may conveniently call it) can be variously understood; I have only tried to contrast it provisionally with "religious faith" in the first, restricted sense. I do not propose to trace the lineage of the concept of existential faith in all its varieties; nor do I wish to imply that there are no other meanings the word "faith" can bear besides the two I have contrasted with each other.[7] The two quotations at the head of this essay signal my limited goal, which is, to invite a comparison between "basic confidence" in the theology of Schubert Ogden and "faith" in the philosophy of F. H. Jacobi (1743–1819), the modern grandfather of those who want to speak of a faith that underlies the whole of human existence. Jacobi's "philosophy of faith" (as it is commonly called) proves Balfour quite mistaken when he wrote: "I regard the belief in an external world as one of a class whose importance has been ignored by philosophy, though all science depends on them."[8]

I

Friedrich Heinrich Jacobi, younger brother of the poet Johann Georg Jacobi (1740–1814), has seldom received his due even in his homeland. There is still no critical edition of his works and no definitive biography of him.[9] It is particularly surprising that, with the exception of the theologians of the Catholic Tübingen School, theologians and historians of theology have hardly ever thought him worthy of their attention.[10] A man of diverse talents and interests, he made significant contributions to German literature and philosophy, and he concerned himself, in addition, with social, economic, and political reform. Together with C. M. Wieland (1733–1813), he founded the journal *Der Teutsche Mercur* ("The German Mercury"), and from 1807 until 1812 he was president of the Munich Academy of Sciences. Philosophically, however, he is usually mentioned merely as the foil to greater minds than his own. He was an astute critic who ventured to take on even Immanuel Kant (1724–1804), and his important, if largely indirect, contributions to the emergence of German speculative idealism are commonly acknowledged. But he produced no system; his philosophical reflections were embodied in his early "romances," *Letters of Edward Allwill* (1776) and *Woldemar* (1779), and in subsequent polemical writings. In the harsh verdict of Johann Wolfgang von Goethe (1749–1832), metaphysical speculation became Jacobi's bad luck; he was neither born nor educated for it.[11]

In the twentieth century, it is true, Jacobi's lack of system has been turned into a virtue, and he has been hailed as a precursor of existentialism and Wilhelm Dilthey's (1833–1911) philosophy of life. There is something to be said for this reappraisal, which we owe particularly to the work of O. F. Bollnow, written under Dilthey's influence. Jacobi held that the true task of the inquirer is to disclose existence in its individuality and concreteness; hence he was suspicious of rationalistic philosophizing that took mathematical reasoning as its ideal in the quest for universal constructs. The idea of a philosophy of life, according to Bollnow, was the original impulse of Jacobi's philosophical concerns, but it became overlaid with traditional questions in his so-called philosophy of faith. Bollnow concentrates on Jacobi as "the philosopher of *Sturm und Drang*," and so as the initiator of the movement that in the twentieth century has blossomed in the philosophy of life or existence.[12] But that still leaves to Jacobi little more than an interesting paragraph or two in somebody else's chapter, and it is hardly surprising that in the English-speaking world he has been lucky to receive as much as a passing mention in a footnote.

There appear to have been hardly any English translations of Jacobi's writings, and few translations of the foreign literature about him. Croce's appreciative essay on Jacobi was made available in English in 1966; Hegel's condescending treatment of him in *Faith and Knowledge* appeared a decade later.[13] Native English and American studies of Jacobi are equally hard to find. Robert H. Worthington hails him (overgenerously) as, next to Kant, the most original thinker of his times; his relationship to Schelling is explored by Lewis Ford, and his relationship to Coleridge by W. Schrickx.[14] More detailed and comprehensive, albeit still quite brief, are two American dissertations on him; both able studies, they merit a closer look for the light they shed on the fundamental problem of his philosophy of faith—and on some of the difficulties of appraising, or even interpreting, him justly.

In his Columbia dissertation, published in 1894, Norman Wilde pictures Jacobi on the dividing line between the first and the second periods of modern philosophy, unable to unite the two. He held tenaciously to God, freedom, and immortality as facts and simply pronounced self-destructive any system that denied them. At the root of Jacobi's life was a mystical sense that defied every attempt at explanation. As he wrote to his friend Johann Georg Hamann (1730–88), there was light in his heart, but when he would bring it to the intellect, it went out.[15]

Wilde cautions us not to seek in Jacobi's writings either precision or system, but he does find there an idea "imperfectly striving for expression." Jacobi's fundamental principle, according to Wilde, can be put like this: "The ultimate standard of truth and falsehood lies outside the concept in the real, which is forever beyond the reach of discursive thought." The epistemology implied in this principle was shaped by Jacobi's religious concerns: he sought the conditions on which alone we can claim a knowledge of God, freedom, and immortality. The theory of knowledge that grew out of this quest Wilde classifies as "natural realism," according to which what is known in cognition is not ideas but things. Jacobi was not a "crude realist"; he did not maintain that a thing must exist exactly as it appears to us, but only that there really is "a somewhat independent of us which determines an object to be this rather than that." In short, "the fact of existence is what he seeks to establish." And Wilde concludes that what Jacobi meant by "faith" or (as Jacobi later said) by "reason" is the "faculty of ratification" that guarantees the reality of the objects known.[16]

The cardinal point in Wilde's interpretation of Jacobi is that faith (to put it in my terms, not Wilde's or Jacobi's) is not a mode of cognition but the conviction of reality that accompanies cognition: that is, the confidence that, in knowing, our minds make contact with a reality independent of our knowing. Consequently, Wilde regrets that Jacobi shifted in his later writings from "faith" to "reason" as his key term and spoke of reason as a faculty analogous to sensation but differing in the sphere to which it is applied: the world not of sensible, but of supersensible, objects. Had Jacobi remained true to his original insight, he would have continued to think in terms of "a faculty of belief, testifying to the existence of a reality which finds expression in the appearance of the senses." All our ideas come by way of the senses; applied to the idea of God, Jacobi's epistemology does not, in Wilde's view, claim any special source of knowledge but simply affirms the power of faith (the *Glaubenskraft*) that accompanies the idea—the immediate certainty of a corresponding reality that meets Jacobi's moral and religious needs.[17]

The estimate of Jacobi's development proposed by Wilde is reversed by Alexander Crawford, who thinks the shift from "faith" to "reason" was an improvement. Perhaps Crawford labors too hard in his Cornell dissertation (1902, published 1905) to correct his predecessor's study of Jacobi as a realist; Jacobi, he maintains, was not a typical realist at all but an idealist who affirmed the rationality of the world and the primacy of spirit. This may well be to confuse the epistemological and the metaphysical senses of "idealism." But, in any case, Crawford thinks that the shift from "faith" to "reason" in Jacobi's later writings was a token of his affinity with spiritualistic idealism and, more importantly, of his claim to be taken seriously as a philosopher.[18]

Crawford's reading of Jacobi presupposes that the terminological shift was a move toward greater appreciation for thought. Jacobi began by trying to give the religious principle of faith the dignity of a philosophical principle, but he later "substituted an intellectual element for the feeling element which characterized his first presentation." Hence the cardinal point of Crawford's interpretation is this: "Only in so far as he got beyond the standpoint of immediacy did he formulate a philosophy at all."[19] That this is in fact the import of Jacobi's later use of the term "reason" is open to question. However, one consequence of a preference for the later Jacobi is clear: it heightens the epistemological dualism in his thinking. It is precisely in the later writings that he differentiates most sharply between knowledge of sensible objects and knowledge of supersensible objects, assigning the latter to the domain of faith (or reason!). Crawford recognizes that sensibility and faith/reason were both, for Jacobi, forms of intuition (that is, immediate knowledge), differing only in the objects they reveal. But because he takes sensibility and

faith/reason for parallel modes of cognition (my expression, not his),
he cannot, like Wilde, represent Jacobi as teaching a unified route to
knowledge.[20] This is not say that Crawford is wrong. But the contrast between his exposition and Wilde's, coupled with the un-
doubted ambiguities occasioned in part by Jacobi's intellectual development, suffice to indicate some of the difficulties of
interpretation. A solution, if one is possible at all, must be sought
chiefly in Jacobi's dialogue, *David Hume on Belief.*

2

When Jacobi turned from his romances to more formal philosophical prose, he still chose letters and dialogue, not the didactic treatise, as his medium of expression. After the letters on Spinoza (1785)
and the dialogue on Hume (1787), his major philosophical writings
were polemical, against Kant (1801) and Schelling (1811); and his
last philosophical testament, often pointed out as the best account
of his thought, took the literary form of an introduction prefixed to
the second edition of the dialogue on Hume (1815). "Of writing a
formal treatise," Wilde remarks, "Jacobi was incapable."[21] Perhaps.
But anyone who turns to *Hume on Belief* expecting truth to emerge
from a lively exchange of conflicting viewpoints will be disappointed. The dialogue begins pleasantly enough, but over the long
haul Jacobi could make a conversation sound very much like a treatise. The visitor's role in the dialogue is mainly passive, to furnish
the puzzlement needed for Jacobi to explain his thoughts more perfectly, or else to offer helpful summaries of what Jacobi has said
more copiously.

Jacobi's interest in David Hume (1711–76) was probably acquired
in part from Hamann.[22] Just how far Hume materially influenced
Jacobi's development is hard to judge, and it would have to be mea-
sured in relation to other influences, such as that of Thomas Reid
(1710–96), the Scottish commonsense philosopher who tried to answer Hume.[23] But what Jacobi discovered in Hume (so he supposed)
was a sense of the word "belief" that justified his own use of the
German word *Glaube.* Since my purpose is to discover what Jacobi
understood by "belief," the dialogue on Hume is plainly a major
source. I shall in fact confine myself, in this essay, to an examination
of the dialogue itself (in this section) and (in section 3) to the fresh
introduction furnished with the second edition, before I attempt a
summary analysis of Jacobi's term *Glaube* (in section 4) and a criti-

cal comparison of it with Schubert Ogden's expression "basic confidence" (in section 5). Indeed, as far as the dialogue itself is concerned, only the first part of it is strictly germane—and perhaps the last few pages. Jacobi originally intended to publish three separate dialogues, to be titled, respectively, "David Hume on Belief," "Idealism and Realism," and "Leibniz, or Concerning Reason." For reasons he does not explain, he decided to combine them in a single publication titled *David Hume on Belief, or Idealism and Realism: A Dialogue.* But he admits that the "or" in the title was not quite justified.[24] And readers can readily verify for themselves that both Hume and belief are almost forgotten in the second and third parts, until belief, though not Hume, reappears at the very end.

The preface briefly sets out Jacobi's design in writing the dialogue. He concedes that in his letters on Spinoza he had employed the word "belief" in an unusual sense. He had wanted to challenge the view that knowledge established by proofs of reason includes certain knowledge of actual existents, of which sense-perception (*sinnliche Erkenntnis*) yields only uncertain belief. His own view is that there are not two kinds of knowledge of existence, one certain and the other uncertain, but only one, and that it comes by way of perception (*Empfindung*); reason (*Vernunft*), by contrast, is confined to the faculty of grasping relationships. Absolute certainty belongs only to the affirmation of purely identical propositions (that is, propositions reducible to instances of the principle of identity); the affirmation that something exists in itself, beyond my idea of it, can never approach such certainty. The idealist, accordingly, can no doubt make Jacobi grant that his conviction of the existence of actual things outside himself is only belief. But, as a realist, Jacobi must then reply: "All knowledge can only come from belief [i.e., *this* belief], since *things* must be *given* to me before I am in a position to perceive relationships."[25]

Both the referent of the word "belief," in Jacobi's sense, and the ground for treating belief as antecedent to reason are thus immediately stated in the short preface. The belief in question is belief in an external world that exists independently of the perceiving mind. There is also at least a hint at what it is that makes "belief" the right word to use in this context: an object of belief cannot be established by rational proofs. On the other hand, there could not be knowledge—or even an activity of reason at all—without it. The dialogue proper, in which the two partners are identified simply as "He" and "I," moves directly into the same circle of epistemological problems.

A visiting friend ("He") discovers Jacobi still in his dressing gown, nursing a cold and chuckling over a book. Jacobi has been reading some thoughts of David Hume on belief. Against belief, then? No, for belief. The theme of the dialogue is Hume as a teacher of belief. Jacobi has been loudly accused of degrading reason and teaching *blind* belief, which is to say, assent based on authority, without proofs or personal insight. And this is to rob Protestantism of its strongest supports—the use of reason and the spirit of free inquiry—and to encourage Catholicism. He is further charged with craftily altering the customary use of the actual word "belief," since he attributes to belief what is in fact a matter of perception: that we have bodies and that there are other bodies and other thinking beings outside us. The suspicion thus arises that a devious attempt is being made to smuggle in specifically religious beliefs.[26]

In reply, Jacobi reveals his "secret"—with obvious glee, since the secret can readily be found in a famous book that has been translated into several languages. He admits that the way he uses the word "belief" departs from *everyday* usage. He means, I take it, that we do commonly use "belief" for "blind belief" (or "blind faith"), assent based on mere authority. In any case, he himself intends a *philosophical* usage, according to which "belief" is a knowing that cannot strictly be proved. And for this usage, as he ironically puts it, he has an "authority" such as his critics, at least, seem to need: he is using the word "belief" as David Hume used it in his *Enquiry Concerning Human Understanding.* Jacobi quotes two well-known passages from the *Enquiry.* The first refers to the belief in external objects, a belief that even animals share with humans: "Without any reasoning . . . we always suppose an external universe, which depends not on our perception." The second passage differentiates belief from fiction (that is, from a product of the imagination) by asserting that there is a special sentiment or feeling annexed to belief, a feeling "which depends not on the will, nor can be commanded at pleasure." "Belief" is indeed, according to Hume, the proper name for this feeling, and everyone knows what is meant by it because everyone is conscious of it. Hard to define, it can nevertheless be described. "Belief is nothing but a more vivid, lively, forcible, firm, steady conception of an object, than what the imagination alone is ever able to attain." It is therefore belief, in Hume's opinion, that gives the ideas of judgment, as distinct from the fictions of the imagination, more weight and influence "and renders them the governing principle of our actions."[27]

Jacobi's visitor is convinced. The quotations from Hume confirm not only Jacobi's use of the word "belief" but also his thesis that belief is the element of all knowledge and activity. Jacobi then moves on to justify another term he is charged with abusing: "revelation." Only here, no appeal to Hume or any other authority is required to support what common usage already warrants; in everyday discourse—whether in German, French, English, Latin, or several other languages—one says that objects are "revealed" by the senses. Jacobi's belief, we conclude, is not assent without evidence, but assent to the evidence that the senses reveal, which is the evidence of the thing itself. If anyone chooses to doubt this evidence and demands proof, there is nothing we can do for him or her, because no other evidence is forthcoming. On the contrary, any proof we might try to construct would already presuppose belief and revelation.

> The decided realist who without doubting accepts external things on the evidence of his senses, views this certainty as an original conviction and cannot but think that every use of the intellect to acquire knowledge of the external world must be grounded on this fundamental experience. What shall such a decided realist call the means by which he acquires the certainty of external objects as things existing independently of his representation of them? He has nothing on which to support his judgment but the matter itself, nothing but the fact that things really do stand before him. Can he express himself by a more appropriate word than the word *revelation*? Is not the *root* of this word and *the source of its use* to be sought precisely here?[28]

Jacobi did not need to be told that a decided realism was not David Hume's conclusion from the phenomenon of belief. Hume inclined more to skeptical idealism; he did not find in the *conviction* that there is an external reality any guarantee that there *is* an external reality, but left open the question whether we really *perceive* things outside us or simply perceive them *as* outside us. Jacobi was content to take from Hume only the sense of the word "belief." And he held it to be a manifest misconstrual of our experience when other philosophers sought to make the conviction that there are objects corresponding to our ideas an inferential rather than an immediate conviction, as though we first had the ideas and then concluded that there must be corresponding objects. As Jacobi makes this point in the dialogue, the visitor announces that he sees the light: "In the same indivisible moment, I experience that I exist and that there exists something outside me. . . . No idea, no inference mediates this double revelation." Jacobi is pleased and assures his friend that, yes, he has got it. "Even in the most primitive and simple perception, the self and the other [*das Ich und das Du*], consciousness within and object without, must be there immediately in the soul, both in the same instant, in the same indivisible moment, without before and after, without any operation of the intellect."[29]

The conversation moves on to Hume's critique of the concept of causality, and once again Jacobi appeals to belief: "If you can let yourself be troubled by such doubt, I don't know how to help you. But I think your belief overcomes it just as easily as mine does." For Jacobi, the assertion that things are interconnected in a causal network is justified, we may say, like the assertion that there are things in themselves, by faith alone. And from there the dialogue passes over into the second and third parts. Neither Hume nor belief is any longer the center of attention. Pertinent to the theme of belief, at least indirectly, is the discussion of reason, which Jacobi ties closely to experience or sense.[30] But what must surely strike the reader is that Jacobi does not attempt to move the discussion of Hume's thoughts on belief out of the technical-epistemological domain into the domain of religion. The boundaries of the theme of belief are apparently set by the epistemological interests of British empiricism.

When he does, finally, come back to belief, it has indeed become belief in God and immortality. But the connection with Humean belief, if in Jacobi's mind there is one, is not explained. To be sure, the visitor remarks that *all* belief must finally rest on fact, experience, perception; and Jacobi agrees that if God does not let himself be perceived or experienced in any way, then belief in God should be given up. But Jacobi does not say what experience of God is; he merely asserts that with the precious gift of reason we receive presentiment of God (*Gottesahndung*). "Thence *freedom* blows upon the soul, and the realms of immortality are opened." The visitor confesses that Jacobi's last discourse has left him all at sea. But Jacobi cuts him off with the announcement that it is late and they must stop. He ends with some choice quotations from J. H. Pestalozzi's (1746–1827) *Leonard and Gertrude* (1781–87), and his friend responds with a couple of allusions to Asmus (Matthias Claudius, 1740–1815). The import of the closing pages appears to be, not that we move from sense perception, through reason, to the idea of God, but rather that in the activity of reason, by virtue of which we distinguish ourselves as persons from the world of mere things, we have a presentiment of the Living God who, like us, is spirit or person. "Humans know God," says Pestalozzi, "only insofar as they know humans, that is, themselves." And it is in deeds rather than words that both humanity and God are made known.[31] But if this is so, we must surely ask, are there not after all *two* sources of knowledge— sense experience and moral experience?

3

The second edition of *Hume on Belief* appeared in Jacobi's collected works largely unchanged, except for the addition of some new footnotes. But the original preface was dropped, and the new preface grew into a general introduction to Jacobi's entire philosophical output; running to 123 pages and published just four years before his death, it is the most important source for understanding his final position. Remarkable is the change from "faith" to "reason" as the key term in Jacobi's philosophical vocabulary: *Vernunft* in the introduction now seems to do duty for what the word *Glaube* did in the dialogue itself. It is perhaps arguable that the terminological shift signals a modification of Jacobi's epistemology, but he denied that the change was substantive. In any case, one may well suspect that the old preface was discarded partly because it asserted a single source of knowledge: namely, perception (*Empfindung*).[32] It does seem clear, however, that already in the dialogue itself Jacobi is stretching the narrow concept of experience he finds in British empiricism; he expressly tells us, for example, that he takes the word "sense" (*Sinn*) "in the whole range of its meaning (as the faculty of perception [*Wahrnehmungsvermögen*] in general)."[33]

The new introduction explains again the purpose of the dialogue. In his book on Spinoza, Jacobi had asserted that all human knowledge comes from revelation and faith. The dialogue on Hume was written in response to the charges of fanaticism and popery that the assertion evoked. It is to be understood as an appendix to the book on Spinoza and was intended to justify the notion of a firsthand knowing (*Wissen*) that conditions all secondhand science (*Wissenschaft*), a knowing without proofs that necessarily precedes all knowing derived from proofs, grounds it, and continually governs it.[34] But Jacobi admits that in the dialogue he failed to distinguish "reason" (*Vernunft*) clearly enough from "intellect" (*Verstand*), which prevented him from giving a properly philosophical account of his fundamental doctrine—that there is a power of faith transcending the capacity of demonstrative science. A distinction between "reason" and "intellect" is actually presupposed in our common speech, which assigns to animals only an intellect or intelligence. Jacobi infers that the difference between animals and humans must be one of kind and not degree; otherwise, if reason and intellect were two names for the same faculty, the difference between an orangutan and a Californian would be less than the difference between a Californian and a Plato, a Leibniz, or a Newton.[35]

What, then, is this special "attribute of reason" which alone raises humanity above brute beasts? Jacobi explains that it is the organ of supersensible perception (*Vernehmung*), as the organ of sight is the eye. Animals perceive only the sensible, whereas humans, endowed with reason, perceive also the supersensible.

> If what we call "reason" were only the product of a faculty of reflection based solely upon sense experience [*Sinneserfahrung*], all talk of supersensible things would be mere twaddle; reason as such would be *groundless*, an inventive fantasy. But if it is truly revelatory, then it brings into being a *human* intellect that *knows* of God, freedom, and virtue, of the true, the beautiful, and the good, an intellect exalted above animal intelligence.[36]

Jacobi does not mean to make a psychological separation of reason from intellect: the revelations of reason are possible only *in* an intellect or, as he puts it, an intellect illumined by reason. But the intellect now takes over the duties that in the dialogue he had sometimes assigned, like every other philosopher of the time, to reason. It is the intellect that is the faculty, hovering over sensibility, of forming concepts, judgments, and inferences, and it can reveal or disclose nothing at all. Reason, by contrast, is the faculty of presupposing the true, the good, and the beautiful with full confidence (*Zuversicht*) in the validity of this presupposition; and this is exactly what he had ascribed in the dialogue to the power of belief, as though it were a faculty *above* reason. Jacobi regrets the confusion to which he has innocently given rise.[37]

Obviously, these remarks do not entirely clear up the confusion. For one thing, in the dialogue Jacobi had concentrated on knowledge of the material world and had not said much about supersensible realities. He had no choice, if he wanted David Hume on his side. It now appears, from the new introduction, that the power of faith (*Glaubenskraft*) is attached to two distinct mental operations—if, indeed, it can seriously be maintained that the duties now assigned to reason represent one operation and not several. In Jacobi's view, there are two faculties of perception, two eyes of the soul, corresponding to two kinds of object: sensible things and supersensible things.[38] Every claim we make to possess knowledge can be substantiated only if we trace our concepts and judgments back to the primary mode of cognition in whichever of the two domains they belong to, which means, if we trace them back to the immediate pronouncements of sense or reason.[39] Jacobi's terminology is alarmingly fluid, and he does not illustrate concretely how either one of these verification processes might work. But, in general, the ideal of justifying cognitive claims by deriving them from basic or protocol sentences is familiar enough, even if its application to supersensible objects is not. And what chiefly interests Jacobi is the status of those initial pronouncements of sense or reason that such a procedure must get back to.

In the opening paragraphs of the introduction, he has already spoken of "firsthand knowing." Further on, he attempts to differentiate the two varieties of firsthand knowing associated respectively with the two faculties of sense and reason.

> The reason creates no concepts, builds no systems, and it makes no judgments, but, *like the outward senses*, it is purely revelatory, making positive pronouncements. . . . As there is a sensible intuition, an *intuition* through *sense*, so there is also a rational intuition through *reason*. The two stand over against each other as actual sources of knowledge; the latter can just as little be derived from the former as the former from the latter. Likewise, each stands in the same relation to the intellect, and to this extent also to demonstration. There cannot be any demonstration of *sensible intuition*, because all demonstration is simply tracing the concept back to the *sensible intuition* (whether empirical or pure) that verifies it: as far as knowledge of nature is concerned, sensible intuition is first and last, the unconditionally valid, the absolute. For the same cause, there cannot be any demonstration of *rational intuition*, or the *intuition of reason*, which gives us knowledge of objects beyond nature, that is, makes us certain of their reality and truth. . . . If anyone says he knows, we rightly ask him how he knows. He must then inevitably appeal in the end to one of these two: either to sense perception [*Sinnes-Empfindung*] or to spiritual feeling [*Geistes-Gefühl*]. Of what we know by spiritual feeling, we say that we *believe* it. That is how we all speak. One can only *believe* in virtue, and so in freedom, and so in spirit and God. But the perception that knowing-in-sensible-intuition establishes (so-called knowing in the proper sense)

is just as little above the feeling that establishes *knowing-in-belief* as animals are above humanity, the material world above the intellectual, nature above its Creator.[40]

Jacobi has by now come to use the words "reason," "belief," and even "feeling" almost interchangeably; and he maintains that reason is a kind of intuition, or a kind of perception,[41] and that it issues in a presupposition or in knowledge. It is easy to see why his critics have found a Babel of terminological confusion in his writings. Even if we confine ourselves, for now, to his use of the term "belief," it may well be impossible to evade all the ambiguities.

Perhaps the most natural interpretation is that in the new introduction he means us to understand belief as the conviction of reality (the *Zuversicht*) that accompanies both modes of primary cognition, sense and reason, and he in fact speaks of a corresponding double *disbelief* that arises from the misuse of the intellect: disbelief in a material world and disbelief in an immaterial, spiritual world.[42] It is true that in the passages just cited belief seems to move over from the side of sense to the side of reason alone. But Jacobi's position is, I think, best expressed when he writes: "Man believes his senses necessarily, and he believes his reason necessarily; and there is no certainty higher than the certainty of this belief." In neither domain can there be proof of the veracity of our ideas; hence one can only speak of "belief." But in neither domain is any guarantee needed beyond the witness of reality to itself.[43] If there is an idea in Jacobi "imperfectly striving for expression" (Wilde), this would seem to be it.

Jacobi developed this fundamental idea in continual debate with Immanuel Kant. His disagreements with Kant were at least as important to his development as his agreement with Hume, who fades into the background in the new introduction.[44] Although such credit as Jacobi has won for himself as a philosopher probably rests chiefly on his astute criticisms of Kant, in some respects he felt an affinity with him, and he came back repeatedly to three cardinal points in the critical philosophy. First, Kant had shown the impossibility of moving deductively from the sensible to the supersensible, or transforming the logic of the intellect into a metaphysics of reality. But, second, his agnosticism about things in themselves was a mere inconsistency in his philosophy: Kant drifts steadily toward subjective idealism, and yet all the while he is making the realistic presupposition that something really appears in the appearances of sense. To resolve the contradiction, Jacobi believed, Kant should have affirmed forthrightly the faith in nature's objectivity that he tacitly presupposed in the first edition of the *Critique of Pure Reason* (1781). For, third, this would be no more philosophically scandalous than the rational faith in God, freedom, and immortality that Kant proposed in the *Critique of Practical Reason* (1788).[45]

The comparison between the critical philosophy and the philosophy of faith cannot be taken any further here. But I think one may justly conclude, without making it a matter of a direct dependence of Jacobi on Kant, that he was trying in effect to strengthen the doctrine of faith or belief that he discovered in the critical philosophy and pronounced "true in spirit." It is particularly instructive to note what he makes of "rational faith" in the Kantian ethics. For Jacobi, as his long discussion of freedom and foresight (both human and divine) makes transparently clear, it was *moral* experience broadly conceived—humans' awareness of themselves as spiritual and personal beings—that opened up the route to supersensible things. It was hard for him to take seriously the Kantian view that the idea of God is not merely indemonstrable but noncognitive, furnishing no information about the Supreme Being. But the heart of Jacobi's faith is disclosed precisely in his fierce insistence that the root of human nature would be a fearful lie if there were no truth in the revelations of the conscience. "Out of man's *willing* springs his truest *knowing*." In the spiritual, and above all the ethical, being of humanity Jacobi claimed to *see* God, though not with the eye of the body.[46]

4

Is there a belief or a faith on which the entire business of being human must ultimately rest? If so, what is it? And in what way is it related to religious faith in general and Christian faith in particular? It would be hard to name any theologian or philosopher who has made these questions more central to his thinking than F. H. Jacobi. It is easy enough to sit in the seat of the scornful as one reads him. He seemed repeatedly to take refuge in edifying rhetoric where one would be happier to have cool analysis; he delighted in provocative paradoxes (a "knowing unknowing" "objective feeling," and the like); and on his side there was no reluctance to heap scorn upon the philosophers. He did not hesitate to confess that his own "philosophy" proceeded from feeling, which it acknowledged as the highest authority. Nevertheless, he protested that his intention was not to disparage reason but to restore it, and that he had never ventured an assertion he did not take pains to establish philosophically. Since he fully accepted the duty to defend his faith before the bar of the philosophical intellect, he thought he deserved a more careful reading than he had received.[47] And he was right.

But can Jacobi's philosophy of faith even be shown to be coherent? His disturbing tendency was to multiply terms that, if not quite synonymous, seem to mingle and merge with one another. Perhaps it is not possible to get complete consistency out of his language, even at a single stage of his development; and it is not surprising that the Jacobi specialists have failed to agree among themselves about his fundamental concepts.[48] But the picture is by no means one of total chaos. On the contrary, the outlines of Jacobi's position are reasonably clear. He did not think that in the religious domain one had to fall back on blind faith and leave reason to the scientitsts and the philosophers. His cardinal point was that *all* factual claims whatever, whether about nature or about God, must in the end be traced back to an immediate awareness. "Intuition" and "feeling" (*Anschauung* and *Gefühl*) are his terms for this immediate, non-reflective awareness. Hence he writes: "Real being [*das reale Seyn*] . . . gives itself to be known only in feeling." It makes no sense to talk about *proving* what immediate awareness *reveals*. But there is no need to prove something that carries its own conviction with it. "All actual being [*alle Wirklichkeit*], bodily (revealed to the senses) just as much as spiritual (revealed to reason), verifies itself to humans only through feeling; there is no verification apart from, or above, this verification." Again: "All human knowledge proceeds from revelation and belief." Why say "belief"? Because the conviction that accompanies the revelations of immediate awareness cannot be proved, and what admits of no proof can only be believed. To distinguish the faculty of immediate awareness or feeling in the so-called supersensible domain by the term "reason" is perhaps eccentric. (Jacobi's use of "reason" was apparently influenced by his reading of Plato.) More eccentric still was the association of reason with feeling; Jacobi could even say that it is feeling that distinguishes humans from animals, since "feeling" and "reason" mean the same thing. But the terminological oddities do not make the substance incoherent.[49]

The divergent interpretations of Jacobi put forward by Wilde and Crawford both have evidence in their support. In part, the difference between them lies in Wilde's preference for the earlier Jacobi, Crawford's for the later. But against Wilde it can now be said that there really *are* two sources of cognition in Jacobi and, according to Jacobi himself, *there always were.* Wilde makes Jacobi do what he denied he had ever done: it never occurred to him, Jacobi expressly says, that he might be accused of making all knowledge the same in kind or, like the philosophers of Locke's school, deriving the entire spiritual life from the senses.[50] It does not follow, however, that Wilde was mistaken about Jacobi's idea of belief, which is not a mode of cognition (though Jacobi sometimes comes close to saying that it is). Belief is rather the confidence that accompanies cognition, or is presupposed in cognition; cognition evokes it, and is in turn sustained and supported by it as immediate awareness passes into reflection. Part of the difficulty arises from the common assumption in the secondary literature that in the later Jacobi "reason" simply replaces "belief" as the word for immediate awareness, at any rate in the supersensible domain. But as Jacobi himself explains it, "reason" replaces one of the meanings of "sense" (*Sinn*), the word wrongly taken for evidence that he must have been an empiricist of the Lockean type.[51] Belief, then, remains as the conviction of reality, the confidence, attached to both kinds of cognition.[52]

Crawford, on the other hand, though he acknowledges two sources of knowledge in the later Jacobi, is clearly mistaken about Jacobi's reinterpretation of the word "reason." Since the effect of the reinterpretation was to detach reason from the intellect and realign it with feeling or intuition, it is hardly possible to seize upon it as evidence of a greater appreciation for thought. Moreover, Crawford speaks as though intuition were not simply a mode of cognition but a method. Jacobi, he says, did not deny the appropriateness of the materialists' methods for dealing with physical phenomena but held that "another method, namely, faith, intuition, and not demonstration" is required to deal with supersensible facts.[53] It is true that Jacobi doubted the possibility of a science of the supersensible.[54] But intuition and belief were, to him, just as much the foundation of natural science as they are of assertions about God and human values. If belief is not stricly a mode of cognition, much less is it a method; and if there is anything like "a form of twofold truth" in Jacobi, as Crawford thinks, it is by no means an opposition between science and faith, seeing that science rests upon faith.[55]

What Jacobi offers is, so to say, neither a monistic nor a dualistic epistemology; it is more like two running-lanes on a single track, which are not identical but must measure up to the same standard. He was the very paragon of those religious apologists who renounce both a theology of proofs and a flight into fideism, and proceed to defend religious faith by showing that formally it has a similar structure to the element of belief in all knowing whatever. Indeed, despite the double-track epistemology, Jacobi was in a position to claim not just that religious faith is *like* nonreligious belief, but that "belief" in both domains means exactly the *same* thing. Of course, the epistemological parallel he draws is not missed by either Wilde or Crawford. But neither of them, it seems to me, quite does justice (for different reasons) to the exact nature of the parallel or its crucial role in his apologetic enterprise, which is, to establish that if belief in supersensible realities has no final defense against radical doubt, at least it is in no worse case than belief in a material world independent of our minds.[56]

5

To argue for the coherence of Jacobi's position, at least in its general features, is not to deny that some tidying up of his leading concepts is desirable. Much less is it to assume that if coherent, his position must be right, or even plausible. It is open, in my opinion, to at least four related questions. I propose now to put these questions to Jacobi, then to ask in conclusion whether Schubert Ogden's notion of "basic confidence" can provide a more satisfactory variation on the theme of existential faith, at least to the extent of not being vulnerable where I think Jacobi's philosophy of faith is vulnerable.

First, even if we allow Jacobi the possibility that there may be two distinct cognitive routes, is the parallel he draws between them a plausible one? His entire case rests upon an alleged, or presumed, analogy between sensing material objects and perceiving spiritual objects. We "see" God, for instance, though not with the bodily eye. Then what exactly is the second, spiritual eye? Jacobi calls it not just a "capacity" or "faculty" but an "organ"—as though, like the organ of literal seeing, it must have a physiological site somewhere on the human body. Yet he calls it an "invisible organ that in no wise presents itself to outward sense."[57] And what kind of organ is that? Of course, it could be replied that reason, in Jacobi's sense, is a function of the brain. In that case, the analogy with the eye would be weakened, but there might still be a valid analogy between two mental *operations*, sensible intuition and rational intuition, and the question of their respective *organs* could be dismissed as philosophically frivolous. We might wish to argue, for example, passing from the psychological to the linguistic mode, that our moral discourse presupposes a basic recognition that there is a difference between good and bad; and we might further argue that this recognition is the sort of operation Jacobi intends by an "intuition" of a supersensible object (in this case, of "the good"). But this then leads to the next question.

Second, granted that there may be something in the spiritual domain analogous to a simple sensation in the material domain, what would the corresponding object be like? Perhaps Jacobi's best candidate for a supersensible intuition is the one just suggested: the simple—that is, irreducible—notion of "good." I do not mean that such a notion is unproblematic (any more than the notions of a simple sensation and a protocol sentence are unproblematic). It is just that Jacobi had a knack for sounding naive, and it is salutary to remember that his questions, even his answers, usually put him in respectable philosophical company. And from the influential work of G. E. Moore (1873–1958) we are at least familiar with the view that "good" is a simple and indefinible property, the presence of which is not seen but intuited. Something like this appears to be what Jacobi had in mind when he spoke of a rational intuition of the good.[58] That we have an immediate intuition of God, however, can hardly be maintained unless Jacobi is ready with a simple definition of the word "God." Apparently he is not. On the contrary, by "God" (der Gott as distinct from das Gott of the speculative philosophers) Jacobi always meant in fact a personal creator outside the material world, endowed with freedom and working by design (Vorsehung), and such a complex idea can scarcely qualify as the referent of a simple intuition or presentiment of God.[59] Jacobi tends to assume he is home, when he has only taken the first cautious step. What corresponds to a simple intuition would surely have to be, or (more correctly) become in reflection, a simple idea, not the full-blown Christian doctrine of God. And if rational intuition is an actual mode of cognition or experience, like sensible intuition, to speak of "intuiting immortality" (in Jacobi's sense of intuiting a future life after bodily dissolution) is still more incongruous: it sounds like mere bad grammar. For what could it possibly mean to claim one has an intuition of something that is neither present nor an object at all, but an abstract noun referring to an anticipated future condition?

Third, there is the closely connected problem of, so to say, knowing when to stop. If belief is the inescapable conviction of reality, of how many things are we inescapably convinced? In a sense, Jacobi's reply is: Just two things, the reality of the material world and the reality of the spiritual world.[60] But he is prepared to itemize the elements of the spiritual world, and he comes back repeatedly (with variations) to the Platonic triad of the true, the good, and the beautiful and the Kantian triad of God, freedom, and immortality.[61] *Belief* in the reality of the supersensible thereby becomes the *beliefs* in God, goodness, immortality, and so on. And once again we must protest that Jacobi's thoughts run ahead of his argument. It will not do for him to tell us what he is personally convinced of. There is a sting in the malicious comment of Arthur Schopenhauer (1788–1860) that Jacobi's little weakness was to take all he learned and approved before his fifteenth year for innate ideas of the human mind.[62] If belief in the supersensible is to have any communicable meaning, the content of the supersensible must be specified; and if belief is thus divided into beliefs, each must be shown individually to be strictly universal, a prerequisite of being human. To attempt such a demonstration is by no means the same as trying to prove the reality of the object of belief. And this brings me to the final question.

Fourth, was Jacobi too apprehensive of anything that smacked of a "science of spirit"? For him, belief passed quickly over into wonder, and he feared that to subject the domain of the spirit to the categories of the intellect was to court disaster. The attitude of wonder would be destroyed, he thought, if some future scientific genius were to demonstrate a mechanics of the human person, as Isaac Newton (1642–1727) had displayed the mechanism of the heavens. For Jacobi, this would be catastrophic for the idea of freedom, the supersensible fact that he made the actual hinge of his entire philosophy.[63] In this sense, he could entertain at least the *hypothetical* possibility of a conflict between science and faith. But his main thought was that the spiritual domain simply eludes, rather than opposes, science; and it was here, I think, that a *real* gap, if not exactly a real conflict, between faith and science opened up.[64] Since belief has a place on both sides of the epistemological paradigm, in the domain of nature as well as in the domain of spirit, to this extent there is no opposition between science and belief. The problem is, however, that on the side of the spiritual realities Jacobi does not complete the paradigm; he does not show how philosophy or theology might correspond to natural science as the parallel activities of the intellect in the domain of the supersensible. He does indeed say that the two kinds of intuition, as two sources of knowledge, stand in a similar relationship to the intellect. But this suggests to him only the impossibility of proving what intuition reveals; he does not see the parallel as a warrant, or a challenge, to develop a science of phenomena in the domain of the spirit.[65] Clearly, what troubles him is the thought of a science of the supersensible objects themselves. But why not a science of religious *belief*? This, in effect, is the question Friedrich Schleiermacher (1768–1834) put to Jacobi—and answered in the system of dogmatics he wanted to dedicate to him.[66]

How does Schubert Ogden's notion of "basic confidence" fare if it is confronted with the four questions I have addressed to Jacobi's philosophy of faith? No lengthy exposition is required, I assume, to establish that the notion of a basic confidence or existential faith in the worth, final meaning, or ultimate significance of life[67] does stand in the lineage of Jacobi's philosophy of faith and Balfour's concept of inevitable beliefs, at least insofar as Ogden's theme is a confidence that is "a necessary presupposition not only of religion but of human existence as such." Ogden's conversation partner, it is true, is neither Jacobi nor Balfour but Stephen Toulmin. Very much in the manner of Balfour, however, he wants to show that theism provides the best reflective account of experiences we all inescapably share; and much like Jacobi, he holds that there is a species of faith that provides the foundations of personal existence.[68] The differences between the three positions, it seems, have more to do with the content than with the function of existential faith. Ogden finds the content in the *secular* affirmation of life here and now. To make his apologetic case, he then needs to provide a link between this affirmation and explicit religious faith in God, so that to profess atheism may accordingly be seen, at one level, as a misunderstanding of one's own existence. The link is forged by the suggestion that the religions of the world can all, including Christianity, be viewed as expressions and re-presentations of the original confidence in the meaning and worth of life.[69]

An important consequence of Ogden's approach is that his final appeal is to just one item of primitive faith, whereas Jacobi struggled to maintain a parallel between two, and Balfour had a whole unwritten creed of inevitable beliefs. Ogden does not deny that there are in fact other existential beliefs; his phrase "reflective inventory of the existential beliefs by which we actually live" could almost stand as an unintended description of what Balfour was about. But Ogden's case actually rests on one belief only: basic confidence in the worth of life. Hence, while he too can see a parallel between confidence in life and experience through sense perception, the kind of epistemological analogy that Jacobi sets up between two sources of knowledge is simply not needed to support his argument; he does not even need to distinguish two mental functions, let alone two organs of knowing. This becomes particularly clear in his criticism of William Christian, who, unlike Toulmin, "fails to see that the religious sort of question is not simply parallel or coordinate to the scientific or moral sorts, but . . . is also fundamental to them." For if the function of religious assertions is to provide reassurance about life's meaning, they are plainly relevant both to scientific explanation and to moral thought and action. Taking morality rather than science as his example, Ogden points out the moral relevance of religious assertions: the original confidence they represent is the necessary condition of all our moral action.[70] In short, the first of my objections to Jacobi's "faith" has no pertinence to Ogden's "basic confidence."

If we turn next from the subjective experience of basic confidence to its objective referent, the advantage of Ogden's unitary approach is confirmed. He expressly indicates that all we can mean by the word "God" at this stage of a case for theism is "the objective ground in reality itself of our ineradicable confidence in the final worth of our existence." Again: "The only God whose reality is implied by a secular affirmation is the God who is the ground of confidence in the ultimate worth or significance of our life in the world." As if this were not already clear enough, Ogden reiterates the point (by way of responding to his critics) in the preface to the paperback edition of *The Reality of God:* "To establish 'the reality of God' in the distinctively theistic sense of that phrase logically requires that one establish more than 'the reality of faith' and its objective ground." Unlike Jacobi, Ogden does not assume he is home once he has taken the first step; accordingly, my second objection to Jacobi also has no pertinence to Ogden's argument, except insofar as one endorses his confession that the argument, as originally stated, was insufficiently clear.[71]

My third objection to Jacobi, too, seems to leave Ogden's position unassailed, and I see no need to consider it more closely. Even if Ogden sometimes indicates an interest in other existential beliefs besides basic confidence,[72] the weight of his argument does not depend on them, and it would therefore be immaterial, as far as the argument is concerned, to ask how many existential beliefs there are, and what they are. I turn, then, to the last of my four questions to Jacobi: whether he was right to surrender the possibility of something like a science of religious belief. No one, I think, will accuse Schubert Ogden of moving too quickly from philosophical to hortatory discourse. His trust in the power of the intellect to illuminate existence is already apparent in the tenacity with which he seeks to establish the concept of basic confidence. He is not content to say that if any should doubt the value of life, he does not know how to help them, but argues forcefully for the presence of a hidden faith even in the person who bows out of life by way of suicide or the person who, like Albert Camus (1913–60), summons us to heroic resistance against life's absurdity.[73] But the point I am more concerned to make now, in comparing Ogden with Jacobi, is that the argument for basic confidence is but half the case he is pleading; the other half is his argument for a revision of classical theism. Whereas Jacobi presupposes the inherited Christian doctrine of God, or defends it at all costs (largely by criticism of the speculative alternatives), Ogden's reduced definition of "God" as "the objective ground of our basic confidence" becomes the point of departure for conceptual or doctrinal change. Although atheism may rest on a misconstrual of the existential affirmations by which even the atheist lives, Ogden grants that it may still be justified as a reflective protest against an untenable variety of theism; and "untenable" is exactly his verdict on conventional, supernaturalistic theism. Hence the discussion of "The Reality of Faith" moves on to a section entitled "Toward a New Theism," which asks plainly: *What* doctrine of God best answers to existential faith?[74] I certainly do not wish to imply that Jacobi would find such a logical move wholly inappropriate. I simply draw attention to the systematic determination with which Ogden carries it out—untroubled that the light of faith might go out if brought to the intellect.

Naturally, to conclude that Schubert Ogden's approach is immune to weaknesses that (in my opinion) vitiate Jacobi's approach is not to say that further analysis of his leading concepts would not be useful, and it does not guarantee that there will be no other objections to which the notion of basic confidence might itself be vulnerable. On the matter of his leading concepts, one might wish to know more about how he conceives of the nonreflective element in basic confidence, and why he qualifies the object of confidence as the "final" or "ultimate" significance of life. He clearly does not regard basic confidence as necessarily reflective, since he holds that one function of the positive religions is to reaffirm it at the level of conscious belief. At the level of an unreflective taking-for-granted, how does it differ from the confidence that appears to activate animal behavior? Or does it become distinctively human *only* when raised to reflective consciousness?[75] And does the qualifier "final" or "ultimate," when attached to the object of basic confidence, perhaps mean no more than the "after all" in the phrase "reassuring us that our life is, after all, worth while"?[76] Indeed, *can* it mean much more than that without jeopardizing the usefulness of the concept of basic confidence to a Christian theologian?

The objection that might be raised against "confidence in the final worth of our existence" from a theological perspective is that it has the appearance of a strongly anthropocentric, even egocentric, notion, and this appearance is heightened by the suggestion that we should so conceive of God as to exhibit him as "the ground of the significance of our life."[77] Now, of course, it could be answered that the notion of the final worth of our existence is purely formal, asserting nothing at all about what the worth of our existing might in fact be; and it would still be possible for a theologian to argue that in actual fact the *final* significance of human existence is a significance *relative* to the actual being of God, which alone has *ultimate* significance.[78] But perhaps a point made initially for theological reasons may occasion another look at the internal logic of basic confidence itself. For, in the first place, confidence of one's individual worth seems to arise from the perception of oneself as a part of a significant whole; and, in the second place, the confidence that our actions "make a difference," while most certainly the presupposition of moral behavior,[79] is surely secondary to the inescapable awareness that we *ought* to make a difference.

If these are sound comments on our confidence in the significance of our existence (and I cannot develop them further here), they may lead us back to thinking again about Jacobi, who discovered *two* irreducible beliefs at the root of human existence: belief in the reality of an ordered world "outside" us, and belief in the authenticity of the voice of conscience. One may wonder if it is possible to defend this double faith without falling into the epistemological difficulties I have pointed out. Be that as it may, Ogden seems to me to provide the happiest formulation of his notion of basic confidence when he writes: "We are selves at all only because of our inalienable trust that our own existence and existence generally are somehow justified and made meaningful by the whole to which we know ourselves to belong."[80] Ogden is not likely to disagree if I venture to add that the whole to which we know ourselves to belong has for us the inescapable character of a *moral* order.[81]

Notes

1. In English usage, "faith" perhaps suggests a greater degree of assurance than "belief" and is often perceived as having stronger religious over-

tones. But there seems to be no agreed differentiation between the two terms in the English authors I shall refer to, and German, like Latin, has only one word for them both. Hence I have used "faith" and "belief" interchangeably in this essay.

2. Thomas's principal discussion of faith appears in *Summa theologiae*, II–II, qq. 1–16; see esp. q. 1, arts. 1–2, 4, 6–7, 9; q. 2, arts. 1, 9–10; q. 4, art. 8; q. 5, art. 2.

3. Anthony Collins, *An Essay Concerning the Use of Reason in Propositions, the Evidence whereof depends upon Human Testimony* (London, 1707), pp. 4–11, 15.

4. Anthony Collins, *A Discourse of Free-Thinking, Occasion'd by the Rise and Growth of a Sect call'd Free-Thinkers* (London, 1713), pp. 16, 37. "Eyesight," in the former passage, is not an expression of a narrow empiricism. Collins's point is that it is absurd to suppress the free exercise of thought or of any human faculty at all; sight is only taken to exemplify the point (see pp. 15, 25).

5. John Locke, *An Essay Concerning Human Understanding*, ed. Peter H. Nidditch (Oxford: Clarendon Press, 1975), IV, xviii, 2, p. 689.

6. Arthur James Balfour, *Theism and Humanism* (New York: George H. Doran, 1915); quotation on p. 263. The theme of inevitable belief appeared already in Balfour's first book, *A Defence of Philosophic Doubt, Being an Essay on the Foundations of Belief* (London: Macmillan, 1879) and its sequel, *The Foundations of Belief, Being Notes Introductory to the Study of Theology* (New York: Longmans, Green, 1895). Balfour actually argued for three classes of inevitable belief—aesthetic and ethical as well as intellectual—and defended theism as supportive of all three. The parallel with Jacobi's position is closer than I need to show in detail here.

7. John Hick mentions Origen (ca. 185–ca. 254) and Arnobius (d. ca. 330) as, so to say, forerunners of Balfour: Hick, *Faith and Knowledge*, 2d ed. (Ithaca, New York: Cornell University Press, 1966), p. 54n. But it is obvious that the notion of existential faith takes on a new dimension in modern times insofar as it is brought into relationship with the scientific concept of nature. Hick makes no mention of Jacobi, and he has little sympathy for the notion of "scientific faith." But his book, first published in 1957, remains an excellent general account of several other approaches to the epistemology of faith that do not concern me here. It will be clear enough, without further comment, that my discussion does not touch the heart of what Luther or Calvin would consider to be "saving faith."

8. Balfour, *Theism and Humanism*, pp. 174–75.

9. A critical edition of Jacobi's writings has been launched (*Gesamtausgabe*, Frommann-Holzboog, 1981–). For the time being, however, we are still dependent on the edition begun by Jacobi himself and continued by Friedrich Köppen and Friedrich Roth: *Friedrich Heinrich Jacobi's Werke*, 6 vols. [vol. 4 in 3 pts.] (Leipzig: Gerhard Fleischer, 1812–25; reprinted, Darmstadt: Wissenschaftliche Buchgesellschaft, 1980), hereafter cited as JW.

10. Reinhard Lauth commented on the absence of theologians in his opening remarks at the Jacobi conference in Düsseldorf in 1969 (the 150th anniversary of Jacobi's death). See Klaus Hammacher, ed., *Friedrich Heinrich Jacobi: Philosoph und Literat der Goethezeit*, Studien zur Philosophie und Literatur des neunzehnten Jahrhunderts, vol. 11 (Frankfurt am Main: Vittorio Klostermann, 1971), p. 4. The interest of the Catholic Tübingen School in Jacobi is noted by Franz Wolfinger, *Denken und Transzendenz— Zum Problem ihrer Vermittlung: Der unterschiedliche Weg der Philosophien F. H. Jacobis und F. W. J. Schellings und ihre Konfrontation im Streit um die Göttlichen Dinge* (1811/12), Theologie im Übergang, vol. 7 (Frankfurt am Main: Peter D. Lang, 1981), p. 3.

11. Goethe, conversation with F. v. Müller, 26 January 1825: Johann Wolfgang Goethe, *Gedenkausgabe der Werke, Briefe und Gespräche*, vol. 23 (Zurich: Artemis, 1950), p. 372.

12. Otto Friedrich Bollnow, *Die Lebensphilosophie F. H. Jacobis*, Göttinger Forschungen, vol. 2 (Stuttgart: W. Kohlhammer, 1933), p. 1.

13. Since the present essay was written, the first English translations of Jacobi (to the best of my knowledge) have appeared: his "Open Letter to Fichte" (1799) and "On Faith and Knowledge in Response to Schelling and Hegel" (1803), trans. Diana I. Behler, in *Philosophy of German Idealism*, ed. Ernst Behler, The German Library, vol. 23 (New York: Continuum, 1987), pp. 119–57. For translations of the foreign secondary literature, see Benedetto Croce (1866–1952), "Considerations on the Philosophy of Jacobi" (1941), reprinted in Cecil Sprigge, trans. and ed., *Philosophy, Poetry, History: An Anthology of Essays by Benedetto Croce* (London: Oxford University Press, 1966), pp. 145–69; G. W. F. Hegel (1770–1831), *Faith and Knowledge*, trans. Walter Cerf and H. S. Harris (Albany: State University of New York Press, 1977). Hegel's *Faith and Knowledge* first appeared anonymously as an article in *Kritisches Journal der Philosophie* (July 1802); from the bad style of the article Jacobi inferred correctly that Hegel, not his coeditor F. W. J. Schelling (1775–1854), must have been the author. The editor of the English translation points out, as does Croce, that Hegel was elsewhere more complimentary to Jacobi. See further n. 81 below.

14. Robert H. Worthington, "Jacobi, and the Philosophy of Faith," *Journal of Speculative Philosophy* 12 (1878): 393–402; Lewis S. Ford, "The Controversy Between Schelling and Jacobi," *Journal of the History of Philosophy* 3 (1965): 75–89; W. Schrickx, "Coleridge and Friedrich Heinrich Jacobi," *Revue belge de philologie et d'histoire* 36 (1958): 812–50. Jacobi occasionally makes an appearance as second fiddle to his friend Hamann: e.g., in Philip Merlan, "Kant, Hamann-Jacobi and Schelling on Hume," *Rivista critica di storia della filosofia* 22 (1967): 481–94; Isaiah Berlin, "Hume and the Sources of German Anti-Rationalism" (1977), reprinted in Berlin, *Against the Current: Essays in the History of Ideas*, ed. Henry Hardy (New York: The Viking Press, 1980), pp. 162–87. Berlin's essay, unfortunately, is mistaken about the thesis of Jacobi's dialogue on Hume, about the date of the first edition, and even about Jacobi's own dates.

15. Norman Wilde, *Friedrich Heinrich Jacobi: A Study in the Origin of German Realism* (New York: Columbia College, 1894), pp. 7, 72. The letter to Hamann, 16 June 1783, is quoted on pp. 52–53 (JW 1:363–67; quotation on p. 367).

16. Wilde, *Jacobi*, pp. 5–8, 42, 57, 60, 63. The expression "natural realism" is borrowed from the Scottish philosopher William Hamilton (1788–1856).

17. Ibid., pp. 64–68, 70–71.

18. Alexander W. Crawford, *The Philosophy of F. H. Jacobi* (New York: Macmillan, 1905), pp. 16, 63–64, 85–86. See also the critique of Wilde's book on pp. 46–47. Crawford does concede that Jacobi may be termed a "psychological realist," insofar as he took what he found in psychology to be real and true (p. 57), or even a "spiritualistic realist" (p. 47).

19. Ibid., pp. 3, 47–50. But Crawford nonetheless does not see the shift as a change of principle (p. 35), and he can still say that Jacobi's service was to show that there is an element of immediacy in thought (p. 50).

20. Ibid., pp. 24–25, 27, 32–38. It is not clear how Crawford relates the epistemological dualism of sensibility and reason to Jacobi's "complete opposition between feeling (reason) and thought (understanding)," or how this "opposition" helps the main thesis that Jacobi moved toward a greater appreciation for thought (see p. 28).

21. Wilde, *Jacobi*, p. 37.

22. Hamann claimed to have studied Hume even before he wrote his *Socratic Memorabilia* (published in 1759). See the editorial comments in *Hamann's Socratic Memorabilia: A Translation and Commentary*, trans. and ed. James C. O'Flaherty (Baltimore: The Johns Hopkins Press, 1967), p. 200, note c. Cf. Ronald Gregor Smith, *J. G. Hamann 1730–1788: A Study in Christian Existence* (London: Collins, 1960), pp. 50–52.

23. See, e.g., Günther Baum, *Vernunft und Erkenntnis: Die Philosophie F. H. Jacobis*, Mainzer Philosophische Forschungen, vol. 9 (Bonn: H. Bouvier, 1969), pp. 17, 42–49, 80–83.

24. Jacobi, *David Hume über den Glauben, oder Idealismus und Realismus: Ein Gespräch* (Breslau: Gottl. Loewe, 1787), pp. iii–iv. I have made no attempt to discuss the interpretations of the dialogue in the secondary literature, some of which is noted by Baum (*Vernunft und Erkenntnis*, pp. 17–22). It should at least be mentioned, however, that Bollnow gives a sensitive reading of Jacobi's first thoughts on *Glaube* in the early romances, where it appeared as a mood without definite object—an affirmation of life and a general sense of happiness in contrast to the sense of meaninglessness and despair in *Unglaube*. But unfaith, Bollnow points out, is not taken by Jacobi for a parallel possibility so much as for the *modus deficiens* of faith itself (*Die Lebensphilosophie Jacobis*, pp. 83–89).

25. *Hume über den Glauben*, pp. iv–vi. Like the English word "perception," *Empfindung* is not necessarily confined to awareness through sensation (see also the first reference in n. 33 below, on *Sinn*). References to the dialogue will be given hereafter to the second edition in JW 2. The text

occupies pages 125–288 and is followed by the original appendix (*Beylage*) "Über den transcendentalen Idealismus" (pp. 289–310). The new introduction, "Vorrede, zugleich Einleitung in des Verfassers sämtliche philosophische Schriften," appears on pages 3–123. Occasionally, the second edition incorporates changes Jacobi alleged to be minor. But see n. 33 below.

26. JW 2:127–29, 137–39, 148.

27. JW 2:129, 143–44, 149–53, 156–63. Jacobi cites section XII, part i, and section V, part ii, of Hume's *Enquiry*, using the 1770 edition and preferring his own translation to the one in common use. Cf. David Hume, *Enquiries Concerning Human Understanding and Concerning the Principles of Morals*, reprinted from the posthumous edition of 1777, ed. L. A. Selby-Bigge, 3d ed., revised by P. H. Nidditch (Oxford: Clarendon Press, 1975), pp. 15–52, 47–50. The *Enquiry Concerning Human Understanding* first appeared in 1748 (as *Philosophical Essays Concerning Human Understanding*).

28. JW 2:163–66. All translations of Jacobi in this essay are mine. Jacobi's "thesis," cited as the first epigraph at the beginning of the essay, was stated in *Über die Lehre des Spinozas, in Briefen an Herrn Moses Mendelssohn* (1785), JW 4, 1:223. In the same work, Jacobi wrote: "Wir alle werden im Glauben geboren, und müssen im Glauben bleiben" (JW 4, 1:210). *Glaube* is here linked with *unmittelbare Gewissheit*, but also with *Fürwahrhalten*.

29. JW 2:165, 173–76; see also pp. 257–58, where the notion of intuitive knowledge of our own existence is documented from G. W. Leibniz (1646–1716). Jacobi's appeal to Hume, I may add, given his limited purpose, does not strike me as wholly farfetched. Whether deliberately or not, Jacobi echoes Humean language at more points than one; besides the phrases I have cited, Hume also writes "to repose faith in the senses" (Selby-Bigge, p. 151), and Jacobi must have noticed his distinction between "definition" or "explanation" and "description" (ibid., pp. 48–49).

30. JW 2:204–5, 225–28, 267–71. *Vernunft* appears here as the mental faculty that processes the data of experience, the role Jacobi later reserves for the *Verstand*.

31. JW 2:279–88; quotations on pp. 285, 287. The dialogue ends with the words that concluded Claudius's short prose piece, "Diogenes von Sinope": "Aber was hilft der blosse Gedanke? *Fussalbe*, Mann von Sinope!" Claudius, *Sämtliche Werke* (Munich: Winkler, 1968), pp. 44–45.

32. Jacobi translates Hume's term "perception" both by *Empfindung* and by *Wahrnehmung*. "Idea," as distinct from the primary "impression" in Hume's vocabulary, he usually renders as *Vorstellung* (see, e.g., JW 2:152–53). For his claim that "in the depths of his soul" his convictions had remained unchanged, see the important footnote added to the second edition of the dialogue on pp. 221–22.

33. JW 2:270. The explanatory parenthesis did not appear in the first edition (*Hume über den Glauben*, p. 184). This is one of the changes that make the reader wary of taking Jacobi's word for it when he claims that he made no corrections that would adulterate the original dialogue's character as a

historical document (JW 2:5). Compare also JW 2:284 with *Hume über den Glauben*, p. 201, and see n. 51 below.

34. JW 2:3–4.

35. JW 2:7–8, 26–28. In English we would be more inclined to speak of animal "intelligence," but "intellect" is usually the best equivalent for the German *Verstand*. Jacobi takes Californians (and the inhabitants of Tierra del Fuego) to exemplify uncultivated peoples.

36. JW 2:9.

37. JW 2:9–11. For reason as a *Voraussetzungsvermögen* (!), cf. JW 2:101. Jacobi similarly speaks of *Glaube* as *Voraussetzung* (p. 20), a notion that might be compared with Hume's construal of belief as "taking for granted." See Hume, *A Treatise of Human Nature*, ed. L. A. Selby-Bigge (Oxford: Clarendon Press, 1888), I, iv, 2 (p. 187) and I, iv, 7 (p. 269).

38. JW 2:74; cf. p. 105.

39. This is what Jacobi means by contrasting the revelatory operations of sense and reason with the reflective operations of the intellect (JW 2:109–11).

40. JW 2:58–60.

41. Sometimes, at least, Jacobi appears to connect *Wahrnehmung* with sensible knowing, *Vernehmung* with supersensible (e.g., JW 2:56); both words are usually translated "perception" in English. But he also speaks of reason as *Wahrnehmung* (pp. 74, 100)—and, indeed, calls reason "the inner sense [*Sinn*]" (p. 107).

42. JW 2:99–100. On *Glaube* as *Zuversicht* in things seen and unseen, see pp. 11, 56.

43. JW 2:107–8. It should be noted that in this passage feeling too, like belief, is located in both domains. But the long footnote on pp. 221–22 describes reason as *the* faculty of immediate certainty, which, if pressed, would imply that there is no immediate certainty in the sensible domain.

44. Jacobi's relationship to Kant is easily misconstrued, if one does not note that the philosophy of faith was conceived before the first edition of the *Critique of Pure Reason* (1781) appeared. Jacobi himself was firmly convinced that the second edition of the *Critique* (1789) owed something to his own work: he believed, in particular, that his formula *Ohne Du kein Ich* was transformed by Kant into a refutation of idealism—and subsequently converted by J. G. Fichte (1762–1814) into the formula *Alles Du ist Ich* (see JW 2:40–41n.; cf. JW 4, 1:211).

45. These are the three main points Jacobi makes in the extended discussion of the critical philosophy in JW 2:14–45. His best-known comment on it was that without *Naturglaube* one cannot get into the system, with it one cannot stay there (JW 2:38; cf. the *Beylage*, JW 2:304). In the preface to the second edition of the *Critique of Pure Reason*, Jacobi points out, Kant admitted that the existence of things outside us must be accepted on faith. But it is surely highly dubious to speak, as Jacobi does, about the "objective validity" of the Kantian ideas of practical reason (JW 2:42).

46. JW 2:44, 120. Cf. the *Vorbericht* to the reprint of *Über die Lehre des Spinoza:* "Durch ein göttliches Leben wird der Mensch Gottes inne. Von dieser Seite ist der Weg zur Erkenntnis des Übersinnlichen ein praktischer, kein theoretischer, bloss wissenschaftlicher" (JW 4,1:xxv). The discussion of freedom and foresight in the new introduction to the dialogue on Hume is given largely in the form of a debate with both materialism and speculative idealism, and it takes up what is actually the longest part of the introduction (JW 2:77–123; cf. pp. 45–55). Jacobi discusses the status of the Kantian postulates further in *Über das Unternehmen des Kriticismus die Vernunft zu Verstande zu bringen und der Philosophie überhaupt eine neue Absicht zu geben* (1801), JW 3:101–5; cf. *Von den göttlichen Dingen und ihrer Offenbarung* (1811), JW 3:362–63.

47. JW 2:20, 61, 109; 99–100, 226, 275–76; 61; 11, 31n., 106–7; 47. Jacobi's claim to be the restorer of reason, not its detractor, rests on his persuasion that since Aristotle (384–322 B.C.), there has been a persistent tendency of philosophers to subordinate reason to intellect, immediate to mediate knowledge, perception to reflection, so that the true has become synonymous with the demonstrable. Jacobi thinks of himself as a real, not merely nominal, rationalist ("philosopher of feeling" is a malicious nickname invented by others), and he believes that his notion of a spiritual eye, a higher cognitive power than sense perception, allies him with Socrates (469–399 B.C.) and Plato (ca. 427–ca. 347 B.C.) (see pp. 11–12, 70–71, 74–76). In actual fact, Plato classified belief as fallible sense-perception, not as knowledge in the proper sense at all, whereas Jacobi's entire endeavor in the dialogue is to show that knowledge rests on belief. But, of course, Jacobi applies the cognitive labels differently than Plato, not meaning by *Glaube* what Plato meant by *pistis;* and he could perhaps claim a genuine affinity between his later use of *Vernunft* and Plato's use of *noesis* for the faculty that grasps the *archai* or eternal forms (ideas). See esp. Plato, *Republic,* 509D–521B; cf. *Theaetetus,* 184B–186E, 200D–201C.

48. See, e.g., Baum, who takes issue with Bollnow at several points and doubts whether Jacobi himself correctly represents in the 1815 introduction what he had said in the dialogue (*Vernunft und Erkenntnis,* pp. 118–23).

49. JW 2:105; 108–9; 3–4; 144 (cf. 146); 61–63.

50. JW 2:221n.

51. Ibid. Jacobi's persistent failure to get his terms straight is betrayed by the fact that he *says* that in the original dialogue he had only the word "sense" for what he now calls "reason": namely, "the faculty of immediate certainty, the faculty of revelation." But "reason" actually became only one kind of revelatory faculty, and he retained "sense" for the other kind, in effect turning "sense" over to the empiricists. The new use of "reason" thus had the consequence that reason became in the later Jacobi exactly what the earlier Jacobi said reason and intellect were not: *besondere [aus sich offenbarende] Kräfte* (p. 284). A further complication is that the phrase I have set in brackets was not in the original edition of the dialogue (cf. *Hume über den Glauben,* p. 201). Jacobi also inserted into the second edition a

sentence that identified sense as the actual revealing faculty, the faculty of perception (*Wahrnehmung*) in general, i.e., presumably, perception of both sensible and supersensible objects. Why did he do that? Apparently, he wished to underscore the very terminological infelicity that he now wanted to renounce!

52. Here, too, Jacobi wavers: in one and the same sentence he speaks of belief as coming from, and being identical with, *ein wissendes Nicht-Wissen*, which means, I take it, immediate knowledge (JW 2:20).

53. Crawford, *Philosophy of Jacobi*, p. 24.

54. I return to this point below; for documentation, see n. 63.

55. Crawford, *Philosophy of Jacobi*, p. 28.

56. Occasionally, Jacobi speaks as though a realistic epistemology were a prerequisite to belief in God: no world, no God (JW 2:37n.).

57. JW2:74. God has no reason any more than he has sense, because he needs no organs (p. 10).

58. George Edward Moore, *Principia Ethica* (Cambridge: Cambridge University Press, 1903), esp. pp. 6–8. It would be harder these days to name a philosopher of aesthetics who thinks similarly of "beautiful" as an irreducible quality, but some recent epistemologists have held that *knowing* is a primitive and indefinable concept, and it might be instructive to compare this view with Jacobi's intuition of the true. See the discussion of John Cook Wilson (1849–1915) and H. A. Prichard (1871–1947) in Anthony Quinton, "Knowledge and Belief," *The Encyclopedia of Philosophy*, ed. Paul Edwards, 8 vols. (New York: Macmillan and The Free Press, 1967), 4:345–52, esp. p. 348.

59. JW 2:83, 93, 114; 285.

60. Bollnow rightly observes that belief directed to the reality of "a certain sphere of objects as a whole" lacks specific content. But I cannot see that belief has to assume the character of a *Modus des Wissens* for its object to become specific (see Bollnow, *Die Lebensphilosophie Jacobis*, pp. 142–45).

61. See, e.g., JW 2:9–11, 55–56, 76–77.

62. Schopenhauer, *Die Welt als Wille und Vorstellung* [1819], vol. 1, based on the 3d ed. [1859], Bibliothek der Gesamt-Litteratur, nos. 491–96 (Halle: Otto Hendel, n.d.), pref. to the 1st ed., p. xiii.

63. JW 2:105–6, 121; 53–55; 46–47. That there cannot be a science of spirit is the burden of Jacobi's brief essay *Über die Unzertrennlichkeit des Begriffes der Freyheit und Vorsehung von dem Begriffe der Vernunft* [1799], JW 2:311–23.

64. Crawford, of course, notes this gap (see, e.g., *Philosophy of Jacobi*, p. 28), but I think he confuses it with a distinction of his own making (not Jacobi's) between faith and science as two methods.

65. JW 2:59. Crawford endorses the view (without any documentation from Jacobi himself) that philosophy for Jacobi was "immediate knowledge of the supersensible" (*Philosophy of Jacobi*, p. 29). But surely philosophy, just as much as science, can only be an activity of the reflective intellect,

and it seems to me unlikely that this is something Jacobi could have failed to notice.

66. Schleiermacher to Jacobi, 30 March 1818, reprinted in Martin Cordes, "Der Brief Schleiermachers an Jacobi: Ein Beitrag zu seiner Entstehung und Überlieferung," *Zeitschrift für Theologie und Kirche* 68 (1971): 195–212; Schleiermacher to Berthold Georg Niebuhr, 28 March 1819, in Heinrich Meisner, ed., *Schleiermacher als Mensch: Familien- und Freundesbriefe*, 2 vols. (Gotha: Friedrich Andreas Perthes, 1922–23), 2:297.

67. Ogden develops this theme, with minor variations of wording, chiefly in the second part of the title essay in *The Reality of God and Other Essays* (1966; paperback ed., New York: Harper and Row, 1977), pp. 21–43. Also pertinent are chapter 3, "Myth and Truth" (pp. 99–119), and chapter 4, "The Strange Witness of Unbelief" (pp. 120–43). The pagination remained the same in the paperback edition except in the new preface, to which my roman numerals refer. See, further, Ogden, *On Theology* (San Francisco: Harper and Row, 1986), pp. 69–84, 106–9, esp. p. 72: "The existential faith by which we live neither needs justification nor can ever be justified. Rather, it is the very ground of justification. . . ."

68. *Reality of God*, pp. xi, 20, 42, 114 (the passage from which my second epigraph is taken). Ogden discusses Stephen Toulmin, *An Examination of the Place of Reason in Ethics* (Cambridge: Cambridge University Press, 1950), on pp. 27–39.

69. *Reality of God*, pp. 20, 23, 33–34. Ogden thus sees human experience as "always essentially religious" (p. 114).

70. Ibid., pp. 37 (cf. p. 43), 115, 34 n. 55, 34–37. Although he focuses on the moral relevance of basic confidence, Ogden takes this as only an illustration of a relevance for life generally (pp. 40, 43, 114). His critical remarks are addressed to William A. Christian, *Meaning and Truth in Religion* (Princeton: Princeton University Press, 1964).

71. *Reality of God*, pp. 37, 43, xi.

72. In addition to the references already given above, see ibid., p. 114: "Man lives and acts, finally, only according to certain principles of truth, beauty, and goodness, which he understands to be normative for his existence. Invariably implied in this understanding is the confidence or assurance that these norms have an unconditional validity and that a life lived in accordance with them is truly worth living." Cf. *On Theology*, pp. 75–76, 106.

73. *Reality of God*, pp. 36, 41–42, 138–40. Ogden does not hesitate to call our existence as such not merely "a standing testimony to God's reality," but "the only really essential 'proof of God's existence'" (p. 43).

74. ibid., pp. x–xi, 24–25, 42, 44–70.

75. Faith *stricto sensu*, Ogden says, is "existential self-understanding" (ibid., p. 93), and "to be a self is not merely to exist, but to understand that one exists" (p. 114; cf. pp. 191, 229). But if even unreflective humans perceive their environment in broader terms than survival and reproduction, it may still be asked whether there is not already a difference between "ani-

mal faith" (George Santayana's term) and unreflective human faith; indeed, whether it can properly be said at all (see *On Theology*, pp. 70, 106) that the former includes "accepting," as well as "adjusting to," the larger setting of life.

76. *Reality of God*, pp. 34–35.

77. Ibid., pp. 37, 47.

78. "God must be conceived as a reality which is genuinely related to our life in the world and to which, therefore, both we ourselves and our various actions all make a difference as to its actual being" (ibid., p. 47).

79. Ibid., pp. 35–36.

80. Ibid., p. 114; cf. pp. 33, 37, and *On Theology*, p. 107.

81. After the present essay was completed, it was brought to my attention that the original edition of Jacobi's dialogue on Hume and the introduction to the second edition have recently been reprinted in Friedrich Heinrich Jacobi, *David Hume über den Glauben oder Idealismus und Realismus (1787) with the Vorrede to the 1815 Edition*, with an introduction by Hamilton Beck, The Philosophy of David Hume [unnumbered series] (New York: Garland Publishing, 1983). To the secondary literature on Jacobi in English can now be added Dale Evarts Snow, "F. H. Jacobi and the Development of German Idealism," *Journal of the History of Philosophy* 25 (1987): 397–415.

New translations of Jacobi himself are given in *The Spinoza Conversations between Lessing and Jacobi: Text with Excerpts from the Ensuing Controversy*, introduced by Gérard Vallée and translated by Vallée, J. B. Lawson, and C. G. Chapple (Lanham, MD: University Press of America, 1988).

Chapter Six

Nietzsche and the
Kantian Paradigm of Faith

VAN A. HARVEY

Introduction

In the last decade, a number of philosophical attacks have been mounted from quite diverse standpoints against anything resembling a traditional notion of truth. Heidegger, Derrida, Foucault, the "hermeneutical tradition," Kuhn, Rorty, Wittgenstein—all have been invoked in the cause of certifying the death of the classical philosophical tradition with its interest in the criteria of knowledge. There are no such criteria, it is argued, there are only interpretations, ways of talking, that given groups find more or less adequate for their own purposes.

Not surprisingly, these arguments have reawakened interest in the philosophy of Nietzsche, especially in that aspect of his thought, his "perspectivism," most neglected by those "gentle Nietzscheans"[1] who, attempting to retrieve him from the hands of the Fascists, have pictured him as a nineteenth-century Socrates attacking the irrationalities of Christian civilization. The newly discovered Nietzsche, by contrast, undermined the rationalistic ideals of knowledge and truth. He argued that the entire apparatus of knowledge is not designed for knowledge but for the "taking possession of things,"[2] to arrange a world in which the species can survive. We do not have a need to know but only to schematize, "to impose upon chaos as much regularity and form as our practical needs require."[3] All so-called knowledge is interpretation from the standpoint of a center of power, a perspective; and there are no limits to the number of possible interpretations. "Truth," then, does not designate the antithesis to error, but "only the posture of various errors in relation to one another."[4] What we call "rational thought" is "interpretation according to a scheme that we cannot throw off."[5] In short, the newly discovered Nietzsche did not attack Christianity so much because it was mendacious but because it undergirded confidence in truth, because it was "Platonism for the masses."[6]

140

In this essay, I wish to explore the significance of Nietzsche's attack for one conception of religious faith that has been influential within Protestantism. I shall call it the Kantian paradigm since its origins lie in Kantian philosophy. Kant argued that religious belief is both rational and responsible because, although there are no objective grounds for belief in God, transcendental criticism can establish that God and the soul are postulates needed by reason and presupposed in our moral life. Therefore, we have a right to believe, or, to use his language, to orient ourselves in thinking by means of a subjective need of reason even though objective grounds are lacking. Nietzsche's critique stands in a paradoxical relationship to this Kantian view. On the one hand, he conceded that the human intellect requires certain basic categories if it is to think at all; on the other hand, he argued that these categories are "fictions" which, if taken seriously, lead to humankind's deepest errors: metaphysics and theism. So regarded, Nietzsche's theory of truth may be understood as an attempt to undermine any reliance by theology upon the transcendental tradition in philosophy.

Because there has been some renewed interest in transcendental arguments, and because one of Schubert Ogden's contributions has been to show that theology is the attempt to thematize what he calls the basic confidence by which human beings live, I hope he will accept this essay as a modest attempt to contribute to that discussion which he has so enriched.

The Kantian Paradigm of Faith

In 1786, five years after the publication of the first but four years before the second of his great *Critiques*, Kant wrote a brief and neglected essay entitled "What Is Orientation in Thinking" in which he delineated a conception of the relationship of faith to reason that has influenced Protestant religious thought.[7] The essay was occasioned by the debate between Mendelssohn and Jacobi concerning the use of the unaided reason in the realm of religious belief, or, as Kant quaintly labels it, the realm of supersensuous objects. He believed that the appeal to religious intuition in that debate once more opened the door to irrationality in religious belief, and, as a true son of the Enlightenment, he wished to reassert that only unaided reason can be the legitimate basis for religious belief. The problem, of course, is how the unaided reason can provide such a basis when Kant had already shown it to be incompetent outside of the realm of sense experience.

Kant approached the issue by exploring the notion of "orientation in thinking." Orientation in its strict sense refers to the ability to find one given direction in the world by reference to another; for example, to locate the easterly direction after having made reference to the known North Star. When we explore the "conditions of possibility" of this simple example of orientation, we discover that we not only must have an objective point of reference, the North Star, but also the subjective capacity to distinguish our right hand from our left. If, for example, a miracle were to occur, and the stars were transposed from east to west but maintained the same pattern relative to one another, only those persons would notice the change who retained the subjective capacity to distinguish their left from their right. "Thus I orient myself geographically by all the objective data of the sky only by virtue of a subjective ground of distinction. . . ."[8]

After considering some extensions of the notion of orientation, Kant proposed that we extend it further and formulate the problem of theology in an analogous fashion: How can we orient ourselves to the supersensuous according to a subjective principle when we know that objective principles are lacking? Kant assumed that there is such a subjective principle that can be described; it is, of course, the structure of reason itself as laid out in the first *Critique*. Moreover, this structure of reason, in the nature of the case, has needs associated with it; and thus the question becomes whether we have a right to orient ourselves in thinking about the supersensuous by means of "nothing else than the feeling of a need belonging to reason."[9]

It could be argued, Kant acknowledged, that in most cases where objective principles of assent are lacking it would be better to suspend judgment altogether. But such would be the case only if it were an arbitrary matter whether one should assent or not. But in cases where a real need is associated with reason itself, judgment is forced upon us even when there is ignorance regarding the details. In such cases, a maxim is necessary to guide our judgment because "reason insists on satisfaction." The maxim is that we should purge such concepts from self-contradiction and then bring them into relation with the objects of experience under the pure concepts of reason. This, to be sure, does not make the supersensuous sensuous; but it does enable us to think instead of rave.

To purge from contradiction the concepts reason needs does not, of course, decide anything regarding the existence of the referents of such concepts; consequently, the real question remains whether reason has any right to assume the existence of that which it cannot claim to know on objective grounds. But Kant argued that there is one concept that may be thought of as possible and that reason also has a need to think of as actual: the concept of a First Being as the supreme intelligence and highest good. Not only does the pure reason need to make the unlimited the basis for the limited, but it requires the existence of a First Being because otherwise

> reason can adduce no satisfying ground for the contingency of the existence of things in the world, least of all for the design and order which is met with everywhere to such a wonderful degree (in the small because it is near us even more than in the large).[10]

Although we cannot prove the impossibility of such design without an original intelligent author, nevertheless there remain sufficient subjective grounds for assuming such an author; namely, "reason's need to presuppose something comprehensible to it in order to explain this given appearance, and nothing else with which reason can connect a mere concept can fill this need."[11]

This need of reason to explain the world and its "organization of ends" is, however, only a theoretical and, hence, a hypothetical or conditional need. It arises only if one feels the need to explain the world. But there is a practical use of reason, Kant argued, where the need to judge is unconditional; namely, in the moral sphere. Here, he claimed, "we are compelled to presuppose the existence of God not just if we *wish* to judge but because we *must* judge...."[12] We are beings who must act, and the demands of the moral law are categorical. Here reason needs to assume that there is "an independent highest good," that is, a correlation between virtue and the greatest happiness, as well as a "supreme intelligence as the highest independent good."[13] Reason does not make these assumptions in order to derive respect for the moral laws, because those laws would have no moral worth if respect for them were derived from anything except the law alone. Rather, reason has a need "only in order to give objective reality to the concept of the highest good, i.e., in order to prevent the highest good, and consequently, all morality, from being regarded as a mere ideal...."[14]

One need not agree with this argument in order to understand why this way of construing the relationship of faith to reason has had an important influence on subsequent Protestant theology. Kant made it seem possible to argue (1) that religious belief was not inherently irrational and reason was driven to postulate the idea of God, and (2) that belief was justified even though it was acknowledged to lack objective grounds. This legitimation came to be extremely important to those post-Victorians who were profoundly troubled, as William James was, by W. K. Clifford's argument that it was immoral to believe anything on insufficient evidence.[15] Since religious believers admittedly lacked any objective grounds for believing in God, Clifford accused them not only of immorality but, more seriously, of abdicating their responsibility as intellectuals (the clerisy) to maintain those rational standards that make civilization possible. Kant, by providing a moral justification for religious belief, in effect provided these Protestant believers with an "ethics of belief."

The very structure of the Kantian paradigm of faith naturally invites certain objections. The first and most obvious is that reason does not, in fact, need the notion of an intelligent first cause in order to account for the design and order in the world. A second is that moral behavior does not necessarily presuppose the coalesence of virtue and happiness. But a more fundamental objection is that, even if the deductions of the categories and the postulates are valid, which is itself problematic, this tells us nothing about the nature of the objective world; it tells us only about the structure of our conceptual scheme.

It is this latter objection that Nietzsche, in principle, advanced. He was willing to concede that the intellect necessarily employs certain categories, but he argued that these so-called necessities of thought give us no right at all to conclusions about the supersensuous world. To assume that they do generates metaphysical and theological illusions. To be sure, the categories tempt us to believe, but to succumb to this temptation leads to a form of life Nietzsche believed to be decadent and sick. This is an interesting argument not only because of its view of reason and language but also because it throws into sharp relief the fact that religious faith, as construed in the Kantian paradigm, itself presupposes a confidence in the categories of reason upon which it rests. Transcendental arguments, in other words, themselves only raise the question whether what we have to think of as true is, in fact, the case.

Nietzsche's Perspectivism

Although Nietzsche's philosophical sensibility was far removed from Kant's, his epistemological concerns were analogous in one important respect: he, too, was a kind of transcendentalist; that is, he wanted to establish those categories that are fundamental to rationality. But whereas Kant assumed that these categories of reason were universal and necessary, Nietzsche, a post-Darwinian, approached the intellect biologically and functionally—with the intent to demystify it. Just as his "immoralism" arises from his willingness to entertain the view that both "good" and "evil" serve the survival of the species, so also his assumption about "knowledge" stems from his conviction that both "truth" and "error" must serve some important biological function. "Truth is the type of error without which a specific type of living being could not live. The value for *life* is ultimately decisive," he wrote.[16] Nietzsche searched for a mode of thought that would embody this functionalism, and the result was his genealogical method, his own unique combination of "natural history" and psychology. This method, as Foucault has shown, enabled him not only to speculate on the origins of moral and religious beliefs but to identify the atavistic survivals in even the highest developments of spirit.[17] He could chart the shifting horizon of every type of evaluation: how a sentiment could be transformed over time and under new conditions into its opposite; how an ancient virtue, cruelty, had become a contemporary vice; and how, too, an ancient vice, such as altruism, had become one of the highest virtues. All virtues, he believed, are intelligible as manifestations of the struggle for survival and as instruments of power.

This genealogical concern is evident in some of the earliest entries in Nietzsche's notebooks. Again and again we find him playing with such thoughts as "life requires illusions, i.e., untruths which are taken to be truths";[18] all that is left for philosophy to do is "to emphasize the *relativity* and *anthropomorphic* character of all knowledge, as well as the all-pervasive ruling power of *illusion*."[19] Every type of culture, he wrote, "begins with the fact of having to veil [*verschleiern*] a great number of things. Human progress depends on this veiling.... Every religion contains such an element...."[20] This view permeates Nietzsche's first published book, *The Birth of Tragedy*, where he argued that the same impulse that had called art into existence was also the source of the Olympian deities.

One of the earliest examples of this distinctive approach to intellect is Nietzsche's unpublished essay "On Truth and Lies in a Nonmoral Sense."[21] It begins with a reflection on the transient and ephemeral nature of the human intellect, which human beings have come to regard pridefully as their finest organ but which from the standpoint of all of nature looks aimless and arbitrary. If we look at the intellect from an evolutionary point of view, we must assume that it was primarily used for dissimulation and lying—in flattery, deluding, wearing a mask—because this is the way an individual preserves itself against another. But if so, whence came the drive for truth? The answer lies in that great evolutionary transformation which took place when societies were first formed. Societies necessarily required promises and agreements, which, in turn, demanded fixed conventions for the uses of language and strict prohibitions against its arbitrary use. And since the first language must have been made up of images and metaphors, Neitzsche theorized, truth itself is basically

> A movable host of metaphors, metonymies, and anthropomorphisms: in short, a sum of human relations which have been poetically and rhetorically intensified, transferred, and embellished and which, after long usage, seem to a people to be fixed, canonical, and binding. Truths are illusions which we have forgotten are illusions; they are metaphors that have become worn out and have been drained of sensuous force, coins which have lost their embossing and are now considered as metal and no longer as coins.[22]

Truth acquired a morally obligatory status even though it was not pure knowledge that was desired but simply the life-preserving consequences of agreement.

In the last of the works published in his lifetime, *The Twilight of the Idols*, Nietzsche drew certain conclusions about religion and metaphysics from this genealogical approach to the intellect. The discussion occurs, significantly, within the framework of his attempts to explain how rationalism became dominant in Western culture and thereby contributed to its decadence. The origin of this decadence, he claimed, is rooted in that fateful change within Greek culture when rationality was elevated to the highest virtue. The perpetrator of this new standard of virtue was none other than Socrates, who equated reason, virtue, and happiness. Socrates not only felt in himself the anarchy of his own instincts but the sickness of the Athenians as well, and he hit upon rationality at any price as the great savior of mankind. By appropriating this faith of Socrates and giving the intellect tyranny over the instincts, Western culture became committed to the priority of form over chaos, being over becoming. A true world was posited over and beyond the apparent world, and from this distinction the religious imagination took its flight.

The basic argument of this text is that the illusion of a true world comes about through the workings of an ancient psychology embodied in reason and language. The inherent tendency of reason is to ignore the senses that perceive becoming and to fasten on certain basic static concepts such as "thinghood," "unity," and "substance." These categories are then elevated to the most abstract and highest level and taken to be unconditional and *causa sui*. The reason, reflecting on the "basic presuppositions of the metaphysics of language," engages in a "crude fetishism" in which the abstractions are reified into agents, which, in turn, are regarded as "wills". The reason "sees a doer and a doing; it believes in will as *the* cause; it believes in the ego [*Ich*], in the ego as being, in the ego as substance, and it projects [*projicirt*] this faith in the ego-substance upon all things—only thereby does it first *create* the concept of 'thing.'"[23] Everywhere "being" is projected by thought, pushed underneath, as the cause; the concept of being follows, and is a derivative of, the concept of ego. This tendency to reify is so pervasive in the human species that it can be found in India as well as in Greece. "'Reason' in language—oh, what an old deceptive female she is! I am afraid we are not rid of God because we still have faith in grammar."[24]

The same "ancient psychology" gives rise to religion. Here the intellect works on the feelings. The reason, inevitably looking for the cause of those moods which unaccountably sweep over the organism, attributes painful feelings to evil causes and interprets those lyrical episodes of joy and ecstasy as gifts of grace. These alleged causes, in turn, are interpreted after the analogy of our own consciousness and agency. Because we believe that we are agents and doers, that we possess consciousness and will, we project these inward facts onto the external world. Everything that happens is considered a doing and the world becomes a multiplicity of doers.

> It was out of himself that man projected [*herausprojicirt*] his three "inner facts"—that in which he believed most firmly, the will, the spirit, the ego. He even took the concept of being from the concept of the ego; he posited "things" as "being" in his image, in accordance with his concept of the ego as a cause. Small wonder that later he always found in things only that *which he had put into them*. The thing itself, to say it once more, the concept of thing is a mere reflex of the faith in the ego as cause.[25]

It might seem that we are dealing here with a relatively simple projection theory of religion, but the theory is much more complex than the metaphor "projection" usually suggests. In traditional projection theories, the projection is said to be "false" because it violates our scientific notions of the real causes of events. For Nietzsche, by contrast, the concept of cause is itself a projection, as are the notions of "thing" and "ego." It is not as though one could simply adopt a nonprojective perspective, because the alleged realities of metaphysics and religion are only the reifications of those basic categories that make thought itself possible. Clearly, more is involved here than any traditional notion of projection.

To understand what more is involved, it is necessary to turn to those extensive and controversial reflections on "knowledge" and "truth" in Nietzsche's notebooks that seem, in many cases, to be preliminary drafts of ideas he intended to incorporate in a major work on nihilism in Western culture.[26] What emerges from these entries looks something like this: The intellect is a biological tool of adaptation and an instrumentality of power.[27] In order for the species to maintain itself, it needed only to comprehend enough to be able to calculate and to base a scheme of behavior on that rough calculation. "The utility of preservation—not some abstract-theoretical need not to be deceived—stands as the motive behind the development of the organs of knowledge—they develop in such a way that their observations suffice for our preservation."[28] What we call knowledge arises out of the need of the human organism to impose order and structure on the chaos of experience, to give as much order as is necessary to survive. The basic need of the species was not to know but "to subsume, to schematize, for the purpose of intelligibility and calculation. . . ."[29]

This view of the intellect enabled Nietzsche to deal with several issues that play a large role in any transcendental analysis of knowing. First of all, he could link "knowledge" inextricably to the sense organs; second, he could concede that there were certain categories of thought more fundamental than others; and finally, he could explain the illusion why these basic categories should seem to be a priori, while casting suspicion on their necessity and universality. Nietzsche was prepared to acknowledge that certain fundamental categories seemed necessary for thought, but he argued that these categories and the modes of judgment they made possible were "habits" that have been acquired over centuries. "Rational thought is interpretation according to a scheme that we cannot throw off."[30] Over time, he argued, the human intellect must have cast up innumerable modes of thought, but only a few have served to preserve the species. Those who hit upon these categories survived and these "articles of faith" became part of the mental furniture of the species.

To write that over millennia there must have been innumerable unsuccessful modes of thought suggests that Nietzsche believed that the categories of reason are not universal even in the human species, a problem to which I shall return below. But it is clear that he believed that creatures with different sense organs than ours will necessarily experience a different world than we. To assume, therefore, that our human interpretations should be universal is one of the "hereditary madnesses of human pride."[31] What the human species can know is only a species-specific "world," a world seen from the "nook perspective" of consciousness. It is this "nook perspective" that decides the character of appearance. How far this perspectival character extends cannot be known. There may be other types of intellects that experience a quite different world from ours.[32]

Nietzsche was prepared to concede that certain categories are fundamental to human rationality, and there are many entries in the notebooks devoted to analyzing them as well as the laws of logic.[33] For example, the notions of essence and form, he argued, result from the necessity of our species with its unique mode of temporality to fasten on something identifiable and enduring.[34] But it is a mistake to think that the essence we abstract is "eternal" or exists apart from our utilization of it. "What appears is always something new, and it is only we who are always comparing, who include the new, to the extent that it is similar to the old, in the unity of the 'form.'"[35] So also, if we employ the concept of species, this only expresses the fact that an abundance of creatures appears and that "the tempo of their further growth and change is for a long time slowed down," so that small variations are not noticed by us.[36] Form, species, law—all these are "fictions"; artificial conventions that enable us to arrange a world for ourselves in which our own existence is assured.

There is a particularly interesting entry written in 1887 and revised the following year in which Nietzsche attempted to deal with logic itself from this point of view. He wrote that if the law of non-contradiction, as Aristotle realized, is the most basic axiom upon which all demonstrative reasoning rests, then it should be rigorously considered what presuppositions lie at the bottom of it. Either it says something true about actuality or it states a rule that one should not both affirm and deny the same thing at the same time. Nietzsche argued that since we have no direct access to actuality except through the mind which adheres to that rule, we cannot confirm the former assumption and so must conclude that logic is "an imperative, not to know the true, but to posit and arrange a world that shall be called true by us."[37] The principle is not so much a measure of reality as it is the "imperative concerning that which *should* count as true."[38] Moreover, the rule itself presupposes a belief in self-identical things which perdure through time. This, in turn, rests on the "coarse sensualist prejudice" that sensations teach us the truth about things, that one cannot at one and the same time call the same thing, say, both hard and soft. Our belief in things, he concludes, is a precondition of our belief in logic.[39]

Nietzsche's attempt to connect the laws of logic with the category of "thing" suggests, as do many other entries, that he believed there to be a systematic connection among the categories constituting the "nook perspective" of the human species. Nevertheless, there is nothing in his writings that approaches a rigorous transcendental deduction of the categories by means of which this systematic connection is exhibited. Nietzsche was not that kind of systematic philosopher. What one does find are numerous entries, varying in length, dealing with such "fictions" as "law," "species," and "thing" that connect these loosely with "causality," "subject," "substance," etc. But despite the unsystematic nature of the entries, the category "subject" or "ego" is obviously regarded as the fundamental category that generates all others. We have already seen in *Twilight* that he had connected the fiction of the willing subject with the error of a "false causality," a world of spirits. But it is also obvious that he believed that the more impersonal notion of causality itself is nothing but a shadow cast by the ghost of the fiction of the subject. In several passages in the notebooks, this connection is spelled out.[40] The belief in cause and effect is said to be a "special case" of the belief that there are subjects.[41] He argues, following Kant and Hume, that since we have no actual experience of cause, we must have derived the conception from a misinterpretation of the muscular activities and tensions accompanying our activity. We invent the notion of cause—we think of ourselves as causal agents—and then project this notion onto things. Thus the notion of causality itself is a deception. We "project it out of ourselves" in order to understand an event.[42] It, too, is simply an "interpretation."

Although it is uncertain how Nietzsche conceived the logical connections among the basic categories of the "nook perspective" of the human species, there can be little doubt that he thought these fictions to give rise to the greatest illusion of all: that there is a true world behind the apparent world. Once we believe in a doer behind the deed and project this subject onto things, we have taken the first step down the garden path to postulating a "thing in itself," a hidden reality behind the attributes that appear to us. It is this postulate which Nietzsche regarded as the source of the sickness of Western culture, a sickness he believed to be exemplified not only in its philosophy and religion but in its science as well. Instead of accepting such fictions for what they are, namely, pragmatic and useful conventions, we have taken them to be the criteria of truth and reality, which is to say, of a world in which there is no deception and change. "In summa: the world as it ought to be exists; this world, in which we live, is an error—this world of ours ought not to exist."[43]

Throughout his writings, Nietzsche was preoccupied with the way in which the human mind was bewitched by the notion of a true world. Again and again he attempted to explain this bewitchment, not always consistently. He finally came to the conclusion that it was rooted in what he called the corrupting pathos of suffering.[44] The human organism, longing for some surcease from the incessant change and perishing of existence, believes that it will find happiness in a world corresponding completely to its desires. It thus recapitulates the inherent "logic of morality": some state of affairs should not have been permitted; therefore, there must be another state of affairs. "It is suffering that inspires these conclusions: fundamentally they are *desires* that such a world should exist; in the same way, to imagine another, more valuable world is an expression of hatred for a world that makes one suffer: the *ressentiment* of metaphysicians against actuality is here creative."[45]

Nietzsche, it needs to be noted, is one of the few atheistic philosophers who has objected to Christianity not because it could not solve the problem of evil but because it believed that evil was a problem that required a solution. It is just because Christians cannot tolerate a world in which there is suffering that they posit the fiction of a world corresponding to their desires. This faith in another perfect world, Nietzsche believed, is the source of all that is wrong with Western culture. This illusion not only is the substance of Christianity but is at the root of the moral prejudices that have corrupted the Western consciousness. This faith essentially represents a rejection of this life and thus appeals to all those weary souls vaguely dissatisfied with it. "Christianity was from the beginning, essentially and fundamentally, life's nausea and disgust with life, merely concealed behind, masked by, dressed up as, faith in 'another' or 'better' life."[46] It has turned existence into a hospital. Consequently, it is the most prodigal elaboration of the moral theme to which humanity has ever been subject, a theme which stands in irrevocable opposition to the aesthetic theme in which life is based on "semblance, art, deception, points of view, and the necessity of perspectives and error."[47] Consequently, the new philosopher, the proponent of the Dionysian wisdom, should resist the twin seductions of reason and suffering and affirm a world of flux, chaos, and suffering. The unknown other world should be rejected as stupid in favor of a ringing affirmation of this world.

Casting Doubt on Our Conceptual Scheme

If we now step back and reflect on the significance of Nietzsche's argument as a whole, we may roughly separate out two basic strands. First of all, he argued that the fundamental categories of our species-perspective are "fictions" that have been acquired over millennia for purposes of schematization and control. It is a mistake, therefore, to think they can be employed to orient ourselves in thought towards the supersensuous. Second, he argued that metaphysics generally and theism particularly are reifications of these fictions which have then been corrupted by the human inability to endure suffering.

It is the first of these strands with which I am primarily concerned in this essay because, as I have suggested, it undermines the Kantian paradigm of faith that has so influenced Protestantism. Kant had argued, it will be remembered, that reason has an inherent structure, a structure such that it is driven to the postulates of "God" and the soul. Although these postulates are such that reason can adduce no objective grounds to justify their referents, nevertheless, because these are reason's own postulates, we have a right to orient ourselves "in the realm of the supersensuous" by means of them. Nietzsche, by contrast, conceded that reason does in fact feel such a subjective need, but this need merely reflects not the inherent structure of reason but millions of years of "habit." The basic categories of reason are simply "conditions of life for us."[48] They do not confer any right to orient ourselves to the supersensuous. Indeed, a belief can be a condition of life and nonetheless be false.[49] "*Ultimate skepsis.—* What are man's truths ultimately? Merely his *irrefutable* errors."[50] It is just by such paradoxical language as this that Nietzsche hoped

to create a vertigo of reason, so to speak; to induce a nauseous diz-
ziness by casting doubt on the very organ that makes doubt itself
possible.

If Nietzsche believed that metaphysics and theism were rooted in
the corruption of specific fictions, and his "Dionysian wisdom" was
intended to be a therapy for the illusions so created, then it is understandable why at least one important commentator should have interpreted him as a forerunner of Wittgenstein. Thus in his book
Friedrich Nietzsche and the Politics of Transformation, Tracy B.
Strong argues that however dissimilar Nietzsche and Wittgenstein
may have been, they nevertheless had deep philosophical affinities.[51]
Not only did they both reject traditional modes of argumentation
but they were led to a very similar picture of the way language and
human activity are related, a picture that looks roughly like this:
Every culture teaches its members to organize their experience in
certain ways by means of language, with its implicit categories and
presuppositions. A common grid, as it were, is fitted over the world,
determining how the things in it will be conceived and related. Thus
the members of each culture acquire a picture of the world, a loosely
connected set of categories, propositions, and beliefs in which the
premises and consequences are mutually supporting. Some of the
categories employed are more basic than others. They are, so to
speak, the hinges upon which the door of rationality swings. They
are so fundamental and taken for granted that it is only against the
background of these categories and the beliefs in which they are
imbedded that doubt can even arise. They are an expression of our
form of life; or, to use Nietzsche's phrase, they are our "most ancient beliefs."

Strong goes on to argue that not only did Nietzsche and Wittgenstein regard language as rooted in distinctive forms of human activity but they also believed that human beings were inevitably bewitched by language, the most common manifestation of this
bewitchment being metaphysical discourse. Certain acoustical illusions are, as it were, set up by the use of language—acoustical
illusions that themselves have become the object of human bewitchment and puzzlement. Wittgenstein argued, for example, that
verbally analogous forms of language seduce us into thinking that
there are common essences, or into thinking that understanding is
an event inside of the head. Both philosophers, Strong claims, regarded philosophy as a means of dispelling these acoustical illusions. And since they regarded language as rooted in a form of life,

they both believed that therapy required a change in that form of life. In Nietzsche's case, his genealogical method was designed to diagnose the illness which the Western psyche had acquired over millennia, and his Dionysian vision was proffered as its cure.

Strong's comparison of Nietzsche and Wittgenstein is undeniably suggestive, but at one important point it rests upon a mistaken view of Wittgenstein that is itself instructive because it throws into relief a basic and important difference between the two thinkers. Whereas Nietzsche was an evangelist for a new and divine way of thinking, Wittgenstein, as Jonathan Lear has recently pointed out, was basically a nonrevisionist in philosophy.[52] In fact, he regarded programs for conceptual revolutions, such as that proposed by Nietzsche, with profound suspicion. This suspicion was not merely attitudinal; it sprang from his own investigations into the nature of language itself. He did not believe that we can step outside of our deeply rooted modes of thought—what Lear calls "our mindedness"—and propose another. The entire point of philosophical analysis is not to prescribe new ways of thinking but, rather, to elucidate how, in fact, we do think. Philosophy, he believed, leaves everything as it is. The attempt to propose a new, revolutionary way of thinking as a cure for an old way is but to infect us with another disease as noxious as that from which the new way promises to deliver us.

Whether Nietzsche's project was, in fact, to propose a new and revolutionary way of thinking is one of the debated points in current Nietzsche scholarship. At the heart of this debate is whether he believed our commonsense conceptual scheme with its categories of self and causality was only one of several schemes possible for our species, or whether he held the quite different view that, although this scheme was the only possible one for us, it nevertheless is only a tool of biological adaption and permits no cognitive access to the inherent structure of things. Was Nietzsche, in short, a cognitive relativist, or was he a pragmatist of some sort? The debate swirls around the interpretation of several crucial Nietzschean terms such as "perspectivism," "power quanta," "nihilism," "the Overman," "the Dionysian wisdom," and "eternal recurrence." On the one side of the debate are those who argue that Nietzsche's significance lies precisely in the radicalness with which he depicted the cognitive situation. They claim that he rejected the essential elements of almost all traditional theories of knowledge: the notion that there is an independent (given) structure of the world apart from any interpretation of it; the notion that truth is some sort of correspondence of thought and being, however specified; the notion that truth is something about which we should seek agreement. The key to Nietzsche's philosophy, it is said, is his view that being is a chaos of centers of power (power quanta) in which each center adopts a perspective toward the remainder, that is, attempts to impose a form upon its immediate environment in order to enhance its own power. Each of these centers of power is nothing other than the sum total of its relationships towards the remainder. "The 'apparent world,' therefore, is reduced to a specific mode of action on the world, emanating from a center."[53] Indeed, interpretation is itself "a form of the will to power."[54] It is an expression of the needs of a center of power to control the environment from its perspective. In short, what Nietzsche called his perspectivism does not refer to anything so bland as the idea that each cognitive center is so situated as to see a common world differently, depending upon its standpoint; rather, he held the view that each center of power constitutes things by means of the act of interpretation. Thus, one commentator writes: "What or how anything is, is a function of this activity and . . . there can be no thing apart from an interpretative act. Thus the interpretative-cognitive act is entirely creative; not only is this act responsible for its contents—it is also identical with them."[55]

If this view of Nietzsche is correct, it follows that there can be no normative cognitive perspective that can be called true; there are only interpretations expressive of the will to power. One should take Nietzsche seriously when he wrote that "The criterion of truth resides in the enhancement of the feeling of power."[56] This is the Dionysian wisdom—the gay science—of which he writes.

On the other side of the debate are those interpreters of Nietzsche who say that the above argument basically misconstrues his position. They argue that it is based on a few cryptic fragments from the *Nachlass* and does not take account of the different levels of analysis of truth found throughout Nietzsche's writings.[57] Although Nietzsche rejected any naive correspondence theory of truth, he did not reject the view that some claims and propositions are more "apt" than others. He even endorsed a certain type of "objectivity."[58] What he meant by saying that a thing is constituted by its relationships, is that the truth about it consists in the form of interactions into which it is capable of entering. He simply wanted to argue, therefore, that the nature of that thing only becomes accessible when viewed from many perspectives. He did not mean to deny that there is a "truth for us"; he only meant to deny that there is some absolute nonhuman perspective, some absolute truth. Indeed, his criticism of Christianity in the *Anti-Christ* is predicated on the assumption that it has falsified the truth. This criticism, as well as much else in his philosophy, would be unintelligible, Richard Schacht argues, if, as has been claimed, Nietzsche had rejected the notion of objective truth.

It is impossible within the limits of this essay to do more than register my own opinion that this debate is possible only because there is a profound tension in Nietzsche's thought regarding the issue of truth. This tension is reflected, for example, in his equivocal use of the term "perspective" itself. Sometimes it refers to the perspective or standpoint of the individual and sometimes to the perspective of the species. Insofar as each individual has a perspective, a relativistic inference can easily be drawn; but insofar as the perspective is that of the species, no relativism need be implied, because "truth" just is what we all are led to think employing the categories and rules of the species. One may contrast one individual perspective with another, but what is it with which the species-perspective is to be contrasted? Insofar as Nietzsche appeals to a universal species-perspective in which there are categories and rules we cannot throw off, then it is possible for him to employ something like a standard view of truth. But insofar as every center of power orders the world from its perspective, then there are any number of possible perspectives and, hence, no truth. This ambiguity is further complicated by Nietzsche's elitism, which leads him to label the species-perspective a "herd perspective" that the creative individual is called upon to surpass and transcend. Moreover, from the standpoint of this latter, highly individualistic perspective, the species-perspective is an expression of conformity and mediocrity. From the standpoint of the former view, truth is "objective," and Christian faith can be regarded as illusion and false. From the standpoint of the latter view, Nietzsche can appear to be arguing for a new and divine way of thinking.

It is precisely at this point that the comparison with Wittgenstein is instructive, because Wittgenstein's analysis not only helps explain how the tension in Nietzsche's perspectivism could arise but shows what confusions result when he tried to propose a new Dionysian mode of thinking as an alternative to the species-perspective. We must remember, Lear points out, that Wittgenstein had begun his own career in the *Tractatus* as a transcendentalist of sorts, attempting to analyze the inherent structure of language and to suggest revisions in the light of it. But in that book he seemed to be on the horns of a dilemma. On the one hand, he wanted to say that the limits of language were the limits of our world and, hence, "of that whereof we cannot speak, we should remain silent." On the other hand, there were occasions when he seemed to violate his own taboo, as when he considered whether God could create anything that would be contrary to the laws of logic. He wanted to communicate transcendental insights but recognized that there was no language in which to communicate them. He recognized that we could not say what an illogical world would look like. It was only later that he came to the conclusion that the illusion that we can transcend our conceptual scheme is created by thinking that our way of conceiving the world is just one empirical possibility among others, when, in fact, all genuine possibilities must occur within the world. The world is the context within which different possibilities make sense.

Although Wittgenstein's views changed considerably after writing the *Tractatus*, he nevertheless retained the view that the aim of philosophy is to bring the presuppositions of language to self-consciousness. He concluded that language is inextricably bound up with distinctively human activities and that one cannot step outside of that form of life with its fundamental categories. The idea that there could be another conceptual scheme utterly unlike our own is an idea that we can imaginatively entertain, perhaps, but to which we can give no determinate content. We may, to be sure, cast up illustrations like those of the mythical tribal chiefs to which Wittgenstein himself sometimes appealed, but these are used merely to throw into relief the structure of our own like-mindedness. It is a mistake to assume that these illustrations can refer to anything of which we can make sense. But by using these illustrations we are seduced into thinking that the proposition "only because we are minded as we are do we see the world the way we do" is an empirical truth, as delimiting one possibility among others. This then prompts us to entertain the proposition "If we were other-minded, we would see the world differently." Although this proposition has the appearance of being capable of being cashed out, all attempts to do so will produce only nonsense or, less pejoratively, mystical poetry. The cognitive relativist is someone who has succumbed to this acoustical illusion. If Wittgenstein is correct, it would be as erroneous to attempt to find a substitute for our way of thinking as it would be to attempt to justify it. We do not need to justify it.

We are tempted to label this view "conventionalism." But conventionalism, as Lear points out, implies that our being minded as we are is contingent, as though the logical rule "if p, then q" was simply a matter of agreement.

> That we feel we are being taken by the throat and forced to a conclusion depends upon the fact that we are minded as we are. But however tenuous a fact our being minded as we are may at times appear, it is not a fact that could genuinely have been otherwise. Of course, the context in which a certain inference can be said to be logically necessary must be a context in which we all tend to "agree." The difference between Wittgenstein and the conventionalists can be summed up as follows: the conventionalists state a falsehood; Wittgenstein tries to point beyond to a transcendental insight.[59]

Nor is this skepticism, since skepticism thrives on the fact that our way of looking at the world is based on beliefs that we can neither prove nor refute.

Insofar as Nietzsche criticized our conceptual scheme because it was inferior to some proposed Dionysian alternative of his own, his position is incoherent and his proposal is not an alternative to our ways of thinking; it is, rather, mystical poetry, a genre with which we are familiar and which is not a cognitive alternative. But does this also mean that we can then dismiss Nietzsche's apparent subversion of the Protestant paradigm of faith? It might initially seem so, for what could it possibly mean, we might ask, to undermine our confidence in the basic categories of our reasoning? Surely any attempt to establish that our basic practice is faulty must itself be wrong, because we could say this only if there was some meaningful alternative for which reasons could be given for and against. But Wittgenstein has convincingly argued that there is no meaningful alternative.

Despite the failure of Nietzsche to provide a meaningful alternative to our conceptual scheme, I think it premature to dismiss as nonsense his attempt to get us to view our basic mindedness as contingent and, hence, to question our right to orient ourselves to the supersensuous world by means of it. What his critique does is to throw into radical relief the species-specific character of our reasoning, which, in turn, reveals that our use of it to orient ourselves to the supersensuous rests on still another deeper belief; namely, that our categories do obtain some sort of purchase on the transcendent. But unlike the belief that accepts the merely pragmatic utility of the categories, this belief, Nietzsche argues, leads to the depreciation of life, a "nay-saying" that ultimately can corrupt the species.

But what can one say to Wittgenstein's argument that it makes no sense to be suspicious of our like-mindedness because there is no meaningful alternative to it for which we could give reasons? We need to recognize that the appeal to a "meaningful alternative" is itself ambiguous. What if we were not to think of Nietzsche's attempt to provide a "gay science" in this connection but, say, we were to reflect on the significance of something like the Madyamika tradition in Buddhism, a theory and practice aimed at casting doubt on and undermining the ultimate validity of the categories of our conceptual scheme: more specifically, the categories of "self" or "subject" of which Nietzsche was also critical? These categories, the Madyamika school has also said, are indispensable and useful at the pragmatic level of dealing with the world but are delusory when relied upon for orienting ourselves in the realm of the supersensuous. Indeed, enlightenment or liberation depends upon embracing this insight into the purely provisional nature of reason and its categories. A Buddhism of this sort, it would seem, does constitute an alternative practice to the Kantian faith in the subjective needs of reason.

We have here, then, a religious version of something like the Nietzschean critique of reason—an alternative to the Protestant paradigm of faith. Or to put it in a slightly different fashion, we might say that the Kantian paradigm of faith itself rests upon a faith in the ultimate trustworthiness of the structures of reason, whereas Madyamika Buddhism rests on the belief, as does Nietzsche's, that this faith in reason leads to a sick form of life. If the issue is put in this fashion, I do not see how one can rationally adjudicate between the two positions. But this is perhaps but another way of saying that Nietzsche's critique throws into relief that theistic belief itself rests upon a deeper but inarticulate belief in reason.

Notes

1. In his translator's introduction to *The Gay Science*, Walter Kaufmann attributes the designation to Crane Brinton, who contrasts "tough" with "gentle Nietzscheans" and includes Kaufmann among the former—"marginally, of course." Some years later, in the *New York Review of Books* (November 5, 1970), Conor Cruise O'Brien unequivocally regards Kaufmann as one of the latter.

2. This and all subsequent references are to the edition prepared by Giorgio Colli and Mazzino Montinari, *Friedrich Nietzsche: Sämtliche Werke: Kristische Studienausgabe in 15 Banden* (Munich, Berlin, and New York: Deutscher Taschenbuch Verlag and Walter de Gruyter, 1980). Hereinafter

referred to as SW followed by the volume and page number. For example, SW XI, 164. In the cases of citations from Nietzsche's notebooks, I have almost always used the translations by Daniel Breazeale (in the work cited in note 18 below) and by Walter Kaufmann and R. J. Hollingdale (in the work entitled *The Will to Power* edited by Kaufmann [New York: Vintage Books, 1968]). This latter work will be referred to as WP, after which follows the section rather than the page number; for example, in this case, WP 503.

3. SW XIII, 333; WP 515.

4. SW XI, 598; WP 535.

5. SW XII, 194; WP 522.

6. SW V, 13; *Beyond Good and Evil*, Preface.

7. In Lewis White Beck, trans. and ed., *Critique of Practical Reason and Other Moral Writings in Moral Philosophy* (Chicago: University of Chicago Press, 1949), pp. 293–305.

8. Ibid., p. 295.

9. Ibid., p. 296.

10. Ibid., p. 298.

11. Ibid.

12. Ibid.

13. Ibid., p. 299.

14. Ibid.

15. See W. K. Clifford, *Lectures and Essays* (London: Macmillan, 1886), pp. 339–63. For an account of the importance of this discussion, see James C. Livingston, *The Ethics of Belief: An Essay on the Victorian Religious Conscience* (Tallahassee, Fla.: American Academy of Religion, 1974).

16. SW XI, 506; WP 493.

17. See Michel Foucault, *Language, Counter-memory, Practice*, ed. with an introduction by Donald F. Bouchard, trans. Donald F. Bouchard and Sherry Simon (Ithaca: Cornell University Press, 1977), pp. 139–64.

18. SW VII, 433. Cf. *Philosophy and Truth, Selections from Nietzsche's Notebooks of the Early 1870s*, trans. and ed. with an Introduction and Notes by Daniel Breazeale (Atlantic Highlands, N.J.: Humanities Press, 1979), p. 16.

19. SW VII, 429; Breazeale, p. 13.

20. SW, VII, 435; Breazeale, p. 18.

21. SW I, 873–890; Breazeale, pp. 79–97.

22. SW I, 880; Breazeale, p. 84.

23. SW VI, 77; see the English translation by Walter Kaufmann in *The Portable Nietzsche* (Middlesex, Eng., Penguin Books, 1977), p. 483.

24. SW VI, 78; *Portable Nietzsche*, p. 483.

25. SW VI, 91; *Portable Nietzsche*, p. 495.

26. Many but not all of these were posthumously collected and placed in Book One of *The Will to Power*.

27. SW XIII, 301; WP 480.

28. SW XIII, 302; WP 480.

29. SW XIII, 333; ibid., WP 515.

30. SW XII, 194; WP 522. "The categories are 'truths' only in the sense that they are conditions of life for us. . . ."

31. SW XII, 238; WP 565.

32. Ibid.

33. SW XII, 417; WP 521.

34. Ibid.

35. Ibid.

36. Ibid.

37. SW XII, 389; WP 516.

38. Ibid.

39. Ibid.

40. Many of these are collected under the rubric "Against Causalism" in WP 545–53.

41. SW XII, 102; WP 550.

42. SW XIII, 274; WP 551.

43. SW XII, 364; WP 585.

44. Ibid.

45. SW XII, 327; WP 579.

46. SW I, 18; see "Attempt at a Self-Criticism," in The Birth of Tragedy, sec. 5.

47. Ibid.

48. SW XIII, 333; WP 515.

49. SW XI, 597; WP 483.

50. SW III, 518; see The Gay Science, bk. III, 265.

51. Berkeley and Los Angeles: University of California Press, 1975, pp. 78–86.

52. "Leaving the World Alone," The Journal of Philosophy 89, 7 (1982): 382–403.

53. SW XIII, 371; WP 567.

54. SW XII, 140; WP 556.

55. Ruediger H. Grimm, Nietzsche's Theory of Knowledge (Berlin: Walter de Gruyter, 1977), p. 185.

56. I am unable to find this sentence in SW although it appears in Karl Schlecta's "Nachlass Out of the Eighties," in Friedrich Nietzsche, Werke in drei Bänden, vol. III, p. 919 (Munich: Carl Hanser Verlag). Cf. WP 534.

57. See Richard Schacht, Nietzsche (London: Routledge and Kegan Paul, 1983), p. 60.

58. Ibid., p. 104.

59. Lear, "Leaving the World Alone,"p. 387.

Chapter Seven

Deconstruction and Reconstruction of "God"

JOHN B. COBB, JR.

The word "God" once held together a multiplicity of denotations and connotations in an effective unity. People were able to discuss God's attributes or whether God existed with some assurance that a common topic lay before them. Today the situation is greatly changed.

There are, of course, militant believers who are very sure what "God" means and resent any use of the word that deviates from their own. There are militant disbelievers who also know exactly what they mean and resent the confusion introduced when believers tell them that they do not believe in such a God either. To learn whether someone affirms God today is little more than to learn whether that person has chosen to use the term "God" in an affirmative way. People with virtually identical beliefs about reality sometimes make opposite choices.

The fact that the word once held together so many denotations and connotations is one reason for the current chaos. For example, "God" long denoted at once Being-Itself and the Supreme Being. That Being-Itself cannot be *a* being, even the Supreme Being, was not widely recognized until it was pointed out forcefully, in their different ways, by Heidegger and Tillich. When "God" is deconstructed in this way, some will identify the God in whom they believe with Being-Itself; others, with the Supreme Being. Still others will try to put the pieces back together.

This is only the beginning of the multiplicity of meanings of "God" in thoughtful usage today. In this essay I will try to sort out some of the most important. There is nothing exhaustive about the list, and many readers will not identify themselves simply and comfortably with any of the choices I offer. This is partly because there are other choices, partly because most of us are vague about what

Note: I am using the term "deconstruction" in this essay in its general usage without specific regard for its function in the French school of deconstructionism.

we mean by "God," and partly because many have either not deconstructed the term fully, or have already begun the task of reconstruction, or both.

Initially, at least, there is no reason to assume that anything other than the word itself now holds these uses together. I am not presupposing that there is somewhere something, an idea, or symbol, or principle, or a being, or anything else to which all of these uses point. Indeed, that is quite unlikely. Hence, there can be no question of truth and falsity in the choice of use. On the other hand, it is quite possible that several of these uses *are* alternate ways of identifying one and the same reality. On this hinges the possibility of reconstruction.

Not only is there a diversity of definitions, there is also a variety of strategies underlying the choices of definition. Some theologians want to define "God" in such a way as to put aside doubts as to God's reality. Other thinkers prefer a rich meaning of "God" leaving open the question of God's existence. Six such strategies for identifying God are briefly described below. Sections VII and VIII introduce considerations relevant to the task of reconstruction.

I

In order to avoid endless debates about the reality of God, some identify God directly with something whose reality can hardly be doubted. For example, one may assert that God means what the New Testament calls *agape*. Then, unless one denies that *agape* has ever been instantiated in the world, the reality of God is established. Of course, many other questions about God remain to be considered.

Another approach is to point out that "God" has at different times and places elicited rich meanings in the minds of the hearers. These meanings or symbols have shaped their lives and human history. By "God" one may refer to these meanings. A change of meanings is, then, without qualification, a change of God. And if these meanings have collapsed or "died," then God has, in a quite intelligible sense, "died." The ontological status of such meanings may not be settled, but it can hardly be doubted that God in this sense has been a reality.

There are others who use the word "God" quite simply to name Jesus. I am not referring to those believers who declare that Jesus is God in a synthetic sense, making metaphysical claims about the historical figure. I mean rather those for whom "God" becomes simply a name for Jesus, so that whatever is learned about Jesus is learned, without qualification, about God. Of course, a few scholars have discussed the possibility that the Jesus of the New Testament may never have lived; so the possibility that God may not have existed also arises. But for most people this appears too unlikely to be interesting.

In addition to those who in these ways identify God with a generally acknowledged reality about which or whom considerable knowledge exists, there are those who identify God with an element in what they find to be a convincing philosophy. For example, for those who are captured by Hegel's vision, *Geist* is self-evidently real. To identify God with *Geist* is, for them, a way of settling the question of God's reality and nature. They can also communicate with other Hegelians in this way. But God's existence is thereby established only for those who share the philosophical vision. It is hard to explain to empiricists what *Geist* means, still harder to convince them of its reality. The confidence that one is speaking realistically when one speaks of God in this sense depends on the general confidence in Hegel's vision.

Similarly, in Whitehead's vision there is required a principle of concretion. Whitehead gives reasons for calling this "God" and Whiteheadian theologians have followed him in this. Once one has entered Whitehead's general vision, the reality of this principle is largely settled. Hence most convinced Whiteheadians are sure of the reality of what they call God. But to explain this to one who does not share the vision is difficult and rarely convincing.

II

A second strategy, which also seeks to defuse the issue of God's reality, is to identify God openendedly. For example, if one says that whatever people place their trust in is their God, this leaves open the question of what their God is. It could be a president or a rabbit's foot. It could also be the Father in Heaven, leaving open for now what actual status this object of trust would have. There could also be people who trust nothing and who, therefore, have no God. This definition leaves all this open.

For many people the use of "God" is tied to religious experience. They may believe that there is a common core to all religious experience. In that case they may assert that God is whatever is experienced in that common element of all religious experience. However, this makes the referent for God dependent on the assumption of commonness.

Others can specify a particular type of religious experience as the experience of God. This may be unitive mysticism, or the sense of the numinous, or the awareness of a spiritual presence, or the sense of the forgiveness of sins. If it is granted that such experiences occur, then the reality of God is established. But what God is, is not established. God may be just what is reported by the subject of the experience, or God may be a neural circuit in the brain. If God is what is experienced in a certain type of religious experience, then empirical research into religious phenomena may throw light on what one or another of these Gods is, or even show that they are all one. But this is very difficult and remains a remote possibility. Henry Nelson Wieman, on the other hand, deserves great credit for a definition of God that, unlike these, successfully opened the way for empirical analysis of God. He defined God openendedly as whatever is creative of human good. He then described a fourfold process that he held could be discerned whenever human good grows. His analysis has held up well under scrutiny. In this case, then, an openended definition led to a convincing description that remains at the empirical level.

III

A third strategy shifts to metaphysics while still trying to overcome any doubtfulness as to God's reality. For some people the meaning of "God" is indissolubly connected with the question of the cause. What makes things happen as they do? The question is most likely to arise intensely in times of tragedy. But in principle it can be asked of anything. By "God" such people mean the efficient cause of all events. However, to fit the present category no unity can be presupposed. If there is no unified causation, then God is the whole complex of factors that led to the result in question. As long as chance is allowed as the answer, or part of the answer, it seems reasonable to assume that God in this sense is real.

For others "God" is indissolubly connected with the idea of totality. God is the Whole. As long as this is loosely understood, it too can be openended. In some sense there is a totality of all things. Whether God is a sheer multiplicity of unrelated items, an organic whole, or a self-conscious person is thus left open by the definition. Whatever the totality is, that is God.

For others, God is not viewed in terms of efficient cause or as the totality, but is rather the ground of all things. Tillich's language and imagery gave currency to this view. In some of its uses "ground" is still colored with notions of efficient causality, but when it is carefully analyzed the central note is that of material causality. God is understood as the answer to the question: what, ultimately, *are* all things insofar as they are at all? This question has been so important in religious traditions East and West, that I will comment on it further.

I noted above that "God" could be used to identify a feature of a comprehensive philosophy, and that the reality of this feature appeared evident within the vision but not to those outside it. The Ground of Being or Being-Itself might be interpreted in that way. Within Tillich's system its reality is certainly indisputable, and the decision to use "God" to refer to it establishes the reality of God. I did not, however, list this as parallel with the systems of Hegel and Whitehead because this question is not so specifically bound to a particular philosophy. It can be asked in the context of many philosophies and can even be rendered intelligible outside philosophical circles. This can be illustrated in relation to physics.

For the most part, if one asks what a physical entity consists of, the scientific answer will refer to that into which it can be analyzed. These parts are metaphysically like the entity with which we begin, in that they have form, or structure, and are composed of subordinate entities as their matter. Cells contain molecules, and molecules contain atoms. But at the end of the line, in electrons or quarks or somewhere, one comes to entities that are not composed of subordinate entities. Of what are they composed? The answer used to be "matter" or "prime matter." Today it is more likely to be "matter-energy" or just "energy." But in any case, that to which these words refer does not have the same status as the entities that are composed of it. They have form or structure, and they exist. "Matter" or "energy" as such has no form or structure, and it does not exist. Yet it is the "ground" of all that exists. It can be called Ultimate Reality.

Obviously, the detour through all the intermediate levels is not important to Tillich. We may quite directly ask what is the ground of our own existence and find that in Being-Itself. For Whitehead, every individual actual entity is an instantiation of creativity. When we look to the East we find the same role being played by Brahman and Sunyata or Emptiness.

The question then for the "ground" is an important one. I have presented it as openended, assuming that there is a "ground" but that how it is to be conceived or named is left open by the question. Is it matter, or energy, or Being-Itself, or creativity, or Brahman, or Sunyata, or something else?

This question is not as openended, however, as most of the others. Although it makes a difference how one names this ultimate, much of what is said of it is similar regardless of the name. It is necessarily beyond all the distinctions expressed by forms. Still, there are deep differences in connotation and religious meaning between its denomination as Being and as matter. In the East the differences between Brahman and Sunyata have led to different meditational disciplines and metaphysical, or anti-metaphysical, sensibilities. Hence I have included this among openended approaches. It is one of the most important in the world history of religious life and thought.

IV

For many people the word "God" is bound up with unity. To use "God" to refer to multiplicities appears erroneous. Yet insofar as the identifications of God above are really openended, multiplicities are included among the possible answers.

An otherwise similar strategy for defining "God" differs from the above at this point. In the case of those for whom God is bound up with the explanation of why things happen as they do, some may use "God" to name the cause of events conceived as a unity. This remains a little ambiguous. It may mean only that the word "God" is a way of ordering the complexity conceptually into a unity. In that case the strategy is hardly different from that discussed in Section III. But it may also mean that one uses "God" in this context because one believes that behind, in, or through the multiplicity there *is* a unity. In that case it is no longer evident, without argument, that God is real.

The situation is similar with those who name the totality or the whole "God." The words they use already suggest unity. Some are genuinely openended, as explained above. But for others it is the totality as a unity that is God. Again, this can mean that "God" is the organizing and uniting concept for whatever may actually be there. But it may also mean that something is being affirmed about the totality, namely, that it is a unity.

Once again, the most interesting case is that of Ultimate Reality or the "Ground." Most of the language used about it, including the terms in the preceding sentence, connote unity. Above I proposed that questions about this ultimate could be genuinely left open. Yet if the connotation of unity were not there, one wonders whether it would be called "God."

The question is acute because this ultimate cannot have unity in the sense that things or beings have unity. It can be said to be beyond the distinction of unity and multiplicity, in the sense that such a distinction, appropriate to things or beings, simply does not apply. Nevertheless, where the account of the ultimate is such as not to suggest unity, as is the case with the Buddhist account of Sunyata, it becomes more difficult to use the name "God." Hence we must say that some who call this ultimate "God" are making a metaphysical judgment that is subject to dispute.

V

We are now ready for the transition to the very different strategy that, until recently, has been more characteristic of Western thought about God. This is to identify God with an entity or being of a certain sort, recognizing the lack of immediate evidence for the existence of this entity. At that point one may either give reasons for believing in God, thus connecting God with what is generally known or believed, or affirm the reality of God on grounds of faith in revelation, or deny God.

For example, God may be held to be the Necessary Being. God is thereby contrasted with all other beings, which are contingent. There is nothing evident here, nor is the meaning of God open-ended, except in the sense that further reflection about God's nature is possible.

From those who approach God in this metaphysical way, normally we can expect an explanation or an argument for (or against) God's existence. If necessary existence is taken as the essence of deity, the positive argument usually consists in an appeal to the meaning of contingency. It is held that contingent existence cannot be simply contingent on other contingent existence ad infinitum. Fundamentally, contingent existence depends for its existence on what is not contingent, namely, necessary existence. The counterargument undertakes to persuade us that the sphere of the contingent can be self-contained or that there is an inner contradiction between necessity and existence.

At the opposite extreme methodologically from this metaphysical approach is the biblicist one. In this case the word "God" names the

One who is called God in the Bible. Believers are then those who believe that the biblical word is true, so that such a One exists and has done and said just what the Bible reports. Insofar as there is argument for God's reality it is more directly argument for the truth of the Bible. Alternately, there may be a call for the leap of faith, with the promise that in the resultant life what appears doubtful from without will be indubitable.

A third group regards as synonymous with the word "God" the word "Creator." This came to the fore as a distinct meaning of "God" largely as a result of modern science. This science presented the world as a self-contained system of physical causes and made belief in God's direct involvement in that world very doubtful. But the same picture emphasized the resemblance of the world to a machine, and common sense insisted that a machine does not make itself. Also, the machine operated in terms of imposed law, and such laws require a law-giver. The One who made the machine and established the laws by which it operates is God.

Abstracted from the matrix of thought in which these three meanings of "God" arise, the meanings themselves may not be mutually exclusive. The God attested in Scripture is, no doubt, a necessary being and is certainly in some way creator and lawgiver. But the biblical God neither functions conspicuously as the ground of contingent events, nor creates and gives laws in a way that correlates with the mechanistic universe. Although reconstruction may be possible, the confusion caused by the merging in "God" of these profoundly different ideas requires an initial deconstruction.

VI

We can distinguish from these rational and fideistic approaches a strategy that identifies God as the correlate of personal or collective experience. This strategy resembles some of those approaches mentioned in Section II, but there the questions were asked with some detachment and objectivity, leaving quite open what God is. For example, to say that God is whatever one trusts is quite different from saying, as a believer, that God is that which evokes and warrants my trust. To say that God is whatever is felt in religious experience is quite different from the statement of the experiencer that God was what was experienced in the experience.

A wide range of aspects of experience leads different people to speak of God. Several were mentioned in Section II. The unitive mystic may say that God is that with which she or he has been united. The one who has encountered the numinous may affirm God as the Holy One. The one who has felt a spiritual presence may declare that God is this Spirit. The one who has experienced, through forgiveness, relief from the burden of guilt may affirm that God is the One who forgives sins.

There are other features of human experience that can determine the use of the word "God." One is moral experience. Many feel an objective rightness about certain actions and feelings that is not dependent on human preference. They may think of this either in terms of general types of action or quite existentially. In either case they find themselves related to something other than themselves and something that must be distinguished from social expectation. God is experienced for them in and through this moral experience.

For others "God" is the One to whom they pray. Insofar as conversational prayer is real to a person, there is implicit in it the sense of being heard. God is the One who hears. Many questions about God are left open by this use of the term, but God must be the Thou to the human I. Hence a strongly personalistic connotation is embedded in this use of "God."

Others experience a power, energy, or process working in and through them which they do not control but on which the good in their lives, their freedom, and even life itself, depends. They adopt toward this process that calls, frees, and empowers them an attitude of trust and expectancy, seeking to let it shape their purposes and actions. This process is, for them, God. Just how it is to be conceived is a secondary question, but it is experienced as having unity and purpose toward good.

Others find within themselves a fundamental anticipation, a hope, or a sense of meaning that is not grounded in the given processes of history or nature. It witnesses to a deep apprehension of a fulfilment of themselves and all things that cannot be in the world of contingent things. That fulfilment is for them God. The language suggests temporal futurity, but this may not be crucial. The distinction between the fulfilment and the meaningfulness it bestows on present actions is.

VII

The intellectual power of our age has expressed itself primarily in analysis and deconstruction. Beside these, the scattered efforts at reconstruction appear halfhearted and often inauthentic. Yet we cannot live by analysis alone. As long as the only choices are to cling to the confusions that precede deconstruction or to live by its results, practical life at all levels will choose the former. This is true of political life and church life as well as of private life. In this situation those who are most sensitive to the validity of deconstruction lack the conviction and therefore the power of those who reject it and live by the blurred meanings of the past. However difficult and uncertain, reconstruction must be attempted.

There are many who would leave "God" out of the reconstruction. This simplifies the task. But the word is not easily excised from our collective vocabulary. It is too central to our heritage, and it arises too naturally from too many features of ongoing experience and thought. Also, if it is left primarily in the hands of those who oppose all deconstruction, its continuing power as a symbol will serve their purposes against the rest. The reconstruction of "God" is urgently needed.

Since there is no one true use of the term, the question of its reconstruction is pragmatic. But this does not set aside questions of truth. "God" can function usefully for us only as we have confidence that what it identifies is real. On the other hand, it can help us only if the reality it identifies has importance and if its import is aligned with what we see as good. And, finally, it can be effective only if it is used in continuity with traditional meanings. These are heavy demands, and there can be no assurance that they can be met. But they do entail some methodological suggestions.

If our concern were exclusively for the assured reality of God, the approaches in Sections I-III above would commend themselves. But they attain this assured reality either by reduction or by openendedness. The result is that they do not assure sufficient importance or continuity with tradition. It is better to begin with the later approaches, despite the questions they raise as to truth, and then to face those questions head-on.

On the other hand, the approaches listed in Sections IV and V pose the question of truth in too unpromising a form. Although there may be good reason for asserting unity at the levels proposed in Section IV, these cannot be formulated apart from a general metaphysics. Similarly, although contingency may require necessity, the task of showing that this necessity has the ontological status of a being can only be carried out in connection with a fully developed philosophical system. This makes the reconstruction of "God" dependent on another, prior, equally problematic reconstruction. This may ultimately be the only option. But this necessity should not be presumed.

To identify God with the One of whom the Bible speaks might

mean no more than the requirement of the continuity with the tradition which is emphatically needed. But as described in Section V this approach is quite different. It requires a refusal of all historical-critical work and of all deconstruction. It cannot be a basis for reconstruction.

The deistic idea of the creator is dependent on a scientific worldview that is rapidly crumbling. It is true that the notion of "Creator" can be generalized into the creative principle or power and so become useful again. But to go beyond extreme vagueness here requires a philosophical reconstruction or commitment to a specific worldview. Although an adequate reconstruction of "God" must show that God is creative, this is not the place to begin.

The most promising point of beginning is with the strategy sketched in Section VI. In these starting points importance and connection with the tradition are assured. The critical question is reality. Reality can be asserted only by moving from personal experience to the truth of the believer's interpretation of the experience. Ours is the age of suspicion of all such moves. Much of the work of deconstruction has focused exactly here. For those whose thought is guided entirely by suspicion, no reconstruction is possible. My suggestion is that reconstruction cannot begin apart from raising suspicion about the extent to which modernity has committed itself to suspicion.

VIII

In its most general form, the suspicion that characterizes modern thought is that the world is not as human beings experience it, or, to put it in another way, that the world-as-experienced does not exist except in the experience of those who share just that experience. That there are grounds for this suspicion is evident. The world presented to us in sense experience is very different from the world described by physics. Also, the world of meanings is a cultural, historical, and psychological product that dominates even sensory experience. All of this is too well established to be challenged.

Now the warranted suspicion of taking the world-as-experienced as independently real has led to unwarranted and confused results. Emphasis is rightly placed on the creative or originating activity of the mind, and this forbids taking the mind's products, including sense data, as having reality independent of the mind. When this point alone is stressed, the implication is that the mind and its world alone exist, that there is no world other than the one created by the mind.

The attribution of that much creative power to the mind should also arouse suspicion. Holding that each person's world is the product of that person's mind, carried all the way, leads logically to solipsism. There are no solipsists, and the fact that there are none strongly suggests that the mind is not as creative as all that. Further, much of the argument for the primacy of the mind's creativity over objective reality is based on historical and cultural differences in the experience of the world. But to appeal to history and culture is to suppose that much is given to us from others. That implies that each individual mind is receptive as well as creative, that it has not created the past persons who have shaped history and culture, that it does not invent its present human companions.

Even those who emphasize the mind's creativity are likely to concede this much. The mind that is creative is rarely thought of as purely private. It is assumed that there really have been and are other people. But little attention has been given to how this confidence in the reality of other people affects judgments about the impossibility of assuming a real world distinct from the experienced world.

If suspicion is turned on the exaggerations of the creativity of the mind and attention is given to the receptive features of the mind, the whole outlook will change. The natural world and the human body will no longer be viewed as the products of human invention alone. Reflection on how the world acts upon mind as well as on how mind creates the experienced world will show that there are positive relationships between the world fashioned by mind and the world that affects and shapes mind. The deep-seated sense that the experienced world is grounded in realities that are independent of human mind will be acknowledged. The broken connection between phenomenology and ontology can be restored. But in the process the truth involved in the hermeneutics of suspicion must not be forgotten. Indeed, any valid reconstruction must build upon it.

The others, from whom we receive so many of the meanings that create our experienced worlds, cannot be identified with those persons as they appear in the world of sense experience. They are not even those persons constructed by imagination as being centers of subjective experience. They were what they were and are what they are independently of how they appear in these constructed worlds. Yet it is reasonable to assume that some beliefs about them are more appropriate than others. They were and are more like the constructions generated by supposing them to be like ourselves in being centers of experience than like they appear to be through sight and touch and hearing alone. This is apparent from the way we receive from them. Our experience not only guarantees the reality of others independent of our experience but also provides information about their nature. The world given in sensory experience can be seen to be a poor clue to the reality that is received and out of which that world is constructed.

In summary, the deconstruction of experience into its receptive and its creative features is a prerequisite of reestablishing the connection between phenomenology and ontology. The constructive aspects of experience must be viewed with suspicion as clues to the independently real. The receptive aspects are the only link to that world. But insofar as the constructive aspects reflect and explain the receptive, they can be used, too.

IX

This general discussion of the suspicion of unlimited suspicion indicates that receptive experience does provide some access to a reality that is independent of our experience of it. This has been argued in relation to other people. There is no need to be suspicious of our strong confidence that we live in a social world in which there are others much like ourselves from whom our own way of constructing our worlds is derived. But it would be arbitrary to limit confidence in the reality of others to other minds. Our own mental constructions depend upon our brain and nervous system and sense organs. To suppose that bodies are themselves constructs of minds is perverse. And to suppose that bodies are the only physical realities that exist apart from mental constructions is equally perverse. We should be profoundly suspicious of attributing such priority to mind.

Section VI referred to subtler elements in receptive experience than those that give rise to confidence that there are other people, bodies, and a physical world. These had to do with moral and religious dimensions of experience. But although the sense of derivation of a sense of rightness from beyond ourselves is subtler than the sense of derivation from our bodies, it is continuous with that. Overcoming the bias toward emphasizing the creative aspect of mind and neglecting the receptive aspect leads to openness to the testimony of all receptive experience. The move from the phenomenology of moral and religious experience to ontology becomes possible. Indeed, when suspicion is rightly applied to the pretense of sense experience to display the objectively real world, and dependence on the receptive aspect of experience for connection to that real world is emphasized, this move from phenomenology to ontology also in reflection about God becomes plausible.

The strong conviction that sensory experience does not give a proper clue to God's reality has led the theological tradition in two directions. One is to seek God through rational conceptual means. The other is to locate God in human receptivity. Ideally these are complementary. Section VIII argued that critical reflection can lead to views of other people in ways that are more appropriate to the inchoate receptive awareness of them than sensory experience is. They are more like ourselves, *having* sensory experience, for example, than like the sensory images we have of them. But the justification of the concepts must lie in their connection with our receptive experience.

My conclusion, then, is that reconstruction of "God" should begin in the phenomenology of receptive experience. We do receive a great deal: from other people, from our bodies, from the wider world. Discrimination among these sources is imperfect, but it works sufficiently well for most purposes. People also find themselves recipients of what does not seem to be from any of these sources. Again, discrimination is imperfect. But if suspicion of the primacy of the sensory world has gone far enough, we need not be more suspicious of such receptive experience than of any other.

Different elements in reception seem particularly important to different people. What seems important, to which elements of reception attention is directed, and how these are interpreted, are all largely shaped by the creative activity of mind. In some cultures people are more attuned to nature, in others to their dreams, in others to the spoken word, in others to their bodily functioning. Hence phenomenological analysis of receptive experience will not be neutral. But all are affected by nature, by dreams, by the spoken word, by bodily functioning. Hence what is experienced by those who are most attentive may inform those who are less attentive about features of reality they have neglected. Cultural differences do not invalidate the experience or raise suspicion about the reality of what is received. Similar differences apply at the level of moral and religious experience. Some cultures attune people to the nuances of moral experience; some stress anticipation; some encourage attention to what can be trusted. Such differences exist also among people in the same culture.

The reconstruction of "God" can begin when people have renewed confidence in their own experience as a source of truth about reality. It will not be reconstruction unless it accepts the deconstruction of experience into its receptive and its creative poles and recognizes the distinct roles they play. The reconstruction must begin with attention to what is received in experience and to the most careful account of what in this reception does not appear to come from fellow creatures. Of every concept one forms of the source of this reception one must be duly suspicious, but not so as to give up conceptual thinking.

As one engages in such phenomenology of reception, one will be attentive to the work of others who focus on other features of experience. Each must begin the reconstruction of "God" with what is most convincing, but even though the other's starting point is less strongly marked in one's own experience, one will not reject it. For example, the question will be whether what is received, on the one hand, in moral receptivity and, on the other hand, in the sense of receiving of life itself, has one source or more. What, then, of the source of meaning, and hope? What of the Thou sensed in prayer?

Any hasty judgment that all of these are truly grounded in reception from the noncreaturely or that they all have a common source must be viewed with suspicion. But where careful phenomenological work and critical ontological reflection can draw together what has been separated in deconstruction, the work of reconstruction will be well on its way.

Chapter Eight

Metaphysical and Empirical Aspects of the Idea of God

CHARLES HARTSHORNE

In this age empirical science has immense and well-deserved intellectual prestige. I have made two attempts myself to contribute to empirical knowledge, at least one of which has met with some recognition by experts.[1] But empirical knowledge is not the only knowledge. Mathematics and formal logic are used by empirical science but are not empirical. Karl Popper has given the right (most useful) definition of empirical knowledge. It is knowledge of propositions that some conceivable observation or experience *could show to be mistaken*, but with which actual experience at least does not conflict. The crucial test of empirical generalizations is not that this or that observation agrees with them but that deliberate and carefully designed observational attempts to falsify them fail to do so. The negative test is the decisive one. Crackpots tell you how experience supports their claims; they do not tell you what conceivable experiences would show the claims to be false. Elementary arithmetic is not empirical, because no conceivable experience could show that its rules are false. In some conceivable world-state perhaps arithmetic would not be very useful, and in some very simple cultures there is no talk of the multiplication table. But this is not evidence that the table is false. Denials of it do not make sense. Nor do denials of elementary formal logic make sense.

I hold that there is a third kind of nonempirical knowledge, and I use the word metaphysics for this third kind. Its propositions, if we get them right, are such that denying them makes no sense. No conceivable observation could contradict them. If any conceivable observation could do this, then they are not metaphysical but empirical. Metaphysical truths (here I differ slightly from Popper) are all extremely general truths, of which any thinkable experience, if we fully understood it, would be an example. For instance, take the truth that the past is settled and definite, whether we know it or not, but the future is partly unsettled and indefinite, since we are now engaged in deciding some aspects of it. The past seems by its very meaning something already settled or decided. I hold that it does not really make sense either to accept the complete definiteness of the future or to deny the complete definiteness of the past. Could any observation upset this? Today many, though not all, physicists admit the contrast between the definite past and the indefinite future.[2] A century ago almost no physicist took this position; and the few I know of who did (only two in fact) were very great men. Today the rank and file tend to have the wisdom that only a few great geniuses had then.

Religion involves both kinds of beliefs, empirical and nonempirical: those that observation could conceivably show to be false and those that observation could not show to be false. For example, religion in most civilized forms accepts the view that God knows your and my existence. This implies something about the nature of God. You and I might not have existed, and once did not exist; for all anyone can show, we might never have existed. Had we never existed, God would not have known of our existence; for there would have been no such thing to know. There is a further contingency. Given an adult, we know that there has been a child, an early phase of that individual; but given a child it is only a guess, hope, or probability that there will ever be an adult phase of that individual. Several times in my early life I came close to dying. I might never have reached adulthood. God, as knowing all that is, might have known of my death long ago. Since there was no such death as mine in 1917, for instance, God does not have knowledge of it.

I have just shown what many theologians have denied, that God has contingent properties not essential to God's existing as God. For, had I died at age twenty, when I was within three minutes of a probable death (I was saved from it by what, much later, was called "the Heimlich maneuver"), God, according to theism, would have known of that death with the unique divine adequacy and certainty. Without this once possible knowledge, God was and still is the all-knowing God.

My proposition then is: Although God only *happened* to know of our existence as it has been, since there might have been no such existence, yet God does not merely happen to exist. The word happen suggests time and change. Accidents do not happen in sheer eternity, but in time. How could it merely happen that God existed? John Hick seems to think it makes sense to say that God eternally exists but might not have existed. I hold that the nonexistence of God makes coherent sense only if the existence of God does not make coherent sense.

"God does not exist but could have existed," might be taken to imply that there is something that could have produced God but failed to do so. Yet the definition of God in high religions contradicts any idea of something producing God, and the idea of a fact that might not have been so, yet lacks any causal explanation of its possibility, is a radical rejection of a basic axiom of our knowledge. Arithmetical truths do not call for causal explanations for they are necessary truths whose denial does not, if their assertions do, make coherent sense. Two and three is five makes sense, two and three is four or six does not. There are truths whose assertion, but not whose denial, makes sense. Formal logic has such truths. I think metaphysics also does. And I think the definition and existence of God must be treated like an arithmetical proposition: if false, it could not have been true, if true it could not have been false.

I have said that metaphysical propositions are extremely general; however, that God exists seems not general at all. Yet consider the way the high religions define God as all-knowing, all-loving, the source of all good and the supreme end of *all* creation. That God exists means that every nondivine actuality is fully known and cherished in an unsurpassable way. This too shows that theism is not one more special, contingent assertion about existence but, if it makes sense at all, is an exposition of what general terms like "existence" or "actuality" imply about things in general.

What could make it false that God exists? Only one thing, as I see it, could do this. If the definition given of God fails to make coherent sense, then the God thus defined does not and could not exist. Some ideas of God seem to me, as they have to many others, including both believers and unbelievers, to be absurdities that could not be true, for they either contradict themselves or have no definite meaning at all—for instance, the idea of God as knowing you and me and yet entirely lacking contingent properties. Contingent simply means, might not have been as it is. If our existence as well as God's is necessary, then "necessary" lacks any distinctive meaning since, for analogous reasons, it applies to everything. This was the view of the Stoics and of Spinoza. Theologians have almost unanimously, and rightly, rejected this view. So, either God does not know us, or God has contingent properties. And if we define God as the all-knowing One, then God will be God whether we exist and God knows we do, or we do not exist and God knows the world that does not contain us. Either way God will be all-knowing. The definition of God is not the specification of all God's qualities, but only of those without which God would not be divine, for instance, would not be all-knowing.

How then do we decide between the necessity and the impossibility of the divine existence? I offer two out of six reasons I have for accepting the former.[3]

1. We have to believe in some kind and degree of order in the world, for no conceivable animal could exist, or really believe it exists, in a pure chaos. Either, then, the world order simply consists in the countless creatures adapting to one another, as we find ourselves adapting, or there is also and primordially a universal orderer giving guidance, directives to all other beings. Adaptation presupposes a reasonably stable environment; one cannot adapt to chaos, hence the adaptation explanation of order begs the question. Darwinism in all forms, and I am a neo-Darwinian, assumes a basic order that is not explained by adaptation but is presupposed by it. To be brief, only a being with supreme excellence in power and wisdom could be the orderer. This may seem to be an empirical argument, but it is not. For any conceivable experience presupposes an ordered world and no experience could show that there is no such order. All our concepts depend on an assumed order.

2. The other of my two arguments is also not empirical. We are mortal, and I have arguments to show that any conceivable being not God must be mortal. Our very species is mortal. In the long run, then, what are we trying to accomplish with our lives? Merely to enjoy them? I agree that this, so far as it goes, is a reasonable aim. But the only enjoyment we have is our present enjoyment, our past enjoyments are now only a faint, vague, memory for us. They are even less than that for others. What meaning, then, does life have? Suppose, however, that God not only knows but fully shares our joys in a consciousness whose memory is complete; so that all beauty once beheld by it is a possession forever, where moth and rust do not corrupt and thieves do not break in or steal. Then all our happiness (and that of those we have helped) becomes an imperishable good in the divine experience. It has been said, "Thou shalt love thy God with all thy mind, all thy heart, all thy soul, and all thy strength." If anyone accepts this, let him not tell us that it does not suffice to give his life meaning to serve God by enriching the divine experience.

I conclude: the arguments sketched show, in outline, that the belief in God explains how world order is possible and how our mortal lives have meaning. What other explanation compares with this?

Could any conceivable experience show us that God does not exist? Some, indeed many, think that the evils of life show this. However, the famous problem of evil rests on an idea of God that, according to the philosophers I trust, does not make sense, even apart from the evils of life. The atheistic argument from evil supposes that God decides everything in the world just as it is, in every detail. Or at least, it supposes that God decides everything except the actions of human beings. But if God decides everything, what do the creatures decide? Apparently nothing. The argument from evil assumes that any decisions made by creatures are also completely made by God. God's own decisions, however—for instance, what the laws of nature shall be—are made only by God, not by anyone else. So we have two sorts of decisions having nothing in common, from a causal point of view, but the word "decision." God decides without any causes back of his decisions, we decide only what God as cause decides for us. I hold that this is nonsense, sheer misuse of words. It implies that our decisions are completely other-determined, God's are not in the least other-determined. Why suppose that this makes sense? Many hold that it does not.

One more step. A human infant shows less sign of intelligence than an adult ape, far less indeed. If the ape has no freedom of decision-making, does the infant? On what ground can we assert this? I see none. To abbreviate a long argument, I hold that the rational view is that all animals have some freedom. Instinct is too vague a term to explain fine points of behavior. Even atoms are not, for current physics, completely determined causally. There is no need to suppose that any creature, however subhuman, is absolutely lacking in decision-making power.

The conclusion is that the details of the world are not divinely determined. There is an element of chance in the way countless creatures partly determine their own behavior and thus, in however slight degree, are co-creators with God in making the world. An English clergyman, Charles Kingsley, who became a Darwinian, put it well; he thinks of God saying, "I make things make themselves." In making themselves, creatures to some extent make their descendants and, in the long run, may make new species. Yet all this presupposes a basic order that is divinely decided. The laws of nature can be divine acts, but they are no longer believed, as in classical physics and biology, to be all-determining, but rather are viewed as statistical regularities, leaving even atoms a modicum of freedom. Thanks to providence and its ordering of the universe, life with its opportunities is made possible. But the same creaturely freedom that makes good possible also makes misfortunes and evils possible.

With opportunities there must also be risks. My view is, without creaturely freedom there could be no creatures, no world; with creaturely freedom there are creatures with both risks and opportunities. Could there be creatures without freedom, how could they have the idea of God, who is supreme freedom? Lesser freedom, supreme freedom—without both of these there could, I hold, be nothing at all. With them there will be some evils. The classical problem of evil is a misunderstanding. The existence of God is either a necessary truth or a logical impossibility. Since without it we can neither understand how cosmic order is possible nor what meaning life can have, we can reasonably reject the divine impossibility and accept the divine necessity.

God is the individual with strictly universal functions, and the only such individual. Tillich overstated this by contending that God is not a being but being itself. God is indeed not merely a being, rather *the* being, indispensable for every other being. To suppose there could be some being or world without God is to suppose that any and every other possible being could also be without God and that the divine existence is an ill-formed concept, lacking in coherent meaning. The division of possible world-kinds into those God could have as their supreme cause and supreme knower and those God could not have has no clear logic that has ever been articulated. I hold that it is a nonidea—except on the assumption that the divine existence is logically impossible, itself a nonidea. In that case the possible worlds God could have is necessarily a null class. The theistic question is linguistically radical; if affirming it is a legitimate language game, denying it is not—and vice versa. Carnap understood this better than some theologians and some atheists have. He refused to call himself an atheist, but rejected theism as without cognitive meaning. Traditional formulations are only too plausibly subject to this charge. But Carnap failed to appreciate the Popperian criterion of nonfalsifiability for the demarcation of "metaphysical" from "empirical," where "metaphysical" is compatible with cognitive meaning and truth.[4]

Concerning the Necessity (N or n) or Contingency (C or c) of God or of nondivine beings, there are sixteen mathematically possible combinations. Three of these are nontheistic (1–3), nine are formally theistic (4–12), four are hard to classify. Column IV in the modal table below stands for the views that take the divine as the only reality (as in the Advaita Vedanta of Hinduism); Column V is the zero case, the view that modal concepts do not apply either to God or anything else.

Modal Table of Theistic and Nontheistic Doctrines

A	I	II	III	IV	V
1. c	4. N.c	7. C.c	10. NC.c	13. N	16. Z.z
2. n	5. N.n	8. C.n	11. NC.n	14. C	
3. cn	6. N.cn	9. C.cn	12. NC.cn	15. NC	

The A or atheistic column shows the modal possibilities for atheism. Lower-case letters stand for modal aspects of nondivine beings: c for contingency, n for necessity; capital letters in columns I, II, III, and IV stand for modal aspects of God, N for necessity, C for contingency. The order NC is reversed in cn to remind us that the two modal categories apply only with a certain difference to God and the creatures. Each individual creature exists contingently in the radical sense that that creature might not have existed at all. God (for views 4, 5, 6, 10, 11, 12) exists necessarily in that the nonexistence of God is not even a conceivable possibility. But the properties that identify the divine being as such, as God, are not (according to views 10, 11, 12) the only divine properties. God, on these views, has a necessarily existing essence, but has also some contingent properties. The sum of these contingent divine properties I call the divine "actuality." The necessary divine existence requires that there must be some contingent divine properties (and, as I interpret view 12, some contingent creatures), but does not require the particular contingent divine properties (or creatures) that there are. Existence is defined as the essence being *somehow* actualized; actuality is defined as *how*, or in *what* divine states or qualities, the essence is actualized. *Actuality* (except in the sense of being *somehow* actualized) *is always contingent*, even in the divine form. This is the truth in the widespread conviction, in both common sense and philosophy, that no mere concept or definition can guarantee concrete actuality. But the word "existence" is misused if this negative statement is applied to God's existence. With ordinary things, all of which lack any necessarily existing essence, it is correct to call their existence contingent, but not with God. The divine essence is infinitely tolerant of diverse possible modes of actualization; but your essence or mine, if one can so use the word "essence," is not so tolerant. In many possible situations you and I would not and could not exist. But God is infinitely able to coexist with possible forms of actuality. Had I not existed, God would have known a world that would not have included me. I would not have known and could not ever know such a world, except in the very partial way in which I know how the world was before I existed.

In the formula cn, what does the n mean? It has two applications.

Granted that I as adult exist, my childhood existence is necessarily included. In general the present requires its past. This is conditional necessity. In addition, according to a reasonable interpretation of views 3, 6, 9, 12, it is unconditionally necessary that there be some world, some set of creatures or other. The only alternative to our world is some other world, rather than God existing alone, or than there being nothing at all, whether divine or not divine. The last, I hold, is not genuinely conceivable, though we can say the words. To refer to absolutely nothing is not to refer.

The table provides a place for every doctrine that definitely denies or definitely admits ontological relevance for modal concepts with respect to God or what is not God. View 16 (Z,z for zero) gives the locus for the currently fashionable view that contingency and necessity—whether in reference to divine or nondivine existence—have no more than logical, linguistic, or syntactical meaning, *modality de dicto*. I hold, with Aristotle and most of the tradition, also with Peirce and Whitehead, that this view is false, indeed incredibly shallow and absurd. If we do not know what we mean by saying that there are contingent options among which at each moment decisions are being made, we know nothing worth talking about. It is not language that makes it impossible for me to feel as a dog feels, but a real lack of this possibility in my nature. My present possibilities are different from any dog's. Each moment we close previously open possibilities. Life simply is that process of deciding among possibilities. If I don't know *that*, I know nothing important whatever.

Modal concepts are not the only ones that can be used to classify the various mutually exclusive views about God and the world. Absolute and relative, infinite and finite, eternal and temporal, object and subject, and still others logically behave in much the same way. In all cases it is the twelfth view, applying both of the two contrasting ideas to God and, also, with a difference in the how of the application, to the world of the creatures.

If there is any device remotely as powerful as the modal table thus generalized for other similarly abstract conceptions, for analyzing the theistic issue, I should be most surprised to hear of it. If I am not remembered for proposing it, my ghost will be disappointed.

I suppose I need to mention the rather obvious truth that there is no contradiction in applying both necessity and contingency to the same being, God, or to the world. As logic books tell us, "S is P and S is not P" is contradictory only if the predicate and its negation are applied "to the same subject in the same respect" or aspect. And this the table does not do. Thus the divine existence is necessary but not the divine actuality. And we have clearly distinguished existence from actuality. Nondivine existence is necessary in that there must be some nondivine beings, but contingent in that there is no one such being or set of beings that must exist. No particular world is necessary; however, some world or other there must be. I challenge anyone to show contradiction in these requirements. But you will not find any very clear anticipation in the older literature for the point I am making. My name for this point is the doctrine of "dual transcendence." God excels by being necessary, absolute, infinite, and so on; but God equally excels by being relative, finite, and so on in an incomparably excellent manner. For example, only God's contingency embraces all other contingency (by adequately knowing and thus possessing it). Similarly with "the divine relativity," on which I wrote a book, recently reprinted after more than thirty years.

It is curious to think that if John Hick is right about heaven he may eventually know by experience that he has been thus right—assuming that his idea of heaven really makes sense, about which I have doubts. On the other hand if I am right about heaven I will never know any better than I do now whether or not I am right about heaven. But I consider that I have rational knowledge right now that the meaning of our lives should not be made dependent on any scenarios about life after death. The ancient Jews and many modern Jews have worshipped God without asking for any rewards for themselves (or punishments for their enemies) after death. Serving God should be its own reward, whether or not our last experience before our death is our last experience altogether. I find life its own reward, provided I can believe that all that is beautiful or good in my earthly living, and in that of those I can influence or help, will be cherished forevermore in the life of God. Loving God with all one's being implies precisely, as I see it, that to have served God is *all* that we seek. If we serve God by being genuinely mortal, then mortal is what we should want to be. It is God who dies not, and I hold that we should leave immortality (other than that of our earthly careers as divinely cherished) to God. Robert Frost put it nicely.

Earth's the right place for love.
I don't know where it's likely to go better.

If we can make a decent society on earth, that's heaven enough. If we don't, we may make hell on earth only too nearly literally. Nuclear warfare could make Dante's Inferno look rather childish. It's time to turn our attention to our known primary problems.

So far I have said nothing about the man in whose honor this essay is being published. I think that he would find much of the above discussion largely familiar and would perhaps for the most part agree with it. He is one of a number of theologically concerned former students of mine who have made effective use of my type of metaphysics. I have long admired his learning in the history of ideas and the closeness of his reasoning. Of all those who have developed a christology on this basis, he is the one whose account of the religious significance of Jesus I find most appealing. I refer here to the chapter on "Jesus Who is Said to be Christ," in *The Point of Christology.* I am grateful to him for this helpful chapter. If I could accept any christology, this would be the one. Comparative religion, the rather dismal record of Christianity (compared to Buddhism) in the war-peace problem, also the anti-Semitism (not in Ogden)—these and other matters continue to trouble me, including the long medieval and still not overcome dalliance with otherworldliness, from which the Jews have been by comparison relatively free.

With one aspect of my neoclassical metaphysics Ogden is unable to agree. It is, however, an aspect that I am unable to give up. Two interconnected points are involved: my (also Whitehead's) psychicalism or theory of the categorial universality of sentience or feeling, and my doctrine of theological analogy. Taking mind as at least sentient, I hold (as Leibniz, Peirce, and Whitehead did) that every single actuality at least feels—where trees and all inanimate objects of magnitudes visible to us are not single (do not act as one) and so by the doctrine need not, do not, feel. Commonsense ideas of wholly dead, mindless matter are explicable, I hold, by this Leibnizian distinction between singly acting actualities and aggregate or composite ones. Apart from this basis for mind-matter dualism I see no positive evidence for the commonsense idea; and I am not aware of any physicist who has recently defended it. Some are materialists and some are psychicalists of one sort or another. Others abstract from the issue.

The connection of psychicalism with the analogy question is as follows. If to be is at least to be sentient, and if all feeling is, as Whitehead holds, feeling *of* (others') feeling, that is, has a social structure, and if this, as I also hold, is the essential, minimal meaning of "love," then every portion of nature that acts as one is a sign by similarity (an icon) of deity as supreme love. Hence the term "love" applied to God is more than a mere metaphor or symbol of God; it is an analogy in the classical sense. For, as Ogden knows, in that classical sense divine properties were also universal categories—provided one abstracts from the "transcendental" form of the properties, including being, unity, goodness, sometimes also power, beauty, and love (in Renaissance thinkers, perhaps also in Bonaventura). Aquinas recognized that if God is supreme goodness there must be some goodness in all that God creates.

For the classical theists, transcendence meant being *without becoming,* unity *without plurality,* actuality *rather than potentiality,* necessity *rather than contingency;* for my "dual" theory, transcendence means a transcendent form of both poles of the categorial contraries. In either case I find transcendence most intelligible if we do not define immanence to mean "in the world" (after all, God is ubiquitous and hence not absent from the world), but to mean the negative of the divine status of surpassing all others. *Exalted beyond possible rivalry* is what makes a property divine. It is not mere infinity that distinguishes God from creatures; it is rather the unique excellence of both the infinity and the finitude of God. Thus the divine finitude is all-embracing, whereas ours is but a fragment of the finite. It is not mere independence that makes God superior to us but the all-surpassing form of the divine dependence. "Surpassing" is a value term in this usage. Before Whitehead, however, scarcely anyone had done much with love as divine property and therefore as, in surpassable form, also universal category.

Ogden fears that psychicalism, with its apparent clash with common sense, is a burden theists as such do well not to bear. I think that dualism is a worse burden, all things considered. Materialistic monism is worse still. Psychical monism is the least troublesome mind-matter doctrine from a theistic standpoint. Love, taken as all-surpassing in God, not zero in any single actuality, generalizes the classical belief that a creature, any creature, is an image, a manifestation, of the divine nature. There are prejudices against psychicalism; but many of the persons with this prejudice have also one against theism.

That we take human love as our primary sample of love rather than any more primitive "feeling of feeling," any sympathy, such as an atom might have, is justified for two reasons: we know the former directly and intimately, as we cannot know the latter; in addition, regardless of how well we knew the feelings of atoms there would be good reason to think ours surpass them in quality and to that extent are better images of the divine feelings. This may not convince Ogden that my analogy theory is acceptable; but it will, I trust, make my unwillingness to give it up intelligible and unsurprising.

Human love between persons as sample of the category needs to be supplemented by human love having human bodily cells as objects of sympathetic concern. God as related to the cosmos as the human mind is related to its nerve cells seems a valuable analogy, strong just where the interpersonal analogy is weak theologically. Modern cell-theory goes better with psychicalism than did older theories of the body. The mind-body analogy also helps against sexism. My feminism is an obstacle for me so far as christology is concerned. The female parent is closer in basic ways to an offspring than the male; but the mind-nervous-system relation is essentially the same for both sexes.

Whereas, for Ogden, psychicalism is at best an unestablished empirical theory, I am forced to regard it as a metaphysical one in good standing as metaphysical doctrines go. Since "empirical" means for me observationally conceivably falsifiable, until I am given a non-question-begging criterion for the total absence of feeling from a portion of nature, psychicalism remains for me metaphysical. In metaphysics truth means, and is shown by, coherence. This is a symmetrical relation of interdependence. There is no linear order, first p is established, then q, then r, and so on. One simply takes all the observationally nonfalsifiable generalizations claiming applicability to everything on the same logical level—such as all concrete entities or all contingent entities and the like—and looks for incompatibilities among the generalizations. By definition "God" is universally applicable if applicable at all since everything not itself divine is divinely known—unless (ontological or Anselmian principle) the idea of God is an absurdity and deity could not, hence does not, exist. For this reason I do not quite understand Ogden's point that we do not have "immediate knowledge" of God but at most only immediate nonconscious experience of God, and so cannot argue for psychicalism from theism or make use of the reverse analogy from divine to human "personality." Divine and nondivine meanings of "person" ("individual with consciousness and sense of right and wrong") are both metaphysical; only "human" brings in an empirical element. Inhabitants of some other planet could have the idea of person and know nothing of our species. I may have missed something here as to what my critic had in mind. I do not hold that God is immediately given in order to prove the divine existence, but only to remove what would otherwise be a lack of coherence and so *dis*prove my doctrine.

What Ogden and I have in common—including acceptance of the two great commandments of love, and belief in the at least symbolic appropriateness of the idea of God as boundless love—is indeed a great deal of agreement between scholars. I am glad that my teaching and writing have contributed to the remarkable achievements of this critical interpreter of my thought. I also appreciate Ogden's thoughtful attention to the practical problems of our time.

Notes

1. I refer here to my books *The Philosophy and Psychology of Sensation* (University of Chicago Press, 1934) and *Born to Sing: an Interpretation and World Survey of Bird Song* (University of Indiana Press, 1974); also to my article "The Monotony Threshold in Singing Birds" which, after thirty years, is still being cited by ornithological specialists. It appeared in the journal of the American Ornithological Union (of which I am an elective member), *The Auk* (1956), vol. 176–192.

2. The famous astronomer Fred Hoyle and a famous physicist, I. I. Rabi, agreed in my presence to a proposition proposed by one of them, as follows: "If we do not know the past, that is our human limitation; if we do not know the future, that is the nature of things." This was in 1940 or 1941. For a recent discussion see Herbert Feigl and Paul Meehl, commenting on Karl Popper's views about the untenability of determinism, and Popper's reply, in *The Philosophy of Karl Popper* (La Salle, Ill.: Open Court, 1974). All three of these authorities (if there are any such) in the philosophy of science agreed that determinism in physics is no longer plausible and that determinism in psychology is at best a vague affair. Popper, to my mind, shows it is either hopelessly so, or clearly wrong. Since Einstein and Planck, defence of determinism has become a rarity in physics.

Popper does defend a mind-matter dualism (which would interest Ogden) but he does it only by showing the implausibility of physical monism or pure materialism, and by ruling out psychical monism because physical theory requires that on the atomic level mind would have to be without memory. Popper knows that Leibniz held mind on its lowest level to be memoryless. I would add that if this means total insensitivity to the past, then it entails also a total absence of causal conditioning, and that this can scarcely be a requirement of physics.

3. My six arguments (I no longer call them proofs) for theism are set forth in Chapter 14 of *Creative Synthesis and Philosophic Method.*

4. For Carnap's misunderstanding of Popper, see *The Philosophy of Rudolf Carnap* (La Salle, Ill.: Open Court, 1963); note Popper's criticism and compare it with Carnap's reply. I add, however, that Carnap's defence of modal logic against Quine's rejection of it opens the door to metaphysics. Popper has shown that any language that excludes metaphysical statements, including the assertion of the existence of God, will also not do for physics, and certainly not for biology and psychology.

Chapter Nine

In What Contexts Does It Make Sense to Say, "God Acts in History"?

MAURICE WILES

I first met Schubert Ogden in 1977. It was my first visit to the United States and he had invited me to come to Dallas. I arrived in his office at 9:30 in the morning to find an array of my writings, heavily underscored, open on his desk. After three hours of vigorous theological exchange, I extricated myself to keep a luncheon engagement. His concluding remark was "When are you coming back for some more?" So began a personal friendship and theological interchange from which I have gained much—and would have gained much more, had the geographical distance between us allowed for more frequent meetings.

In my writings I have not often found myself wanting to make any direct retraction of things that I have written earlier. The nearest I have come to it was in an article on "Farrer's Concept of Double Agency" where I wrote:

> It is precisely the notion of God's particular action that I find particularly difficult. I now think that in the past I have overreacted to those difficulties and written too exclusively of a divine purpose for the world and for mankind in general terms. I think that what I have said before can and should be extended to speak of particular divine purposes for individuals in their specific situations. But even to say that is still (ostensibly at least) to say a good deal less than is being said by talk of God's particular actions.[1]

The source of that change of heart was a conversation with Schubert Ogden in which he had vigorously challenged me with the need and possibility for the theologian to speak in such individual terms.

When the invitation to share in this well-deserved tribute arrived, I was just embarking on the preparation of a special course of lectures, now published as *God's Action in the World*.[2] That book owes a great deal to Schubert Ogden, for he is one of those who have most helped me through writing and through conversation in my struggles with this central but difficult topic. In the preparation of those lectures, I had to wrestle again with the issue of God's partic- ular action, which had been the subject of that earlier conversation between us and about which he has written in so thought-provoking a manner in his essay "What Sense Does It Make to Say 'God Acts in History'?"[3]

Ogden begins that essay by justifying his choice of title in prefer- ence to an alternative form of the question, namely: "Can one make sense of the statement 'God acts in history'?" We ought not, he ar- gues, to expect to be able to pronounce, as that way of posing the question suggests we can, between the possibility and impossibility of making sense of the statement—except by actually making some particular sense of it.[4] But his own formulation of the question could also suggest a sharper dichotomy than is appropriate—either succeeding or failing to make sense of the statement.

For we sometimes use the language of "making sense" in a graded way. We speak of "making good sense" or "making some sort of sense." So there are perhaps mediating forms in which the question might usefully be posed, such as: "Is the sense it makes to say 'God acts in history' such that we might reasonably prefer to express it in some other way?" That is a formulation with which Ogden himself might have some sympathy. For in speaking of Bultmann's doubt "whether mythological statements make *theological* sense," he ap- pends his own comment "or, better said, whether they are an appro- priate way of expressing the sense or meaning that theological state- ments are supposed to express."[5] Moreover, his own affirmation that "God's action, in its fundamental sense, is not an action in history at all"[6] suggests that there could be grounds for saying something similar about the inappropriateness, though not the vacuity, of speaking of God's action in history—despite his own unequivocal conclusion that the historical event of Jesus' life and ministry "stands before us as itself God's act in a sense that we both can and *must* affirm."[7]

We also speak of things making sense in one context but not in another. To say that "stars in their courses fought against Sisera" (Judg. 5:20) makes good sense in a song of victory, but it would make no sense in a treatise on astronomy, even though there is no equiv- ocation in the use of the word "stars." So there is another formula- tion of the question, which again encourages the expectation of a more qualified, but still positive, answer to the underlying question, namely: "In what contexts does it make sense to say 'God acts in history'?" And it is this formulation that I have chosen for the title of this essay.

The most obvious contrast of contexts within which we might want to speak of God acting in history is that between religious and theological utterance. The difference between the two is not absolute. Most religious utterances embody, albeit often unconsciously, the fruit of some prior theological reflection, and theological reflection can be carried out in a variety of ways, some more and some less distanced from the forms of direct religious utterance. Nonetheless there is an important difference between the two, not altogether unlike the difference between the two contexts in the case of the stars. Religious utterance uses the vigorous and concrete imagery characteristic of the song-writer or the poet. The theologian seeks to clarify, coordinate, and work out the implications of this basic religious awareness, as the astronomer seeks to clarify, coordinate, and work out the implications of the varied human observations of the stars. The idiom appropriate to the more reflective task is very different from that appropriate to the more immediate and primary activity.

The work in which both Ogden and I have been engaged has been firmly at the theological end of the spectrum. And the theological answers that we have given to the question of how to understand the language of God's action are very similar in structure, even though we operate with significantly different analyses of action. Ogden allows three senses in which one may speak of God acting. First, as we have already seen, there is the fundamental sense which transcends history, "whereby he [God] ever and again actualizes his own divine essence by responding in love to all the creatures in his world."[8] Second, "every creature is to some extent God's act—just as, by analogy, all our bodily actions are to some extent our actions as selves."[9] And third, "there are certain distinctively human words and deeds in which his [God's] characteristic action as Creator and Redeemer is appropriately re-presented or revealed"; these are in a special sense "acts of God analogously to the way in which our outer acts *are* our acts insofar as they re-present our own characteristic decisions as selves or persons."[10] I have not found it so congenial to distinguish those inner decisions whereby we constitute our own selves and regard them as the primary form of human action. Working rather with an understanding of action as "a piece of intentional behaviour initiated by an agent," I have nonetheless proposed a similar threefold structure for the understanding of divine action:

first, a fundamental sense in which there is only one act of God, namely the continuing creation of the universe; second, the regular patterns according to which the physical world operates, which by their very constitution are elements within the divine activity but not, in my judgment, to be spoken of as distinguishable acts of God in themselves; and, third, actions by human agents, who freely intend to further the purposes of God, seek God's grace to enable them to do so, and do in fact achieve their intended goal, which may in a secondary and highly qualified sense be allowed the designation "acts of God."[11] I do not intend to argue here the relative merits of these two ways of conceiving action in attempting an interpretation of God's acts. That has been interestingly done in comparisons of Ogden and Kaufman, to whom on this issue I stand much closer.[12] I want rather to stress the measure of substantive agreement between us, and go on to consider the implications of such a theological understanding for the actual use of the language of God's action in its original, that is to say, its religious, context.

The primary task of theological reflection is to understand and clarify existing religious usage. Often it will have achieved its goal if it leads to modifications in the way in which the traditional religious language is understood. But its outcome need not always be to leave things where they were linguistically. Its reflections may point to particular religious contexts within which certain widely accepted forms of religious language are inappropriate, misleading, or straightforwardly false. Is that the case in this instance? Does the theological analysis give the language of God's action in history a clean bill of health and underwrite its use in all circumstances? Or does it suggest the desirability of some modification in the way it is used or some restriction on the contexts in which it is employed?

The first issue that I want to consider is the fact that there is one class of special divine action clearly affirmed in Scripture for which our theological analyses allow no place. The Assyrian is the rod of God's anger; it is God who sends him and bids him spoil and plunder the land of Israel (Isa. 10:5–6). Similarly, it is God who gives Cyrus the victories that lead to the restoration of Israel and the rebuilding of Jerusalem (Isa. 44:28–45:3). These are as clear and as significant examples of God being said to act in history as any to be found in Scripture. Yet the action of the Assyrian warlord can hardly be said to re-present the characteristic action of God as Creator and Redeemer whereby he continually responds in love to all the creatures in the world. The Assyrians' intention is explicitly described as an evil intention for mass-destruction (Isa. 10:7–8). Nor can Cyrus be said to be aiming to further God's purpose or to be seeking his grace to do so. He is explicitly stated to have no knowledge of God (Isa. 45:4). If the imperialistic adventures of the Assyrians and the Babylonians were done in response to the lure of the divine love, then God employs the principle that the end justifies the means in a way more cynical than that of the most cynical of politicians.

Does our inability to make theological sense of the scriptural accounts of God's action in relation to the Assyrians or to Cyrus mean that we should abandon all talk of God acting in history in such cases? If we can make no sense of the statements theologically, then it does surely follow that they should have no place in our theological speech. But that does not necessarily mean that the language was being improperly used in the first instance. It is no coincidence that so much of Hebrew prophecy (including both the passages that we have been discussing) is in the form of poetic diction. Nor does it necessarily mean that such language should have no place in any contemporary equivalent of the prophetic context. The aim of such prophetic language is to bring home to its hearers the seriousness of the situation that they are in and its potentiality for a response that will significantly re-present God's action or forward God's purposes. There is no lack of contemporary examples (the inner-city riots in Britain at the time at which this is being written is an obvious one) which call for that kind of prophetic interpretation. To speak of them in terms of what God is doing and saying to us in history is a legitimate form of such speech.

But what is the reflective theologian to make of it? Austin Farrer uses the description of the Assyrian as the rod of God's anger as an example of his concept of "double agency." He reflects on how the ancient prophet may have conceived "the mechanism of the divine control" as lying "in the openness of men's thoughts to pressures of which they are unaware." But in the end he concludes that the Hebrew prophet and the modern Christian stand together. They can be sure the Assyrian action is a "divine effect." But they neither can, nor need, know anything about "the causal joint (so to speak) between infinite and finite action" because such knowledge "can play no part in our concern with God and his will."[13] There may be contexts in which this combination of strong affirmation of the fact and reverent, but total, agnosticism of the mechanism or manner of its operation is appropriate. But this is not one of them. If a theological analysis of the kind that both Ogden and I have put forward is on the right lines, we ought to be prepared to say that the language of divine action in a case like that of the Assyrians is not to be taken to imply that the Assyrian action is a "divine effect" in anything more than that limited sense in which everything that happens is a divine effect. There is no hidden causal joint, not even a "causal joint (so to speak)." If religious devotion can flourish without knowing the manner by which the divine effect is supposed to be achieved, it can get on fine without affirming that it is a specific divine effect at all. The prophetic language has an altogether different rationale.

This distinction between prophecy and theology is not without its own difficulties. As was recognized at the outset, the frontier between religious and theological speech cannot be drawn in any absolute or clear-cut way. Theologies of liberation provide an example of just such a difficult, borderline case. As Ogden himself has expressed it, such "theologies typically are not so much theology as witness." [14] Such a remark is descriptive rather than evaluative. Theology is not superior to witness; the difference is one of function. The claim, made to me in conversation by one American theologian, that "all theology should be prophetic theology" only holds true insofar as we also allow that "all prophecy should be theological prophecy." To demand such a union of the two in practice is a false, utopian demand. What we should be striving for is not their conflation or their identity, but a recognition of their mutual interdependence and therefore of the importance of their listening to each other. For the present we are better served by acknowledging the need for both direct prophetic proclamation and sustained critical reflection. Despite the existence of borderline cases, we need the variety of their different vocations with their different vocabularies.

The concept of "vocation" suggests another, smaller-scale aspect of our central problem. History is not a matter only of battles and royal decrees, of the decisions of warlords and emperors. It is a matter also, as a good deal of modern historical writing emphasizes, of the more ordinary lives of individual men and women. So any sense that we are to make of God acting in history must relate not only to the broader sweep of historical development but also to the lives of individuals.

In secular usage "vocation" is a dead metaphor. How its significance is understood in religious usage is more uncertain. It is not always clear whether someone using the term in that context understands it in some quite literal sense or at least intends the metaphor to be taken as a living one, implying something more than would be intended in secular usage. There are two components which might go to make up that something more. First there is the conviction that there is a particular role or purpose which God has for me to

fulfil. Secondly there is the further point of there being some specific call whereby God has made or is making known to me what
his will for me is. In other words, in addition to God's particular will
for me, there may also be some particular action of God whereby he
communicates that will to me, though not in a way that removes
my freedom to refuse. Many biblical stories speak of such a particular will, and indeed the communication of it, as preceding even the
birth of the person concerned. Such accounts cannot be taken at
their face value. To do so would involve far too predetermined a conception both of the way we grow as human persons and of the circumstances within which any lifework will have to be played out in
the future. Such language can only coherently be understood as a
vivid way of expressing retrospectively the significance of a person's
life in relation to God's purpose in the world.[15] But those objections
do not apply in the same way to the concept of God having a particular purpose for me now. That is a concept, as I acknowledged earlier, which Ogden has helped persuade me must not be eliminated
from the theologian's purview. But I still have difficulty in determining just what the theologian ought to make of it. How, then, is it to
be understood in relation to vocation?

To speak of God's particular purpose for me now may suggest that
there is one, and only one, specific way in which my life can be lived
in line with the will of God. The use of language about testing
whether a person "really has a vocation or not" (regularly used in
relation to the ordained ministry or the religious life) easily lends
itself to that sort of interpretation. It can sound as if we are trying
to decide between two possibilities: either the person has been
called, in which case he or she must be ordained, or the person has
not been called, in which case he or she must not be ordained. But
it does not need to be and should not be understood in that way. It
smacks too much of a divinely preprogrammed destiny. There are
normally a variety of ways in which our lives could be lived in line
with the will of God. Testing a vocation is the process of trying to
determine whether the proposed course of action is or is not one
such way. Similarly the idea of a particular divine "call" may suggest
that we ought to give extra weight to any unusual inner experiential
evidence, over and above the criteria that might usually be employed
for determining appropriateness for the proposed work. An inner
conviction about what decision to make may arise intuitively and
unexpectedly in any walk of life, without involving any particular
religious understanding or implications. The concept of a particular
divine call ought not to be allowed to give any additional signifi-

cance to that sort of experience. Many great wrongs, as a book like William James's *Varieties of Religious Experience* vividly illustrates, have been done through failure to heed that danger.

If the language of vocation, when treated as something more than a dead metaphor, has such inherent dangers, what is its value? The question needs to be answered on the basis of our theological analysis of the concept of God's action. Seen in that light it serves primarily as a forceful reminder of the setting within which our lives are lived. We live in a world in which God is continually active as creator and redeemer, a world of whose existence he is the purposive initiator and continuator. And it is in relation to this continually God-given reality, with its rich range of future possibilities, that any determination of our own actions needs to be seen. Moreover, it is what we understand to be the character and goal of that divine action, as we see them re-presented in Christ, that should provide the criteria of our choosing. To allow the language of vocation to become an utterly dead metaphor would be to weaken that all-important religious context within which our lives are to be lived and our choices to be made.

The language of vocation, therefore, remains important, but it is equally important that its continuation goes hand in hand with critical reflection about its proper understanding. And such reflection may lead us to suggest that within religious usage there are different contexts within some of which it is appropriate to talk of "what God is calling us to do" or of "what the Holy Spirit is showing us to be the will of God," and other contexts in which such language cannot properly be used. I can best indicate the kind of distinction I have in mind by reference to an aspect of moral discourse discussed by Stephen Toulmin in his book *The Place of Reason in Ethics*. Toulmin distinguishes between the appropriate contexts for the deontologist's appeal to moral principles and the utilitarian's consideration of consequences. In reasoning about the rightness of particular actions in normal circumstances, the former reasoning is appropriate. In that context, "because it was a promise" is a sufficient answer; to offer any further, more general reason would be out of place. Consideration of consequences is appropriate in contexts where there is a conflict between accepted principles or where a generally agreed social practice is called into question. The two different kinds of reasoning are seen not as conflicting rival explanations for the same situation but as appropriate in different contexts.[16] May not something similar be true also in the case that we are considering?

I have argued that the significance of the language of divine vocation lies in its reminder of the wider setting in relation to which our decisions are to be made and of the criterion for making such decisions provided by the Christian understanding of God's continuing action as creator and redeemer. To ask "What is the will of God for me?" or "What is the Holy Spirit saying to me?" is a way of ensuring that our deliberations are pursued in that full context. Such phrases cannot properly by used to justify the particular decision reached. They make no sense as justifying reasons for particular decisions—even about our choice of vocation. That has to be done in terms of the particular criteria for decision which our reflection on the nature of God's action has led us to adopt in the particular case. The Council of Jerusalem (or the author of the Book of Acts, if he is the real originator of the phrase) has a lot to answer for when it employed the words "It is the decision of the Holy Spirit, and our decision . . ." (Acts 15:29). For if that is intended as a reason why the Gentile churches should accept the decisions of the council, it smacks more of authoritarian manipulation than of acceptable religious reasoning. It is even more dangerous as paving the way for claims about the inerrancy of councils, so rightly contradicted by the Articles of the Church of England.[17] The action of the Holy Spirit makes sense as a reminder of the full context of Christian decision-making or as a justification of the general style of such decision-making. It does not make sense as a reason for particular decisions.

The kind of reflection that I have been pursuing here in relation to prophetic affirmation of God's hand in an Assyrian invasion or an inner-city riot and in relation to the understanding of "vocation" could be widely extended. There are hardly any aspects of Christian religious practice itself, or of Christian understanding of the world, in which the language of God's action is not both central and problematic. An obvious further example that I have discussed elsewhere is the practice of prayer.[18]

But the purpose of this essay is not so much to solve such problems as to make a plea for serious engagement with them. The most sophisticated theological reflection and the most ordinary forms of religious practice need to be carried on in conscious relationship to one another. For me one of the most significant features of Schubert Ogden's work has been his determination to combine the two. Few theologians have attacked the problems facing them with the same measure of unrelenting rational inquiry, and few theologians have been more concerned about the implications of that inquiry for ordinary religious practice. Without that dual commitment our theology runs the risk of sterility and our religious practice that of the corrupting suspicion of bad faith. What our theological analysis of how and where it makes sense to say "God acts in history" implies for religious practice needs more careful and thorough exploration than it commonly receives.

Notes

1. *Theology* 74 (July 1981): 245.
2. Maurice Wiles, *God's Action in the World* (SCM Press, 1986).
3. Schubert Ogden, *The Reality of God* (SCM Press, 1967).
4. Ibid., pp.164–65.
5. Ibid., pp.167–68.
6. Ibid., p.179.
7. Ibid., p.187.
8. Ibid., p.179.
9. Ibid., p.180.
10. Ibid., p.184.
11. See my *God's Action in the World*, especially chapter 8.
12. See David R. Mason, "Selfhood, Transcendence, and the Experience of God," *Modern Theology* 3 (July 1987): 293–314, and Thomas F. Tracy, "Enacting History: Ogden and Kaufman on God's Mighty Acts," *Journal of Religion* 64, 1 (January 1984): 20–36.
13. Austin Farrer, *Faith and Speculation* (A. & C. Black, 1967), pp.61–67.
14. Schubert Ogden, *Faith and Freedom* (Abingdon, 1979), p.33.
15. See my *God's Action in the World*, chapter 6.
16. Stephen Toulmin, *The Place of Reason in Ethics* (Cambridge University Press, 1960), pp. 145–51. The book is one much drawn upon by Schubert Ogden, especially in *The Reality of God*.
17. Article XXI: "General Councils ... may err, and sometimes have erred, even in things pertaining unto God".
18. See my *God's Action in the World*, chapter 8.

Chapter Ten

Metaphysics and the Moral Law:
A Conversation with Karl-Otto Apel

FRANKLIN I. GAMWELL

I

Nothing could be "more fatal to morality," wrote Immanuel Kant, "than that we should wish to derive it from examples. For every example of it that is set before me must be first itself tested by principles of morality, whether it is worthy to serve as an original example, that is, as a pattern, but by no means can it authoritatively furnish the conception of morality. Even the Holy One of the Gospels must first be compared with our ideal of moral perfection before we can recognize Him as such" (Kant, 26). With these words, Kant provided an early formulation and defense of the claim that moral conclusions cannot be derived from existential propositions or descriptions alone. Such putative derivations are fatal to morality, Kant held, because they contradict the autonomy of the moral law. A rational will can only be bound to principles which reason itself legislates, and the moral law must be a priori in the sense that rational subjectivity as such presupposes or implies it. As Karl-Otto Apel has recently formulated the same point, "any one who is interested philosophically in grounding the basic norm is able to appreciate through transcendental reflection that he is already presupposing this norm" (1980, 296). For Kant, then, obligations which are derived from examples or from the existential propositions which describe them are heteronomous and, therefore, not moral in character.

Schubert M. Ogden agrees that moral claims cannot be justified by appeal to "the Holy One of the Gospels." To be sure, Ogden holds that "the constitutive Christian assertion," namely, that Jesus is the Christ, is true and, moreover, that this claim, because it is not only a claim about Jesus but also a claim about authentic human existence, includes or implies moral claims (see Ogden, chap. 2). As readers of Ogden well know, however, he has insisted throughout his theological achievement that there is a logical distinction between making a claim and validating that claim and, therefore, between the meaning and truth of Christian convictions. No theologian, in my judgment, has been as thorough and as systematic as has Ogden in formulating this distinction and clarifying its importance for Christian theology. One of its important implications is that the moral claims of the Christian faith are justified only if reasons for them can be given which are independent of the making of those claims in the apostolic witness to Jesus (see Ogden, 2–4). In this sense, we may say that Ogden, with Kant, holds that a law of the will is moral only if it is one which reason gives to itself and which is, therefore, autonomous.

Because the Christian claim refers to the authentic existence of humans as such, Ogden also holds, with Kant, that a law is shown to be autonomous only by reflection upon the a priori presuppositions of human subjectivity. But Ogden does *not* agree that the justification of the moral law is logically independent of all existential propositions. For the constitutive Christian assertion about Jesus is a claim about authentic human existence only because it is also a claim about the ultimate or divine reality which authorizes authentic humanity. To say that this claim is true is to imply that transcendental reflection, through which the moral law is justified, must include transcendental metaphysics, that is, an inquiry into the presuppositions of being or reality as such (see Ogden, chap. 2).[1] Of course, Kant cannot accept this condition for practical reason, because he insists that an inquiry into the nature of being as such is impossible. *The Critique of Pure Reason*, whatever else it includes, is an attempt to show that the putative claims of transcendental metaphysics fall beyond the limits of reason.[2]

For anyone who agrees with both Kant and Ogden that morality is autonomous and, therefore, that the justification of moral claims requires transcendental reflection, the difference between these two authors begs for further examination. The purpose of this essay is to contribute to that examination. I propose to do so by engaging in conversation with the attempt of Karl-Otto Apel to justify a basic ethical norm. At least with respect to ethics, Apel's work may be understood as an attempt so to transform Kant's argument as to achieve the success which, Apel believes, Kant was denied. The revision which Apel introduces is, in one respect, fundamental and may, as I will seek to explain, be summarized in the change from Kant's "transcendental" to Apel's "transcendental pragmatic" argument. But this does not gainsay that Apel's argument is Kantian in the sense that he seeks a transcendental justification of ethical norms that is independent of metaphysics. I will prepare for the assessment of Apel's proposal with a briefer interpretation of Kant's own argument, as this is found in the *Fundamental Principles of the Metaphysic of Morals*, in order to show why this argument did not achieve its purpose and, therefore, why some transformation is required. In doing this, I will seek to relate Kant's failure to his denial of transcendental metaphysics, because I subsequently wish to show that Apel's transformation fails to appreciate just this aspect of Kant's difficulty. Whatever the importance of the transformation which Apel effects, I will argue that he remains unable to justify the moral law because he seeks to do so independently of metaphysics. Of course, that conclusion will not establish the possibility of transcendental metaphysics and, therefore, will not imply the divine reality which Ogden affirms. One might hold, to the contrary, that there is no transcendental moral law. In conclusion, however, I will suggest that Apel's transformation of Kant is important, precisely because it offers reason to assert that subjectivity is morally bound and, therefore, that our authentic existence is authorized by ultimate reality.

II

"Nothing can possibly be conceived in the world, or even out of it, which can be called good without qualification, except a *good will*" (Kant, 11).[3] This famous introductory assertion of the *Fundamental Principles* may be read with two different meanings, and the difference turns upon how the two uses of "good" are understood. On the first reading, a "good will" is a will that chooses as morality requires. In saying that this will alone is good without qualification, Kant makes the important point that moral praise and blame in the strict sense refer only to volition, since this is the only thing for which one can be responsible. Thus, for instance, moral goodness cannot be constituted by the consequences to which action in fact leads (although it might be constituted by the choice to pursue those consequences), because the actor does not necessarily control the results of his or her deeds. Given the first reading, then, the two uses of "good" are identical, referring to the strict sense of moral goodness in accord with which the exercise of freedom alone can be moral or immoral. As a consequence, the assertion does not answer the question: In what does a moral exercise of freedom consist?

On a second reading, however, the identity of moral goodness is addressed, and it is this second reading which accounts for the abiding philosophical fascination of Kant's claim. The two uses of "good" are now different. A "good will" continues to mean morally good in the strict sense. In contrast, something is now "good without qualification" in the sense that it provides the terms with which moral goodness may be identified, that is, choice which is moral may be distinguished from choice which is immoral. For instance, one might claim (although Kant does not) that the actor's own happiness is unqualifiedly good, so that action is moral if the actor chooses to pursue for its own sake his or her own happiness and immoral if the actor does not. In general, we may say that moral goodness in the strict sense implies that something is unqualifiedly good in the sense just described, because only so can moral and immoral volition be distinguished. Henceforth, I will consider this second reading of Kant's introductory assertion, because it then expresses the singular thesis of Kant's ethics—namely, the different meanings of "good" notwithstanding, nothing can be good without qualification except a good will.

In so introducing the *Fundamental Principles*, Kant may seem to assume that something is unqualifiedly good, such that he then derives his understanding of the moral law or categorical imperative on the basis of this assumption. But this is so only in the sense that he seeks the necessary conditions of moral goodness and seeks to argue that these conditions obtain. It must not be supposed, in other words, that Kant's argument is open to the objection of the amoralist, who claims rationally to refuse all moral imperatives because he or she declines to accept the prior premise that something is good without qualification. Kant recognizes that this refusal, were it rational, would mean that the premise is necessarily false. Anything said to be unqualifiedly good would be so only given the qualification that one chooses to affirm that there is such a thing (and, therefore, would not really be good without qualification), so that any imperative subsequently derived would be, in Kant's famous distinction, hypothetical rather than categorical. For Kant, in other words, one of the necessary conditions of moral goodness is that the principle of such goodness, the moral law, is rationally necessary, such that practical reason cannot consistently refuse it. If there is no moral law which is rationally necessary, then it is rationally necessary that there is no moral law, and, for Kant, this simply explicates the meaning of "moral." It is his intent to show that the categorical imperative is implicitly affirmed by the practical reason of human subjectivity as such, that is, by any chooser or actor who reasons about his or her choices, and it is in this sense that his categorical imperative may be called transcendental.[4]

We may begin to clarify Kant's argument by noting that his assertion regarding the unqualified goodness of the will has a negative as well as a positive meaning. Positively, it claims that the will is good in a sense which identifies the moral law, and this is precisely what Kant's subsequent argument is designed to establish. Negatively, Kant claims that nothing other than the will can be unqualifiedly good, by which he means that the moral law cannot be defined by a purpose or telos which choice or action ought to pursue. "The purposes which we may have in view in our actions, or their effects regarded as ends and springs of the will, cannot give to actions any unconditional or moral worth" (17). This follows for Kant because the definition of a purpose or telos is an existential proposition (that is, a proposition regarding what does or might exist), and all existential propositions are rationally contingent. "It is clear that all moral conceptions have their seat and reason completely *a priori* in the reason, . . . ; that they cannot be obtained by abstraction from any empirical, and therefore merely contingent, knowledge" (29; see also 35). Given that the moral law must be implied by rational choice as such, a telos could be good without qualification only if it too were so implied. Since a choice is simply the affirmation of one among more than one possible states of affairs, a telos which identifies moral goodness must be implied by all possible states of affairs. Some have held, for instance, that the divine purpose is so implied, because the divine being is the creator and telos of all things. But a telos implied by all possible states of affairs could itself be defined only by a rationally necessary existential proposition. Because, for Kant, all existential propositions are rationally contingent, it follows that no telos or purpose can be essential to the identification of the moral law.

Kant illustrates this point by attending to the claim that humans are sensuous or desiring beings and always desire their own happiness, so that happiness is unqualifiedly good. Precisely because happiness is a state of affairs or telos to be pursued, it is rationally contingent and, therefore, cannot be necessarily affirmed by rational choice as such. One need not choose to affirm or pursue what one always desires. Thus, when Kant says that the sensuous character of human beings is itself empirical, he means that not only desiring but also all possible objects of desire (e.g., happiness) are contingent phenomena. Accordingly, he also says that the moral law "must be valid, not merely for man, but for all *rational creatures generally,*" and we cannot "bring into unbounded respect as a universal precept for every rational nature that which perhaps holds only under the contingent conditions of humanity" (26), that is, desire with its pursuit of some telos.

It is worth noting that morality cannot be derived from examples, not even from "the Holy One of the Gospels," precisely because all existential propositions are rationally contingent, so that nothing defined by an existential proposition can be good without qualification. In the context of the present essay, it is even more important to note that, for Kant, all existential propositions are rationally contingent precisely because transcendental metaphysics is impossible. Rationally necessary existential propositions would require that transcendental inquiry might discover not only the character of our subjectivity as such but also the nature of being or reality. Accordingly, we may say that the negative meaning of Kant's singular introductory assertion expresses his intent to justify moral claims independently of metaphysics.

The same intent may be formulated by saying that choices or actions can be morally good only if practical reason as such implies a moral law that is formal rather than material. Since the "matter" of a choice is the state of affairs which it affirms, its moral goodness "must be determined by the formal principle of volition when an action is done from duty, in which case every material principle has been withdrawn from it" (18). Kant does not mean to say that there can be an action without some telos or state of affairs which it affirms. His point is rather that the morality of an action can never be identified as the pursuit of this telos; a moral person does not choose a purpose because he or she desires that state of affairs but because choice of that purpose conforms with the formal principle by which a good will is determined. With this conclusion, Kant turns directly to the positive meaning of his introductory assertion. The formal principle required by morality is, he claims, given in the strictly formal universality of practical reason itself, that is, in the self-legislation of practical reason. Just because reason itself is a principle to which the will of any rational being is bound, there is a moral law which may be formulated: "Act only on that maxim whereby thou canst at the same time will that it should become a universal law" (38; emphasis deleted), that is, a law for all rational beings.

To be sure, it might be questioned whether the argument has led to the formulation of a *moral* law. Granted that a rational will is bound by the principles of practical reason as such, it may seem to remain an open question whether any one of those principles is moral. The possibility of hypothetical imperatives also involves,

Kant argues, a universal and strictly formal principle. "Whoever wills the end wills also (so far as reason decides his conduct) the means in his power which are indispensably necessary thereto" (34). This proposition, which Kant calls "analytical" (34), may be reformulated as the strictly formal principle of practical reason: Whoever wills the end ought also to will the means in his or her power which are indispensably necessary thereto. But if this is so, then a principle of practical reason as such is not necessarily a moral law or categorical imperative. On the contrary, an additional condition of the latter is that reason as such provides a distinction among the ends or purposes which humans might will (or, as Kant has it, among the maxims in accord with which human ends are chosen), such that some are categorically proscribed and others are categorically required. The further condition for a moral law, in other words, is that practical reason as such identify something as good without qualification, and one might doubt, at least initially, whether the formal universality of practical reason does so.

But Kant also argues that this further condition is fulfilled in the self-legislation of practical reason. The concept of such legislation, he claims, implies that "any rational being *exists* as an end in himself, *not merely as a means* to be arbitrarily used by this or that will, but in all his actions, whether they concern himself or other rational beings, must be always regarded at the same time as an end" (45). Given that no telos can be unqualifiedly good, a rational will cannot properly understand itself as merely a means to some state of affairs but necessarily affirms itself (and, therefore, any other rational will) as "something *whose existence* has *in itself* an absolute worth" (45). Thus, the formal universality of practical reason legislates for the human will the categorical imperative expressed in Kant's famous "second" formulation: "So act as to treat humanity, whether in thine own person or in that of any other, in every case as an end withal, never as means only" (46, emphasis deleted). It is this formulation, generalized, which results in Kant's notion of a "kingdom of ends." Moreover, "we . . . now end where we started at the beginning, namely, with the conception of a will unconditionally good" (54). But the end differs from the beginning in that the unqualified goodness of the will has been demonstrated and, therefore, the necessary conditions for morality have been established.

What is immediately striking about Kant's argument as I have presented it is the apparent contradiction between the negative and the positive meanings of his claim that the rational will alone is unqualifiedly good. Nothing else can be good in this sense, he argues, because all states of affairs are rationally contingent, and, therefore, no existential propositions can provide the definition of unqualified goodness. But the positive meaning asserts that the existence of a rational will "has *in itself* an absolute worth" (45). Thus, the apparent contradiction obtains between the denial that any state of affairs can be, and the affirmation that the existence of rational being is, good without qualification. We may also say that Kant's insistence upon a strictly formal categorical imperative seems to contradict the "material principle," the reference to rational beings as ends in themselves, with which moral goodness is identified. The question, then, is whether Kant's singular introductory assertion is self-consistent. Because something unqualifiedly good must provide a distinction between moral and immoral choices or maxims, it seems to be necessarily material. But the rational will, in the sense of a will bound by principles of practical reason as such, is one from which every "material principle" has been withdrawn.

If this contradiction is more than apparent, Kant's attempt to derive the positive meaning from the negative must be unsuccessful. Assessing that attempt requires clarity about what argument is proposed. One might think that Kant intends the following: Since no state of affairs in pursuit of which a rational will might be treated solely as a means can be unqualifiedly good, a rational being must be treated as an end withal. So stated, however, the argument seems to beg the question at issue—namely, whether anything at all is good without qualification, such that the will is morally bound. Given that (1) nothing other than a rational will is good without qualification, it follows that a rational being is an end in itself only if one assumes that (2) something is unqualifiedly good. Absent the assumption, the claim that there is no state of affairs to which a rational will might be treated as a means implies only that one is never morally bound to treat a rational being in this way. But this does not entail that one is morally required to treat rational beings as ends withal. On the contrary, there is a third alternative, namely, that one is not morally required to treat rational beings in any way at all, because the will is not morally bound. Since it was precisely the necessary conditions of morality that the argument was designed to establish, its need to assume such conditions would beg the question.

But Kant's argument cannot be so readily dismissed. As I have mentioned, he is not only aware but insistent that the moral law must be transcendental, so that his argument intends no gratuitous assumption. As one would expect, he argues that there must be something unqualifiedly good, because freedom which is rational implies the self-legislation of morality. "Although freedom is not a property of the will depending on physical laws, yet it is not for that reason lawless; on the contrary, it must be a causality acting according to immutable laws, but of a peculiar kind; otherwise a free will would be an absurdity" (63). The point here, if I understand Kant correctly, is that freedom to choose between alternatives is not rational unless there is a rational law binding the choice; reasoned choice is absurd if it is solely hypothetical. We need not pause to decide whether Kant is correct in this claim, although it is worth noting that anyone who affirms a transcendental moral law cannot consistently deny it. Let us grant Kant the point and ask whether it now follows that a rational will alone is good without qualification. Given that (2) something is unqualifiedly good, Kant's conclusion follows only if (1) nothing other than a rational will can be so. Kant believes he has shown the validity of (1), because all existential statements are rationally contingent. But if this is the grounds for (1), then it also follows that the existence of a rational will cannot be of absolute worth, since statements which assert such existence must also be rationally contingent. In other words, (1) is inconsistent with (2), and Kant's argument is not successful.

Some may wish to object that this criticism misses Kant's fundamental point—namely, that the existence of rational freedom is relevantly different from the existence of possible states of affairs. In one passage, Kant argues that an actor necessarily endorses the existence of his or her own freedom regardless of what state of affairs he or she chooses to pursue and is, therefore, bound to endorse the freedom of all other rational beings. "Man necessarily conceives his own existence as being [an end in itself] . . . ; so far then this is a *subjective* principle of human actions. But every other rational being regards its existence similarly, just on the same principle that holds for me; so that it is at the same time an objective principle from which as a supreme practical law all laws of the will must be capable of being deduced" (46). In response to the charge of contradiction, this argument might be read as follows: Just because freedom is endorsed regardless of the state of affairs which the action pursues, its existence is necessarily different from the existence of states of affairs and, accordingly, existence of the former kind can be good without qualification notwithstanding that existence of the latter kind cannot.

In my judgment, however, this defense of Kant fails, because it requires that freedom be conceived independently of *all* possible states of affairs. Since no possible purpose or telos can be unqualifiedly good, the existence of freedom can be unqualifiedly good only if its conception requires no reference to the possible existence of states of affairs. But choice simply is the affirmation of one among more than one possible state of affairs. Even if freedom may be conceived regardless of *which* telos or purpose is chosen, it cannot be conceived without *any* purpose.[5] Thus, if no state of affairs is good without qualification, then it is impossible to conceive of the freedom which, it is said, an actor necessarily endorses. Thus, the term "existence" cannot have a relevantly different meaning in reference to freedom than it has in reference to those states of affairs without which freedom cannot be conceived.[6]

I conclude that the contradiction is genuine. To say that a rational will is unqualifiedly good is to say that an existential proposition defines the good. But Kant also says that nothing other than a rational will can be good without qualification precisely because *no* existential proposition can define the good. It then follows not only that Kant has failed to establish the necessary conditions of morality but also that he cannot do so. If neither something other than the rational will nor that rational will itself can be good without qualification, then nothing can be good in this sense. Given the insistence that the moral law must be strictly formal, in the sense that every "material principle" has been withdrawn, there can be no moral law. Strictly formal principles of practical reason cannot distinguish between ends which might be willed, and therefore, are restricted to such nonmoral, analytic principles as "whoever wills the end ought to will the means which are indispensably necessary thereto."

It is now important to recall that, for Kant, the moral law must be strictly formal because transcendental metaphysics is impossible. Morality cannot be derived from material examples because all existential propositions are contingent. But if a strictly formal principle cannot be a moral law, it then follows that moral claims cannot be justified without metaphysics. In other words, nothing can be good without qualification except a telos that is implicitly affirmed whenever a rational will chooses to affirm one rather than another possible state of affairs, that is, a telos implied by any possible state of affairs and, therefore, defined only by a rationally necessary existential proposition. This conclusion may be summarized as follows: Because unqualified goodness cannot be defined by a rationally contingent existential proposition, there can be no moral law in the absence of transcendental metaphysics. Whether a metaphysical telos is indeed conceivable is, of course, another question. But if Kant is correct in saying that morality cannot be derived from contingent examples, the only alternative to metaphysics is no morality at all.

III

We are now in a position to engage in a conversation with the "transformation of Kant's transcendental philosophy" presented by Karl-Otto Apel (see Apel 1984, 232). For Apel holds that Kant's failure does not derive from a denial of transcendental metaphysics but rather from a misunderstanding of transcendental subjectivity. Specifically, Kant did not understand that subjectivity as such is intersubjective. For Apel, Kant's critical philosophy assumes that the transcendental subject is solitary and, therefore, that subjectivity as such has no relation to other subjects. As a consequence, it is impossible for Kant to derive an obligation to treat other rational beings as ends in themselves, and the practical principles to which reason as such is bound cannot be moral. In contrast, Apel argues that the transcendental subject is intersubjective, and it is this relationship which he expresses in the phrase "transcendental-pragmatic philosophy." Moreover, as I will try to show, he holds that an ethic may be justified by reflecting upon the nature of this transcendental relationship, and, so justified, the ethic remains independent of metaphysics (on the independence from metaphysics, see 1984, 209–42).

With Kant, then, Apel attempts explicitly to understand the presuppositions or necessary conditions of valid cognition or rational subjectivity as such. Valid cognition, he insists, means that human subjectivity is self-reflective, for the subject's claim to validity is a judgment or assertion about itself, that is, about its own thought. Never merely the occurrence or passive entertainment of a proposition, cognition is also an action in relation to this thought. "Possible *propositions* are dependent, in principle, on possible *acts of assertion;* and correspondingly, possible *truth* is dependent on possible *truth-claims*" (1979a, 315). Only this understanding of cognition, Apel contends, permits an understanding of the predicate "is true," as it is used in such phrases as, "I hereby assert that p is true" (or, if assertion is a claim to truth, as implied in, "I hereby assert p"). Absent the self-reflective character of subjectivity, the predicate "is true" is redundant, such that the factual occurrence or entertainment of a thought or proposition and the validity of the thought would be identical: if entertained, then valid. In the nature of the case, however, the validity of a proposition is not assured by and, in that sense, transcends the here and now, contingent entertainment of the proposition; the latter is never a sufficient condition of the former, and this is what we mean in saying that validity is objective. In other words, any given validity claim can be questioned, so that the predicate "is true" cannot be redundant and cognition must include the judgment upon one's thought or assertion of validity claims that occurs in self-reflection.

To judge or assert that one's thought is valid is, Apel continues, to claim that it conforms to the necessary conditions of valid subjectivity. Thus, every validity claim presupposes and implicitly claims to understand valid subjectivity as such, and philosophy seeks to understand transcendental subjectivity explicitly. Since all validity claims presuppose these necessary conditions, the peculiar character of philosophical claims is that they presuppose themselves. They are, as Apel also puts it, "self-referential" (1979a, 316). It then follows that the denial of a valid philosophical claim must be self-contradictory. Because such a denial is itself a claim which presupposes the necessary conditions of valid cognition, it presupposes the very claim which it denies and, therefore, denies itself.[7] "If I cannot challenge something without actual self-contradiction and cannot deductively ground it without formal-logical *petitio principii* [that is, the claim presupposes itself], then that thing belongs precisely to those transcendental-pragmatic presuppositions of argumentation which one must always have accepted" (1975, 264; see also 1980, 263).

As I have mentioned, Apel says that cognition as such is transcendental-pragmatic because self-reflection implies intersubjectivity. A relation to other subjects follows, if I understand Apel rightly, because the subject which reflects is not only the same as but also different from the subject upon which it reflects. The two must be the same, because the reflection is *self*-reflection. But the two must be different, because "I hereby assert that the thought which I entertain is valid" implies that the "I" which asserts is not identical with the "I" which entertains. Apel insists that this two-in-one can only mean that the active assertion differs from the entertainment as the offering of something differs from the something offered. Self-reflection is a self-expression, in which a subject offers his or her thought to others, so that human cognition is by nature a communicative performance. Self-reflection is a public act and can only be understood in this way because it claims validity, that is, a character for which the contingency of the self is not a sufficient condition. Validity claims involve the *"performative-propositional double-structure* of sentences which express whole speech-acts" (1979b, 50), so that "the performative speech-act . . . expresses the actual act of thought" (1979a, 332; emphasis deleted). It is the performative or communicative character of thought as such to which Apel refers in calling it pragmatic, and the same character explains in what sense subjectivity implies intersubjectivity.[8]

The communicative offer is made with the expectation that other subjects will agree with one's thought, again because "is true" attributes to one's thought a character that is public. The objectivity of truth commands intersubjective agreement. Moreover, the offer with this expectation is made in principle to any and all other subjects. A limitation upon the public whose confirmation one expects would in principle identify validity with the contingent entertainment of thought by some limited community of subjects. But no contingent entertainment of a thought can be a sufficient condition of validity. Given such identity, it would be impossible to question any claims upon which all members of that community agree. Thus, Apel holds that a validity claim is in principle an offer to communicate to and an expectation of agreement from an indefinite communication community. "The *semantic* notion of *truth*, as well as that of *propositions as truth-bearers*, can only be understood philosophically . . . if one reflects on the (*transcendental-pragmatic*) fact . . . that there are human beings that *claim* truth for their knowledge and are able, in principle, to express their truth-claims by *performative* (and self-reflective) phrases such as, e.g., 'I hereby state, that. . . .' through which the *propositions* claimed to be true are communicated as parts of illocutionary speech acts and thereby exposed, in principle, to the possible assent or contestation of an indefinite argumentation community" (1979a, 315). That the communication community is an argumentation community also follows from the attribution to one's thought of a character which transcends any contingent subject or groups of subjects. A validity claim implies that all subjects *should* confirm or agree with the thought. But this is to say that reasons can be given for the claim, that is, communication can include grounds which will elicit the assent of all rational subjects. In sum, the claim can be defended by argument or, as Apel also says, redeemed. Consequently, Apel can say that philosophy is an attempt to understand the nature of argumentative discourse as such (see, e.g., 1982, 99).[9]

It should be clear from what has been said that Apel's transcendental-pragmatic philosophy includes a consensus theory of validity. Because a validity claim is the expectation that argument or good reasons would command the agreement of any and all rational subjects, valid claims may be defined as those which would enjoy the consensus of all rational subjects. "The possibility of creating consensus in an unrestricted communication community must, in principle, be included among the conditions of the possibility of truth" (1984, 239). In the nature of the case, however, this consensus cannot be an arbitrary one, that is, the agreement of others cannot be caused by any accidental character of their subjectivity nor be the consequence of their arbitrary choices but must be based upon grounds which transcend, in a manner consistent with the claim to validity, all such contingencies. It must be a consensus of all *rational* subjects and, therefore, achieved by the "force" or persuasion of the better argument. To be sure, one might hold that the agreement of any and all potential subjects could be based only upon reasons, since the unrestricted or indefinite character of the communication community prevents the controlling influence of subjective contingencies. Still, the statement that consensus is *not* based upon subjective contingencies is a negative characterization, and this negative implies a corresponding positive. Agreement that transcends subjective contingencies is itself meaningless unless one can state positively upon what such agreement is based. In other words, there must be transcendental conditions of valid argumentation, and philosophy must be able to inquire into the valid forms or methods of reasoning, theoretical and practical. Thus, Apel cites approvingly the claim of Hans Lenk that "at least some logical rules are basically removed from rational revision," because they are presupposed in any argument at all (cited in 1980, 266).

Apel's attempt to justify a basic ethical norm is a part of his philosophic inquiry into practical reasoning. Only if there is some norm which any subject presupposes or implicitly affirms, he insists, can morality be possible at all. This is just to say again that Apel, with Kant, holds that the moral law must be transcendental. The requirement that "one must justify the basic moral norm without being permitted to presuppose any norm at all" is impossible to fulfill, and any attempt to meet it yields either an infinite regress of norms or sheer moral dogmatism. "Anyone who is interested philosophically in grounding the basic norm is able to appreciate through transcendental reflection that he is already presupposing this norm" (1980, 296). Of course, one might assert that it is not possible to justify moral claims, that is, a basic norm is never presupposed. But Apel argues that this claim is self-contradictory, because the self-reflection of subjectivity is an act in which the subject evaluates itself according to a norm, that is, claims that its own thought conforms to the necessary conditions of valid cognition. One might respond that this is a theoretical norm, not a practical or ethical one, but, for Apel, this response forgets that self-reflection is an act in which one offers to communicate and to provide argument for one's claim. Implied in this performance, he contends, are "*universal pragmatic* rules that constitute the conditions of the possibility of . . . illocutionary effects" of communicative acts (1979b, 51). These rules may be summarized as the norm of respect for the rational subjectivity of one's communication partner or partners, where "respect" means that one will not destroy the conditions under which the partner(s) may respond to one's validity claim on the grounds of reason alone. One is committed to acting toward or treating one's communication partners as participants in an argumentative discourse and, therefore, as independent subjects of reasonable evaluation. Validity claims imply "the norm of reciprocal acknowledgment of persons as equal partners and hence the norm of equal rights and duties in using argumentative speech-acts for proposing, defending, explicating and possibly questioning validity claims" (1979b, 51).

To this argument it may be objected that a person is committed to such respect for his or her communication partners only if he or she actually chooses to argue. In contrast to an ultimate norm, this objection asserts, Apel's norm of argumentation is, in Kant's sense, a hypothetical imperative: *If* one chooses to argue, then there are certain rules which one ought to observe. But this objection misses Apel's point. Since making a validity claim *is* an act in which one offers to redeem that claim in communication, the absence of respect for one's communication partners is in effect a denial that one makes such a claim and is, therefore, self-contradictory. At this point, the objection might be radicalized by insisting that the subject might choose not to make validity claims. Perhaps a given subject simply chooses to pursue his or her perceived interest or whim and refrains from the whole sphere of validity claims. Given this putative possibility, the ethics of communication remains a hypothetical imperative: *If* one chooses to make validity claims, then one is committed to norms of respect. Apel responds that the putative choice not to make validity claims is the self-contradictory notion of a choice not to be a cognitive subject. It is self-contradictory, because it cannot be "understood as a meaningful act of decision"

(1979b, 48; emphasis deleted). Subjectivity *is* the making of validity claims, so that one cannot choose to avoid them. "Everyone, even if he merely acts in a *meaningful* manner—e.g., takes a decision in the face of an alternative and claims to understand himself—already implicitly presupposes the logical and moral preconditions for critical communication" (1980, 269). Since the ethic of "reciprocal recognition of communication partners" (1978, 97) is implied by any thought about alternatives, it is categorical or transcendental.

Because the ethic of communicative respect follows from the transcendental fact that thought as such is an offer to communicate, one might wonder how *immorality* is possible. If all subjects *do* offer to communicate, how can they fail to respect their communication partners? But this apparent dilemma can be displayed as merely apparent if one underscores that the ethical norm prescribes respect for *all* other subjects, actual and potential. Since a validity claim is the offer to give reasons that one expects would command the agreement of all other subjects, one is normatively committed to communicative respect within the indefinite or ideal communication community. "All persons who are capable of linguistic communication must be recognized as persons since in all their actions and utterances they are potential participants in a discussion, and the unlimited justification of thought cannot dispense with any participant" (1980, 259). "In the situation of argumentative discourse we must suppose an 'ideal speech situation' and thereby adjudicate equal rights and duties of asking and answering all kinds of questions concerning any conceivable topic to all possible members of the argumentation-community" (1982, 100). One may say, then, that cognition is actual respect for at least some other subjects and is the implicit commitment to respect for all potential communication partners. Hence, in contradiction to the presuppositions of making a validity claim, immorality arbitrarily limits the communication community which one respects.[10] Moreover, the implicit commitment to all subjects allows Apel to conclude that his transformation of Kant has redeemed Kant's moral claim: All rational subjects should be treated as ends withal, participants in a "kingdom of ends."

Although Apel claims to derive a transcendental ethic of ideal communication, it is not a materially comprehensive norm. It is not, in other words, a norm in relation to which the morality of all choice alternatives can be evaluated. That this is so may be confirmed by the following consideration: Were the ideal communication community realized, so that there obtained in fact full communicative competence in all individuals and full reciprocal recognition of persons as equal partners in argumentative discourse, the participants in this community would have to communicate *about something.* Ideal communication cannot simply be about the "equal rights and duties" of ideal communication. But, then, ideal communication cannot be a norm in relation to which one might morally evaluate all things· about which communication does or might occur. Alternatively stated, human subjects have not only a transcendental interest in the ideal communication community but also a diversity of individual interests or purposes which they seek to fulfill in their lives, and a comprehensive ethic must include norms in accord with which choices among these interests may be evaluated and conflicts among them adjudicated.

But Apel argues that the materially noncomprehensive norm of ideal communication prescribes the manner in which other material norms should be decided. It is "a meta-norm of norm generation" (see 1979a, 335). His meaning, if I understand him rightly, may be explicated as follows: Any purpose chosen, if the choice is indeed a meaningful or intelligent one, involves validity claims. With respect to ethics, one claims that one's purpose is at least morally permissible and, therefore, if one's purpose conflicts with the purposes of others, that it is not morally wrong for the conflict to be resolved in one's favor. Accordingly, one is transcendentally committed to the ideal communicative or argumentative resolution of conflicts of interest or purpose. One presupposes in choosing any purpose at all that norms in accord with which conflicts of interest may be adjudicated can and should be consensually established through argumentative discourse. "If and when a person *seriously* enters an *argumentative discourse,* then he not only accepts the rules and presupposed ethical norms of an argumentation-community, but he also expresses his *presupposition that it is possible and necessary in principle to solve the conflicts of practical life by argumentative discourse....* Now this presupposition of every *serious* argumentative discourse implies that one has not only accepted the formal ethical norms of fair discussion . . . but that one supposes, in principle, that the argumentative discourse qua 'practical discourse' may and should lead to an *agreement about concrete material norms*" (1979a, 335).

Given that the material norms are properly achieved by argumentative consensus, it follows, for Apel, that the interests of individuals are justifiable when they accord with what he calls a "universalization principle." "These concrete norms must result from examining the *claims* of all participants by means of a *universali-zation principle* that takes into account the *compatibility of the interests of all people who are potentially affected by the question under discussion.* It is essentially this principle of an argumentative mediation of all normatively relevant claims of all virtual members of the argumentation community, and hence of the human com-munication-community, that makes up the *fundamental norm* of an ethics of communication" (1979a, 335). Or, again: "It is in principle necessary to acknowledge all those claims of one's communication partners that can be shown through argument to be compatible with the claims of all other members of the communication community. In this sense, all individual *interests* and *needs* that are compatible with those of all others can be validated as argumentatively defen-sible claims" (1978, 97). In sum, the ethic of communication is a "regulative principle" (1982, 103). "Our fundamental norm is not a material norm to be related to a special type of situation but a 'meta-norm' that prescribes the ideal procedure of . . . legitimating mate-rial norms . . . by seeking a consensus of all affected people by an argumentative mediation of their interests" (1982, 100–101).

We may also say that the ethic of communication *must* prescribe the argumentative or consensual legitimation of material norms, be-cause the ethic would otherwise make no sense. Were it not possible to legitimate material norms, any interest claim or purpose would be morally permissible, so that, in a situation of conflict, discussion could only be a strategic aspect of the pursuit of one's own particular interest. Thus, one would be bound by the basic norm of commu-nication only if one's particular interest were in the pursuit of truth or in the redemption of validity claims—or, better, only if such pur-suit could be a particular interest rather than a commitment presup-posed by all interests. But the redemption of validity claims is a pursuit necessarily presupposed in choosing any purpose at all. As a consequence, argumentative mediation of conflicts of interest must be possible.

Finally, it should be noted that the ideal communication com-munity is a telos or ideal-to-be-pursued rather than an ideal-to-be-illustrated in all of one's actions toward other persons. In any given situation of interaction, some of one's actual communication part-ners may not be "thoroughly competent subjects of communicative understanding" and/or may choose to be immoral, so that some "will not behave purely *consensually* but rather *strategically* with respect to their own and other people's interests" (1979a, 337). To act "purely consensually" in such an actual community, and thereby to presume that the ideal community is an ideal-to-be-illustrated, could be immoral, because the basic norm prescribes respect for the subjects of an indefinite communication community. In other words, a consensus reached in any given situation may be the result of "repressive" or "systematically distorted" communication or, more generally, be contingent or arbitrary in character. To respect this consensus may have consequences which violate one's obligation to respect all actual and potential subjects. Thus, the ideal is a "regulative principle of progressively realizing standards of an ethics of consensual communication" (1982, 103). It is an ideal-to-be-pursued, such that the categorical imperative is "that of *realizing in the long run the ideal communication-community within the real communication-community*" (1979a, 338).

IV

I turn now to an assessment of Apel's claim that human subjects as such presuppose or implicitly affirm a meta-norm or regulative principle in accord with which all conflicts of interest should be argumentatively mediated, so that all material norms are justified or legitimated by consensus within the ideal communication community. I begin by emphasizing that the consensus to which any putative material norm appeals cannot be an arbitrary or contingent one. It is, rather, a rational or grounded consensus, and this is what is meant when one says that the communication community is ideal or that interests are argumentatively mediated. In accord with the earlier discussion of the consensus theory of validity, then, the legitimation of material norms implies appropriate transcendental standards of practical discourse by which consensus due to the persuasion of good argument may be identified. To be sure, it can be said that agreement which is not arbitrary or contingent can be only a rational one. But this does not gainsay that there must be standards for argumentation in practical discourse, if the term "rational" is to have any positive meaning.

Consider the consequences were there no such standards. Because discussion can never be in fact completely ideal, that is, cannot in fact include all potential subjects of communication or persist indefinitely, the absence of standards of practical argumentation would make it impossible to judge (that is, to argue) that any given consensus regarding material norms is the one which ideal communication would fully validate. Moreover, in the absence of argumentative standards, there would be no way for each participant in the discussion to assess the arguments that others advance, so that even a consensus within an indefinite community would, if possible at all, be accidental. Both of these considerations are expressions of the fact, mentioned earlier, that unlimited communication is a negative characterization; if it is a transcendental condition for the full redemption of validity claims, this is so only because there is also a corresponding positive characterization of the grounds upon which ideal consensus is achievable, that is, a transcendental form or forms of good argument.

Now, the form of good practical argumentation is one in which evaluation is defended by appeal to a rationally justifiable norm. To be sure, Apel's project does purport transcendentally to justify the norm of ideal communication, but this norm is a regulative principle or meta-norm prescribing the argumentative or rationally consensual establishment of specific material norms. Accordingly, we may ask: By appeal to what rationally justifiable norm or norms does practical discourse adjudicate conflicts of interest and purpose, that is, legitimate specific material norms? Assume that we all agree to mediate our conflicts of interest or purpose argumentatively. What shall we now do; that is, by appeal to what shall we assess arguments? One would only beg this question if one were to reply that practical argument appeals simply to the norm of argumentative consensus, and this is just to say again that the ethic of communication is not a materially comprehensive norm.

Perhaps Apel's answer is his "principle of universalization," that is, arguments are good ones when they take into account "the compatibility of the interests of all people who are potentially affected by the question under discussion" (1979a, 335; emphasis deleted). But this answer either is false or again begs the question. It is false if the interests whose compatibility is required are the perceived or chosen interests of the individuals involved. On this reading, the principle would not provide grounds for an adjudication of conflicts, because conflict among perceived interests means precisely that the interests are not compatible. Further, the basic norm prescribes that the relevant individuals include all actual or potential subjects and, therefore, all future subjects, and there is no way to know what the perceived interests of future subjects will be. But these problems are expressions of the fact that compatibility among perceived interests cannot be a rational ground for practical discourse, because any consensus thereby achieved is an arbitrary or accidental one. Any relevant subject could destroy the consensus by changing his or her perceived or chosen interests, and consensus that may be destroyed by arbitrary choice is not based upon the force or persuasion of reason alone.[11]

Alternatively, Apel might contend that argumentative discourse about interests will persuade at least some individuals that their perceived interests are not their real or genuine interests, with the consequence that argument changes the interests of individuals, so that a compatibility of genuine or legitimate interests is achieved. Depending upon what is meant by "genuine or legitimate interests," some may doubt that a compatibility among them is possible, because this notion seems to imply some kind of "preestablished harmony" that will be difficult to prove. Be that as it may, this reformulation of Apel's meaning begs the question. For individuals can be persuaded about their genuine interests only if there is some rational ground on the basis of which to assess arguments in this regard, that is, some rationally justifiable norm in accord with which to distinguish in principle between genuine and perceived interests.

I conclude that Apel's ethic presupposes and, therefore, is incomplete without a materially comprehensive norm, that is, a norm in relation to which all conflicts of interest may be argumentatively mediated. Because such rational adjudication is implicitly affirmed by subjectivity as such, this materially comprehensive norm must also be transcendental in character or presupposed in making any validity claim at all. Given that the ideal communication community is itself transcendentally presupposed, it is true that the materially comprehensive norm can only be such as to include this teleological ideal. But the fundamental norm cannot be *exhausted* by indefinite or ideal communication, since this ideal itself presupposes grounds upon which practical reason may adjudicate conflicting interests. In accord with this conclusion, we may speak of the "compatibility of interests" as the principle for grounding specific material norms only if this phrase refers to a teleologically *comprehensive* interest which all subjects presuppose in choosing any interest at all. Thus, a particular interest is shown to conform to this principle when it is shown to be compatible with the interests that all others would have were they fully informed about each other and informed by the teleologically comprehensive norm. But this is just to say that an interest is moral if it can be defended by appeal to that same comprehensive norm.

I also conclude that Apel's ethic is incomplete in the absence of transcendental metaphysics. This follows, I believe, because a norm by virtue of which all conflicts of interest may be morally evaluated must be a principle or variable in relation to which all possible or conceivable human interests can be exhaustively compared. Were this not the case, some human interests in some respects could not be morally evaluated, and, because those interests in those respects could also conflict with others, the principle could not serve as the basis for adjudicating all conflicts of interest. In the respects in which they are not morally evaluated, in other words, interests are declared to be morally irrelevant; but that assertion is itself a moral evaluation of those respects, so that the principle in question would presuppose another, all-inclusive principle. It is just for this reason that a materially *non*comprehensive ethic of ideal communication presupposes a comprehensive norm. But possible or conceivable human interests, to complete the argument, include interest in anything at all. Indeed, to be conceivable is to be something in which human subjects might be interested, even if this interest is simply in thinking about it. Accordingly, we may say that Apel's ethic presupposes a principle or variable exemplified in and comparative of all possible concrete things as such. The transcendental subject which thinks about and acts within a world can only mean by "world" a plurality of actual and possible concrete things all of which exemplify a variable in terms of which they can be exhaustively evaluated. The transcendental or necessary conditions of subjectivity as such include transcendental conditions of reality as such. If Apel denies the possibility of transcendental metaphysics, he thereby contradicts the presupposition of his own ethic.

V

If the preceding assessment of Apel is correct, then Apel's attempt to redeem Kantian moral philosophy by transforming Kant's argument into a transcendental-pragmatic one does not succeed. We may now recall the summary conclusion of the earlier discussion of Kant: Because unqualified goodness cannot be defined by a rationally contingent existential proposition, there can be no moral law in the absence of transcendental metaphysics. The antecedent of this summary expresses, Kant claims, the transcendental or autonomous character of the moral law. Although Apel agrees that morality must be autonomous, his transformation of Kant attempts, in effect, to deny Kant's expression of this truth, that is, to deny that unqualified goodness cannot be defined by a rationally contingent existential proposition. Because Apel rejects transcendental metaphysics, the ideal communication community which he asserts to be the morally prescribed telos of all human action can only be so defined. Notwithstanding its indefiniteness, this community is constituted by a plurality of subjects each of whose existence or possible existence is rationally contingent. The ideal communication community is, in other words, thoroughly human in character. If, as I have argued, this telos itself presupposes a materially comprehensive or metaphysical principle of evaluation, then Apel's attempted transformation only succeeds in illustrating Kant's claim.

I am persuaded that Apel's project does not in this respect improve upon Kant, because the claim in question is one of Kant's most important philosophical contributions. Because choice is nothing other than the affirmation of one rather than another possible state of affairs, an existential proposition cannot identify what is unqualifiedly good unless it is presupposed by any possible existential affirmation and is, therefore, a rationally necessary existential proposition. If, as I have also argued, Kant's own attempt to derive a strictly formal moral law contradicts precisely this claim, then the importance of Kant's contribution is formulated in the consequent of the summary conclusion repeated above: There can be no moral law in the absence of transcendental metaphysics. In any event, we may say that Apel's proposal, whatever its importance in other respects, does not give reason to reject this conclusion.

It remains, as it did after the earlier discussion of Kant, that the possibility of metaphysics has not been established. Kant and Apel may both be correct in rejecting an inquiry into reality as such, so that we must also reject all transcendental moral laws. But I am also persuaded that Apel's transformation of Kant is itself a contribution precisely in this respect. I find convincing the claim that there can be no moral obligation if the transcendental subject is solitary, and, moreover, I am inclined to think that transcendental intersubjectivity does imply a moral commitment to all other subjects. If this is so, then Apel's argument for the pragmatic character of subjectivity as such offers reasons to affirm the moral enterprise. It then follows, given Kant's contribution, that Apel also offers, contrary to his own intention, implicit reason to affirm transcendental metaphysics. It is, to be sure, yet another step to Christian theism. But Apel's achievement, if my judgment about it is correct, argues implicitly for agreement with Schubert M. Ogden at least to this extent: Authentic human existence is authorized by ultimate reality.

Notes

1. At least generally speaking, Kant reserves the term "transcendental" for the justification of a priori synthetic knowledge of objects, so that moral philosophy does not belong to transcendental philosophy. Still, the moral law is for Kant, justified a priori, so that, in the context of the present inquiry, no injustice is done to the substance of his thought by using the term "transcendental," as Apel does, in a wider sense. I will use that term to refer to inquiry which seeks the presuppositions or necessary conditions of subjectivity as such, either theoretical or practical, and I will also speak of these conditions as transcendental presuppositions of subjectivity. Transcendental metaphysics, then, is the process or product of inquiry into the necessary conditions of reality as such, conditions which are, if they are at all, included within but do not exhaust the transcendental conditions of subjectivity.

2. It is true that Kant spoke of "the metaphysics of morals" and, moreover, that he advanced a moral argument for the affirmation of God. But it is also clear that neither of these verbal similarities alters the substantive difference between his position and that of Ogden. Kant's use of the term "metaphysics" in this regard does not refer to the process or product of reflection upon reality as such; on the contrary, the impossibility of such inquiry is precisely what the transcendental dialectic in the *Critique of Pure Reason* is designed to establish. The metaphysics of morals, then, refers to the a priori principles of moral philosophy, which are justified without appeal to any existential propositions. Similarly, Kant's affirmation of God is not a part of a transcendental inquiry into the nature of reality but a practical postulate which, he argues, follows from our recognition of the moral law. I shall not seek to pursue here the precise meaning of Kant's claim nor his argument for it. However those should be understood, it was Kant's clear intention to assert that the postulate of God's reality follows from a prior recognition of the moral law or autonomy of the will, such that the justification of moral claims is no more dependent upon the existence of God than it is upon "the Holy One of the Gospels." "But where have we the conception of God as the supreme good? Simply from the *idea* of moral perfection, which reason frames *a priori* and connects inseparably with the notion of a free will" (26).

3. I should underscore that the present section of the essay seeks to interpret Kant's argument for the moral law as this is found in the *Fundamental Principles*. Whether the interpretation is adequate to other works in which the same matter is discussed, I do not pretend to judge.

4. I recognize that the sense in which the moral law is, in Kant's thought, rationally necessary is problematic. Kant holds that this imperative is synthetic a priori rather than analytic. With respect to the categorical imperative, he makes this distinction because humans are sensible as well as rational beings. The categorical imperative is not possible unless human reason can be practical, which, for Kant, means that the will is free, and the

affirmation that the will of a sensible creature is free is not analytic. As a consequence, the difficult third section of the *Fundamental Principles* seeks to justify this affirmation. But it then follows, I believe, that the moral law *is* analytic if one assumes that the will is free. Given practical reason, that is, a being who reasons about choices or actions, the will is bound by the moral law in the sense that its denial involves practical reason in logical self-contradiction. For the purposes of this essay, I will assume that the will is free and, therefore, equate Kant's use of a priori with rational necessity in the logical sense. Accordingly, I will use "rationally contingent" in the logical sense as equivalent to Kant's use of a posteriori. On the use of "transcendental" in reference to Kant's ethics, see n. 1, above.

5. Were it the case that the exercise of freedom is morally good regardless of what state of affairs one chooses to pursue, this would not imply that *no* state of affairs identifies the moral law but rather that *all* states of affairs do so.

6. On my reading, it is Kant's distinction between phenomenal and noumenal existence which, in his own mind, allows him to avoid a contradiction between the negative and positive meanings of his famous introductory assertion in the *Fundamental Principles.* When he says that no end can be good without qualification, he refers to phenomenal existence; when he says that rational being is an end in itself, he refers to noumenal existence. It is, of course, this same distinction that is expressed in Kant's insistence that the transcendental law of practical reason must be identified independently of transcendental metaphysics: All statements about states of affairs are rationally contingent because they are statements about the existence of phenomena. An adequate assessment of this distinction would require extensive attention to the *Critique of Pure Reason.* But if I am correct in the claim that freedom cannot be conceived independently of some state of affairs which is affirmed, then the distinction is, I believe, indirectly called into question. Another way to formulate that claim is the following: Kantian assertions regarding the existence of something which is not phenomenal are solely negative in character and, therefore, could not refer to something which identifies the positive difference between moral and immoral choices, that is, could not refer to something good without qualification.

7. Thus, for instance, one might deny that the conditions of valid cognition are transcendental and thereby deny that philosophy in Apel's sense is possible. But Apel holds that this denial is self-contradictory. Because the denial claims to be valid, it implies the positive claim that conditions of validity are in some manner and in all respects always relative to the subject in question. But this implicit positive claim is a claim about subjectivity as such, that is, a transcendental claim. "Thus, for example, in the sentence, 'in principle, we cannot abstract from the fact that we are individuals conditioned by different forms of life,' the first part contradicts the second on the level of philosophical discourse. The first part implicitly views the 'we' as the subject of the intersubjectively valid insight into the limits of the possibility of the abstraction; hence, it attributes to the 'we' precisely that transcendental function disputed by the second part" (1984, 238).

8. It might be objected that cognition as such cannot be an offer to communicate, because it is evident to any thinker that he or she has many thoughts which he or she does not attempt to speak or otherwise to communicate to other individuals. Surely it will not do to say that cognition is a *potential* offer of communication, for then the offer to communicate cannot define the *actual* self-reflectiveness of thought. Apel does hold that the solitary thinker is one who "is able to internalize the dialogue of a potential community . . . in the critical 'discourse of the soul with itself' (Plato)" (1980, 258; see also 1984, 274 n. 14). In itself, however, this begs the present question. Solitary thought cannot be so described unless one can first know how such thought *is* an offer of communication. I am not clear about Apel's response to this problem, and I suspect that resolution of it is not possible if communication occurs only between human individuals. In contrast, the self-reflective subject might be understood as a momentary act, so that an individual is a temporally enduring sequence of such subjects. Accordingly, the actual offer of communication might be made to the succeeding moment of the same individual. If, as the next paragraph in the text goes on to say, the claim to validity is in principle the offer to communicate with all potential subjects, then one might say that solitary thought cannot be understood independently of those speech-acts which constitute communication among individuals. Thus, solitary thought may be described as the internalization of the dialogue of a potential community. As this discussion may suggest, I judge that a potentially fruitful comparison may be drawn between Apel's claims about the self-reflectiveness of thought and Alfred North Whitehead's claim that all concrete subjects are both subjects and superjects (see, e.g., Whitehead, 29).

Of course, if Apel is correct in saying that thought is necessarily an offer to communicate, then it follows from the self-referential character of philosophy that the denial of this transcendental claim must be self-contradictory. Apel calls this denial "methodological solipsism." "By . . . 'methodological solipsism' I mean the belief . . . that even if a human being, viewed empirically, is a social being, the possibility and validity of forming judgments and intentions can still be basically understood without the *transcendental-logical presupposition of a communication community*" (1980, 287). Given that the pragmatic character of subjectivity is constitutive of Apel's program, that program also includes a continuing criticism of methodological solipsism as self-contradictory (see, for an especially important statement, 1975).

9. Because the claim to validity is the offer to communicate and argue, Apel continually insists that rationality cannot be exhaustively differentiated into scientific rationality, which seeks causal explanation, and practical reason, which mediates between either ethical norms or prerational ends and particular situations of practice. To make this distinction exhaustive is, for Apel, to agree with Kant's assumption that the transcendental subject is solitary. Given that subjectivity as such is intersubjective, we must also distinguish hermeneutic rationality as a complementary type that is presupposed by both scientific and practical reason. Hermeneutic

rationality is the capacity to understand the validity claims and the arguments for them which are offered by others, that is, to understand the thought of other subjects. Since valid cognition is the offer to communicate, in other words, it presupposes the capacity to receive communication, that is, to understand another. This insight, Apel contends, permits a resolution of the so-called *Erklären-Verstehen* controversy, such that the human sciences can never be adequately reduced to a specific example of the sciences which seek causal explanation. On the contrary, the *Geisteswissenschaften* include a methodical attempt to understand the judgments and intentions of other subjects, that is, they exemplify a hermeneutic rationality which is presupposed by all forms of rationality as a condition of their own validity claims (see, for an extended statement, 1984; see also 1979a, 1979b).

Another way to express the fact that rationality presupposes communication and, therefore, includes hermeneutic rationality is to say that cognition cannot be conceived independently of language. All cognition is "bound up with the use of publicly understandable signs" through which it may be understood by another individual and, therefore, "must constantly presuppose the communicative processes of fixing the nominal value of our concepts by sign-interpretation" (1979b, 46). Thus, cognition not only is an offer to communicate but also presupposes prior communication in order to occur. Even "a man who, by accident, was the last representative of the communication-community and thus was alone in an empirical sense. . . . would have to presuppose 1) that there must have been a real communication-community, and 2) that there might be an unlimited ideal communication-community, both capable in principle of confirming his certain insight" (1975, 267). To insist upon the inseparability of thought and language does not deny that cognition is in some sense thought about experience. It is rather to say that thought is always a linguistically mediated interpretation of experience, the claim to validity of which is a claim about the potential agreement of all subjects of cognition. Accordingly, Apel also calls his transcendental pragmatic philosophy a transcendental pragmatics of language (see, e.g., 1975, 246).

10. The normative commitment to respect for all other subjects is, I believe, the precise meaning of Apel's assertion that cognition is *in principle* an offer to communicate with "an indefinite argumentation community" (1979a, 315). Self-reflection is, by definition, an actual offer of communication to at least one other subject (see n. 8, above). In principle, however, no limited consensus is a sufficient condition of validity, so that one's claim commits one to respect for—and, in that sense, is an offer to communicate with—all other subjects. Thus, any validity claim which implies respect for less than the indefinite community of subjects insofar is self-refuting, because it denies the possibility of a sufficient condition of its own validity. Such limited respect, then, is insofar immoral.

11. One makes the same point in saying that there is no reason to call the perceived interests, among which compatibility is achieved, good ones. Just as the predicate "is true" cannot be redundant, the same is the case with

the predicate "is good" or "is legitimate." The factual perception or choice of an interest does not make it good any more than the factual entertainment of a proposition makes it valid. A compatibility among perceived interests, then, is a circumstance in which a certain combination of factual choices obtains, and to move from that state of affairs to the claim that it is good is to identify goodness with the contingent characteristics of a community of subjects. In sum, on this reading, Apel's universalization principle cannot itself be defended by argument and, therefore, is false.

Works Cited

Apel, Karl-Otto

1975　"The Problem of Philosophical Fundamental-Grounding in Light of a Transcendental Pragmatic of Language." *Man and World*, 8, 239–75.

1978　"The Conflicts of Our Time and the Problem of Political Ethics." *From Conflict to Community.* Ed. Fred K. Dallmayr. New York: Marcel Dekker, 81–102.

1979a　"Types of Rationality Today." *Rationality Today.* Ed. Theodore Geraets. Ottawa: University Press, 307–40.

1979b　"The Common Presuppositions of Hermeneutics and Ethics: Types of Rationality Beyond Science and Technology." *Research in Phenomenology*, 9, 35–53.

1980　*Toward a Transformation of Philosophy.* London: Routledge and Kegan Paul.

1982　"Normative Ethics and Strategic Rationality: The Philosophical Problem of a Political Ethics." *Graduate Faculty Philosophy Journal*, 9/1 (Winter), 81–107.

1984　*Understanding and Explanation: A Transcendental-Pragmatic Perspective.* Cambridge, Mass.: MIT.

Kant, Immanuel

1949　*Fundamental Principles of the Metaphysic of Morals.* Indianapolis: Bobbs-Merrill.

Ogden, Schubert

1982　*The Point of Christology.* San Francisco: Harper and Row.

Whitehead, Alfred North

1978　*Process and Reality*, corrected edition. Ed. David Ray Griffin and Donald Sherburne. New York: The Free Press.

Appendix

Published Writings of Schubert M. Ogden

Abbreviations

BCS	*Buddhist Christian Studies*
CA	*Christian Advocate*
CC	*The Christian Century*
C&C	*Christianity and Crisis*
C&S	*Christianity and Society*
CTSR	*The Chicago Theological Seminary Register*
DSN	*The Divinity School News*
JAAR	*The Journal of the American Academy of Religion*
JBR	*The Journal of Bible and Religion*
JR	*The Journal of Religion*
PS	*Process Studies*
PSTJ	*The Perkins School of Theology Journal*
RE	*Religious Education*
RL	*Religion in Life*
USQR	*Union Seminary Quarterly Review*
WB	*The Westminster Bookman*
ZThK	*Zeitschrift für Theologie und Kirche*

1953a "Time, Eternity, and a New Liberalism." *Quest*, 2, 1: 1–14.
   b "Creation, Redemption, and the Divine Dependence: A Reply." *Quest*, 2, 2: 6–8.

1954 Review: George F. Kennan, *Realities of American Foreign Policy*. *C&S*, 19, 4: 29–31.

1955a " 'Every One Who Is of the Truth. . . .' " *DSN*, 22, 1: 1–8.
   b Review: E. La B. Cherbonnier, *Hardness of Heart: A Contemporary Interpretation of the Doctrine of Sin*. *C&S*, 20, 4: 26–28.

1956a "Davida Boyd Lewis *in memoriam*." *DSN*, 23, 2: 17–18.
   b "Reflections on Parish Week." *The Log*, 7, 4: 3.

c Review: Friedrich Gogarten, *Demythologizing and History.* *CTSR*, 46, 2: 80–81.

1957a "Bultmann's Project of Demythologization and the Problem of Theology and Philosophy." *JR*, 37: 156–73.

b Review: Martin J. Heinecken, *The Moment before God: An Interpretation of Kierkegaard. PSTJ*, 10, 2: 22–24.

c Review: Hans Hofmann, *The Theology of Reinhold Niebuhr. JR*, 37: 131–32.

d Review: Geraint Vaughan Jones, *Christology and Myth in the New Testament. CTSR*, 47, 5: 17–19.

e Review: Paul Tillich, *Systematic Theology*, 2. *The Dallas Times Herald*, "Roundup," 28 July: 19.

f Review: Arthur F. Smethurst, *Modern Science and Christian Beliefs. JR*, 37: 267–68.

g Review: Samuel M. Thompson, *A Modern Philosophy of Religion. PSTJ*, 11, 1: 42–43.

h Review: Roger L. Shinn, *Life, Death, and Destiny. PSTJ*, 11, 1: 43–44.

i Review: David E. Roberts, *Existentialism and Religious Belief. PSTJ*, 11, 1: 44–46.

j Review: Gustaf Wingren, *Luther on Vocation. PSTJ*, 11, 1: 46–47.

k Review: Leslie Newbigin, *Sin and Salvation. PSTJ*, 11, 1: 47–48.

1958a "Destiny and Fate." In *A Handbook of Christian Theology*, ed. Arthur A. Cohen and Marvin Halverson. New York: Meridian Books, 77–80.

b "The Concern of the Theologian." In *Christianity and Communism*, ed. Merrimon Cuninggim. Dallas: SMU Press, 58–74.

c Review: George W. Davis, *Existentialism and Theology. JR*, 38: 66–67.

d Review: David E. Trueblood, *Philosophy of Religion. PSTJ*, 11, 2 & 3: 52–53.

e Review: George C. Hackman, et al., *Religion in Modern Life. PSTJ*, 11, 2 & 3: 53–54.

f Review: William Ernest Hocking, *The Meaning of Immortality in Human Experience. JR*, 38: 141–42.

g Review: Albert Camus, *Caligula and Three Other Plays.* *The Dallas Times Herald*, "Roundup," 14 September: 16.

h Review: F. D. Maurice, *Theological Essays. CC*, 75: 1081–82.

i   Review: William Inge, *Four Plays. The Dallas Times Herald,* "Roundup," 12 October: 17.

j   Review: Louis Schneider and Sanford M. Dornbush, *Popular Religion. The Dallas Times Herald,* "Roundup," 26 October: 21.

k   Review: Martin Buber, *I and Thou.* 2d ed. *The Dallas Times Herald,* "Roundup," 23 November: 10.

l   Review: Martin Werner, *The Formation of Christian Dogma. CC,* 75: 1513–14.

1959a   "The Situation in Contemporary Protestant Theology, 4: Systematic Theology." *PSTJ,* 12, 2: 13–20.

b   "The Debate on 'Demythologizing'." *JBR,* 27: 17–27.

c   "May a Christian Smoke?" *The Log,* 9, 14:2.

d   "The Quest for Theological Adequacy." *Letter to Laymen,* 5, 9: 1, 5–6.

e   "The Old Meaning in New Words and the New Meaning in Old Words: A Conversation with Schubert Ogden." *Letter to Laymen,* 5, 10: 5–6.

f   Translation: Rudolf Bultmann, "Eternal Light of Christmas." *CC,* 76: 1465–466.

g   Review: William Temple, *Religious Experience and Other Essays and Addresses. CC,* 76: 19–20.

h   Review: Nathan A. Scott, Jr., ed., *The Tragic Vision and the Christian Faith. JR,* 39: 65–66.

i   Review: John C. Bennett, *Christians and the State. Dallas Times Herald,* "Roundup," 15 March: 19.

j   Review: R. J. W. Bevan, ed., *Steps to Christian Understanding. PSTJ,* 12, 3: 26–27.

k   Review: Emile Bréhier, *The Philosophy of Plotinus. PSTJ,* 12, 3: 27.

l   Review: A. Roy Eckardt, *The Surge of Piety in America. WB,* 18, 2: 24–25.

m   Review: Henri de Lubac, S.J., *Catholicism. CC,* 76: 923.

n   Review: Martin Heidegger, *An Introduction to Metaphysics. CC,* 76: 1056.

o   Review: Walter Leibrecht, ed., *Religion and Culture: Essays in Honor of Paul Tillich. PSTJ,* 13, 1: 27–28.

p   Review: Paperback publications in the general field of religion, Spring-Summer, 1959. *PSTJ,* 13, 1: 41–42.

1960a   "An Adequate Theology for Our Time." *CA,* 4, 18: 7–8.

b   "The Lordship of Jesus Christ: The Meaning of Our Affirmation." *Encounter,* 21: 408–22.

c   "The Right to Celebrate the Reformation." *The Pulpit,* 31: 302–4.

d   Edition and translation: *Existence and Faith: Shorter Writings of Rudolf Bultmann.* New York: Meridian Books.

e   Translation: Rudolf Bultmann, "On Behalf of Christian Freedom." *JR,* 40: 95–99.

f   Translation: Rudolf Bultmann, "Is Exegesis without Presuppositions Possible?" *Encounter,* 21: 194–200.

g   Review: F. H. Cleobury, *Christian Rationalism and Philosophical Analysis. CC,* 77: 192–93.

h   Review: Paul Hessert, *Introduction to Christianity. JR,* 40: 53–54.

i   Review: Robert M. Grant, *Gnosticism and Early Christianity. CTSR,* 50, 1: 2–3.

j   Review: Langdon Gilkey, *Maker of Heaven and Earth. PSTJ,* 13, 2: 43.

k   Review: William Strunk, Jr., *The Elements of Style. PSTJ,* 13, 2: 48–49.

l   Review: L. Malevez, S.J., *The Christian Message and Myth. CC,* 77: 949–950.

m   Review: Carl Michalson, *The Hinge of History. JR,* 40: 217–219.

n   Review: Rudolf Bultmann, *This World and the Beyond. CA,* 4, 26: 17.

o   Review: Rudolf Bultmann, *This World and the Beyond. WB,* 19, 4: 8–9.

p   Review: Dagobert D. Runes, *Pictorial History of Philosophy. PSTJ,* 14, 1: 42.

1961a   *Christ without Myth: A Study Based on the Theology of Rudolf Bultmann.* New York: Harper & Brothers.

b   "Liturgical Worship?" *Motive,* 22, 1: 14.

c   Edition and translation: *Existence and Faith: Shorter Writings of Rudolf Bultmann.* London: Hodder and Stoughton.

d   Translation: Rudolf Bultmann, "Children of Light." *Motive,* 22, 3: 6–9.

e   Review: Franklin H. Littell, *The German Phoenix. The Dallas Morning News,* Sec. 5. 15 January: 6.

f   Review: Jaroslav Pelikan, *Luther the Expositor. PSTJ,* 14, 2: 49–50.

g   Review: Theodore G. Tappert, ed., *The Book of Concord. PSTJ,* 14, 2: 51–52.

h   Review: Giovanni Miegge, *Gospel and Myth in the Thought of Rudolf Bultmann. PSTJ*, 14, 2: 54–55.
i   Review: Paperback publications in the general field of religion, Fall-Winter, 1960–61. *PSTJ*, 14, 2: 57–58.
j   Review: William A. Christian, *An Interpretation of Whitehead's Metaphysics. PSTJ*, 14, 3: 49.
k   Review: Rollo May, ed., *Symbolism in Religion and Literature. JR*, 41: 325–326.
l   Review: John W. Doberstein, ed., *Minister's Prayer Book*, and Robert N. Rodenmayer, ed., *The Pastor's Prayer Book. PSTJ*, 15, 1: 64–65.

1962a   *Christ without Myth: A Study Based on the Theology of Rudolf Bultmann.* London: Collins.
b   "The Significance of Rudolf Bultmann." *PSTJ*, 15, 2: 5–17.
c   "Wie neu ist die 'Neue Frage nach dem historischen Jesus'?" *ZThK*, 59: 46–87 (with Van A. Harvey).
d   "Bultmann and the 'New Quest'." *JBR*, 30: 209–18.
e   " 'You Also Should Do as I Have Done to You'." *Perkins Perspective*, 5, 1: 1, 3–4.
f   Translation: Rudolf Bultmann, "On the Problem of Demythologizing." *JR*, 42: 96–102.
g   Review: Harold E. Fey, ed., *How My Mind Has Changed. CC*, 79: 17.
h   Review: Wilhelm Pauck, *The Heritage of the Reformation.* 2d ed. *PSTJ*, 15, 2: 38–39.
i   Review: John Macquarrie, *The Scope of Demythologizing. PSTJ*, 15, 2: 40–41.
j   Review: Paperback publications in the general field of religion, Fall-Winter, 1961–62. *PSTJ*, 15, 2: 60–61.
k   Review: June Bingham, *Courage to Change: An Introduction to the Life and Thought of Reinhold Niebuhr. PSTJ*, 15, 3: 45–46.
l   Review: Gerhard Ebeling, *The Nature of Faith. PSTJ*, 15, 3: 46–47.
m   Review: H. R. Niebuhr, *Radical Monotheism and Western Culture. PSTJ*, 15, 3: 48–49.
n   Review: Carl E. Braaten and Roy A. Harrisville, eds., *Kerygma and History: A Symposium on the Theology of Rudolf Bultmann. CA*, 6, 20:17.
o   Review: Carl E. Braaten and Roy A. Harrisville, eds., *Ke-*

rygma and History: A Symposium on the Theology of Rudolf Bultmann. PSTJ, 16, 1: 52–53.

1963a "The Understanding of Theology in Ott and Bultmann." In *New Frontiers in Theology, 1: The Latter Heidegger and Theology,* ed. James M. Robinson and John B. Cobb, Jr. New York: Harper & Row, 157–73.

b " 'This Generation Will Not Pass Away. . . .' " In *Sermons to Intellectuals from Three Continents,* ed. Franklin H. Littell. New York: Macmillan, 123–34.

c "What Sense Does It Makes to Say, 'God Acts in History'?" *JR,* 63: 1–19.

d "Who Represents Christ?" *C&C,* 23: 115–18.

e "Honest to God." *CA,* 7, 14: 7–8.

f "Beyond Supernaturalism." *RL,* 33: 7–18.

g Review: Robert W. Bretall, ed., *The Empirical Theology of Henry Nelson Wieman. Theology Today,* 20: 424–25.

h Review: Kenneth Cauthen, *The Impact of American Religious Liberalism. PSTJ,* 17, 1: 42.

i Review: Charles Hartshorne, *The Logic of Perfection. PSTJ,* 17, 1: 47–48.

1964a "Theology and Philosophy: A New Phase of the Discussion." *JR,* 44: 1–16.

b "How New Is the 'New Quest of the Historical Jesus'?" In *The Historical Jesus and the Kerygmatic Christ,* ed. Carl E. Braaten and Roy A. Harrisville. New York: Abingdon, 197–242 (with Van A. Harvey).

c "Zur Frage der 'richtigen' Philosophie." *ZThK,* 61: 103–24.

d "Der Begriff der Theologie bei Ott und Bultmann." In *Der spätere Heidegger und die Theologie,* ed. James M. Robinson and John B. Cobb, Jr. Zurich: Zwingli Verlag, 187–205.

e "The Temporality of God." In *Zeit und Geschichte, Dankesgabe an Rudolf Bultmann zum 80. Geburtstag,* ed. Erich Dinkler. Tübingen: J. C. B. Mohr, 381–398.

f "Bultmann's Demythologizing and Hartshorne's Dipolar Theism." In *Process and Divinity: The Hartshorne Festschrift,* ed. William L. Reese and Eugene Freeman. LaSalle, Ill.: Open Court, 493–513.

g Edition and translation: *Existence and Faith: Shorter Writings of Rudolf Bultmann.* London: Collins.

h Review: John A. T. Robinson, *Honest to God. The SMU Campus,* 49, 30: 4.

i   Review: Paul M. van Buren, *The Secular Meaning of the Gospel. RE,* 59: 184–185.

j   Review: Carl Michalson, *The Rationality of Faith. WB,* 23, 1: 9–10.

k   Review: Gerhard Ebeling, *Word and Faith. CA,* 8, 14: 15–16.

l   Review: Kenneth Cauthen, *The Impact of American Religious Liberalism. The Church School,* 17, 11: 17.

m   Review: Carl Michalson, *The Rationality of Faith. PSTJ,* 17, 2 & 3: 45–46.

n   Review: Paul M. van Buren, *The Secular Meaning of the Gospel. PSTJ,* 17, 2 & 3: 50–51.

o   Review: John F. Porter and William J. Wolf, eds., *Toward the Recovery of Unity: The Thought of Frederick Denison Maurice. CA,* 8, 25: 18–19.

p   Review: Wilfred Cantwell Smith, *The Meaning and End of Religion. PSTJ,* 18, 1: 41–42.

q   Review: Frank N. Magill, ed., *Masterpieces of World Philosophy in Summary Form* and *Masterpieces of Christian Literature in Summary Form. PSTJ,* 18, 1: 44.

r   Review: Ninian Smart, ed., *Historical Selections in the Philosophy of Religion. PSTJ,* 18, 1: 44–45.

1965a   "Myth and Truth." *McCormick Quarterly,* 18, Special Supplement: 57–76.

b   "The Possibility and Task of Philosophical Theology." *USQR,* 20: 271–79.

c   "Intercessory Prayer in the Life of the Church." *The Log,* 14, 5: 7–8.

d   "The Christian and Unbelievers." *Motive,* 25, 8: 21–23.

e   "Theology and Objectivity." *JR,* 45: 175–95.

f   "Welch's Polemic: A Reply." *Theology Today,* 22: 275–77.

g   "Faith and Truth." *CC,* 82: 1057–1060.

h   Review: William A. Christian, *Meaning and Truth in Religion. PSTJ,* 18, 3: 57.

i   Review: John B. Cobb, Jr., *A Christian Natural Theology. CA,* 9, 18: 11–12.

1966a   *The Reality of God and Other Essays.* New York: Harper & Row.

b   "The Significance of Rudolf Bultmann for Contemporary Theology." In *The Theology of Rudolf Bultmann,* ed. Charles W. Kegley. New York: Harper & Row: 104–26.

c "Love Unbounded: The Doctrine of God." *PSTJ*, 19, 3: 5–17.

d "The Christian Proclamation of God to Men of the So-Called 'Atheistic Age'." In *Is God Dead?*, ed. Johannes Metz. New York: Paulist Press: 89–98.

e "The Permanent Reformation." *Classmate*, 74, 2: 30–32.

f Review: William A. Christian, *Meaning and Truth in Religion*. *PSTJ*, 19, 1 & 2: 64–65.

g Review: John B. Cobb, Jr., *A Christian Natural Theology*. *RE*, 61: 146.

1967a *The Reality of God and Other Essays*. London: SCM Press.

b *Theology in Crisis: A Colloquium on the Credibility of "God."* New Concord, Ohio: Muskingum College (with Charles Hartshorne).

c "Faith and Truth." In *Frontline Theology*, ed. Dean Peerman. Richmond, Va.: John Knox Press, 126–33.

d "How Does God Function in Human Life?" *C&C*, 27, 8: 105–8.

e "On Demythologizing." *Pittsburgh Perspective*, 8:2: 27–35.

f " 'Ask and It Will Be Given You'." In *Rockefeller Chapel Sermons*, ed. Donovan E. Smucker. Chicago: University of Chicago Press: 98–109.

g "Karl Rahner: Theologian of Open Catholicism." *CA* 11, 17: 11–13.

h Translation: Rudolf Bultmann, "General Truths and Christian Proclamation." *Journal for Theology and the Church, 4: History and Hermeneutics*. New York: Harper & Row: 153–62.

i Review: Karl Rahner, S.J., and Herbert Vorgrimler, S.J., *Theological Dictionary*. *PSTJ*, 20, 1 & 2: 57.

j Review: John Macquarrie, *Principles of Christian Theology*. *USQR*, 22: 263–64, 267.

k Review: Larry Shiner, *The Secularization of History: An Introduction to the Theology of Friedrich Gogarten*. *The Church School*, 20, 12: 29.

l Review: Ronald Gregor Smith, *Secular Christianity*. *RL*, 36: 478–79.

m Review: Fritz Buri, *Theology of Existence*. *PSTJ*, 21, 1: 50.

1968a "God and Philosophy: A Discussion with Antony Flew." *JR*, 48: 161–81.

b "The Challenge to Protestant Thought." *Continuum*, 6: 236–40.

c "Theology and Objectivity." In *Philosophy and Religion:*

Some Contemporary Perspectives, ed. Jerry A. Gill. Minneapolis: Burgess, 205–27.

d "Glaube und Wahrheit." In *Theologie im Umbruch, Der Beitrag Amerikas zur gegenwärtigen Theologie.* Munich: Christian Kaiser Verlag, 130–37.

e Review: Mortimer J. Adler, *The Difference of Man and the Difference It Makes. PSTJ,* 21, 2 & 3: 63–64.

f Review: Hans Jonas, *The Phenomenon of Life: Toward a Philosophical Biology. PSTJ,* 21, 2 & 3: 64–65.

g Review: René Marlé, S.J., *Bultmann and Christian Faith. RE,* 63: 415.

1969a "Present Prospects for Empirical Theology." In *The Future of Empirical Theology,* ed. Bernard E. Meland. Chicago: University of Chicago Press: 65–88.

b "Theology and Metaphysics." *Criterion,* 9, 1: 15–18.

c "On Perkins and Theological Education." *The Perkins Newsletter,* 3, 3: 1, 9–12.

d Review: Rudolf Bultmann, *Faith and Understanding. PSTJ,* 22, 2 & 3: 118–20.

1970 *Die Realität Gottes,* trans. Käthe Gregor Smith. Zurich: Zwingli Verlag.

1971a "A *Christian* Natural Theology?" In *Process Philosophy and Christian Thought,* ed. Delwin Brown, Ralph E. James, Jr., and Gene Reeves. Indianapolis: Bobbs-Merrill, 111–15.

b "Toward a New Theism." In *Process Philosophy and Christian Thought:* 173–87.

c "The Task of Philosophical Theology." In *The Future of Philosophical Theology,* ed. Robert A. Evans. Philadelphia: Westminster Press, 55–84.

d "On Thinking Historically about Christ." *CA,* 15, 11: 7–8.

e "Truth, Truthfulness, and Secularity." *C&C,* 31: 56–60.

f "Lonergan and the Subjectivist Principle." *JR,* 51: 155–72.

g "The Reality of God." In *Process Theology: Basic Writings,* ed. Ewert H. Cousins. New York: Newman Press, 119–35.

h "Prudence and Grace." *Criterion,* 11, 1: 6–8.

i Review: Charles Hartshorne, *Creative Synthesis and Philosophic Method. RE,* 66: 296.

1972a "What Is Theology?" *JR,* 5: 22–40.

b " 'The Reformation That We Want.' " *The Anglican Theological Review,* 54: 260–73.

c "Response to Jürgen Moltmann." In *Hope and the Future of*

Man, ed. Ewert H. Cousins. Philadelphia: Fortress Press, 109–16.

d   "Lonergan and the Subjectivist Principle." In *Language, Truth, and Meaning*, ed. Philip McShane. Dublin: Gill and Macmillan, 218–35.

e   Recording: "What Is Process Theology?" *Thesis*, 3, 9.

f   Translation: Rudolf Bultmann, "Protestant Theology and Atheism." *JR*, 52: 331–35.

g   Review: Joseph Maréchal, S.J., *A Maréchal Reader. JR*, 52: 103–4.

h   Review: Levi A. Olan, *Judaism and Immortality. PSTJ*, 25, 2: 40–41.

1973a   "What Is Theology?" *PSTJ*, 26, 2: 1–13.

b   "Response." *PSTJ*, 26, 2: 45–57.

c   Review: Frederick Herzog, *Liberation Theology. RL*, 42: 434–35.

d   Review: John A. T. Robinson, *The Human Face of God. RE*, 68: 756–57.

e   Review: Lyman T. Lundeen, *Risk and Rhetoric in Religion: Whitehead's Theory of Language and the Discourse of Faith. PSTJ*, 27, 2: 44–46.

1974a   "Faith and Secularity." In *God, Secularization, and History: Essays in Memory of Ronald Gregor Smith*, ed. Eugene Thomas Long. Columbia: University of South Carolina Press, 26–43.

b   "Falsification and Belief." *Religious Studies*, 10: 21–43.

c   "'Love Divine, All Loves Excelling': Theological Reflections." *United Methodists Today*, 1, 9: 68–71; 1, 10: 84–85.

d   "Doctrinal Standards in the United Methodist Church." *PSTJ*, 28, 1: 19–27.

e   "Response to Professor Connelly, 1." *Proceedings of the Catholic Theological Society of America*, 29: 59–66.

f   Review: Richard R. Niebuhr, *Experiential Religion. JAAR*, 42: 568–70.

1975a   "On Revelation." In *Our Common History as Christians: Essays in Honor of Albert C. Outler*, ed. John Deschner, Leroy T. Howe, and Klaus Penzel. New York: Oxford University Press, 261–92.

b   "A Colloquy on Bernard Lonergan, B. 3." *PSTJ*, 28, 3: 35–37.

c   "'Theology and Falsification' in Retrospect: A Reply." In *The Logic of God: Theology and Verification*, ed. Malcolm L. Diamond and Thomas V. Litzenburg, Jr. Indianapolis: Bobbs-Merrill, 290–97.

d   "The Criterion of Metaphysical Truth and the Senses of 'Metaphysics'." *PS*, 5: 47–48.

e   "The Meaning of Christian Hope." *USQR*, 30: 153–64.

f   "Christliche Theologie und die neue Religiosität." In *Chancen der Religion*, ed. Rainer Volp. Gütersloh: Gütersloher Verlagshaus Gerd Mohn, 157–74.

g   "The Point of Christology." *JR*, 55: 375–95.

1976a   "The Meaning of Christian Hope." In *Religious Experience and Process Theology: The Pastoral Implications of a Major Modern Movement*, ed. Harry James Cargas and Bernard Lee. New York: Paulist Press, 195–212.

b   "The Authority of Scripture for Theology." *Interpretation*, 30: 242–61.

c   "Christology Reconsidered: John Cobb's 'Christ in a Pluralistic Age'." *PS*, 6: 116–22.

d   "'I Believe in': Theological Brief." In *Christian Theology: A Case Study Approach*, ed. Robert A. Evans and Thomas D. Parker. New York: Harper & Row, 41–45.

e   "Sources of Religious Authority in Liberal Protestantism." *JAAR*, 44: 403–16.

1977a   *The Reality of God and Other Essays.* 2d ed. New York: Harper & Row.

b   "Linguistic Analysis and Theology." *Theologische Zeitschrift*, 33: 318–25.

c   "Prolegomena to a Christian Theology of Nature." In *A Rational Faith: Essays in Honor of Levi A. Olan*, ed. Jack Bemporad. New York: Ktav Publishing House: 125–36.

d   Translation: Charles Hartshorne, "Whitehead's Metaphysical System," *A Rational Faith: Essays in Honor of Levi A. Olan*: 107–23.

e   Review: Antony Flew, *The Presumption of Atheism and Other Philosophical Essays on God, Freedom and Immortality. Religious Studies Review*, 3: 142–44.

1978a   "Theology and Religious Studies: Their Difference and the Difference It Makes." *JAAR*, 46: 3–17.

b   "An Outline Still to Be Filled Out." *CC*, 95: 538–39.

c   "The Books That Shape Lives: Schubert M. Ogden." *CC*, 95: 571.

d   "Evil and Belief in God: The Distinctive Relevance of a 'Process Theology.' In *PSTJ*, 31, 4: 29–34.

e   "A Free-Church Answer." *Why Did God Make Me?*, ed. Hans Küng and Jürgen Moltmann. New York: Seabury Press, 67–73.

f   "Response to Peter Berger." *Theological Studies*, 39: 497–502.

g   Review: Jon Sobrino, S.J., *Christology at the Crossroads. PSTJ*, 31, 4: 47–49.

1979a   *Faith and Freedom: Toward a Theology of Liberation.* Nashville: Abingdon.

b   *Faith and Freedom: Toward a Theology of Liberation.* Belfast: Christian Journals.

c   *Christ without Myth: A Study Based on the Theology of Rudolf Bultmann.* 2d ed. Dallas: SMU Press.

d   "Ethical Queries about Modern Science." *Anticipation*, 25: 15–17.

e   "The Emancipation of Theology." *The Circuit Rider*, 3, 2: 3–5.

f   "Theology in the Modern World." *JR*, 59: 472–76.

g   " 'Theological Education and Liberation Theology': A Response." *Theological Education*, 16,1: 48–50.

h   Review: Alfred North Whitehead, *Process and Reality: An Essay in Cosmology.* Corrected ed. *PSTJ*, 33, 1: 57.

1980a   "On the Trinity." *Theology*, 83: 97–102.

b   "Christian Theology and Neoclassical Theism." *JR*, 60: 205–9.

c   "Faith and Freedom." *CC*, 97: 1241–44.

d   "The Church and Homosexual Persons: The Issue of Ordination." *Perkins Newsletter*, 13, 19: 7.

1981a   "Theology in the University." In *Unfinished Essays in Honor of Ray L. Hart*, ed. Mark C. Taylor. *Journal of the American Academy of Religion Thematic Studies*, 48/1: 3–13.

b   "Jews and Christians: Do We Live in the Same World? A Christian Asks the Question." *PSTJ*, 34, 4: 34–43.

c   "The Concept of a Theology of Liberation: Must a Christian Theology Today Be So Conceived?" In *The Challenge of Liberation Theology: A First World Response*, ed. Brian J. Mahan and L. Dale Richesin. Maryknoll, N.Y.: Orbis Books, 127–40.

d "Response to Dorothee Soelle." In *The Challenge of Liberation Theology: A First World Response:* 17–20.

e "Faith and Freedom." In *Theologians in Transition: The Christian Century "How My Mind Has Changed" Series*, ed. James M. Wall. New York: Crossroad: 100–106.

1982a *The Point of Christology.* San Francisco: Harper & Row.

b *The Point of Christology.* London: SMC Press.

c "Prolegomena to Practical Theology." *PSTJ*, 35, 3: 17–21.

d "Reader's Response." *Church Divinity 1982*, ed. John H. Morgan. Notre Dame, Ind.: Church Divinity Monograph Series, 128–29.

e "*Adversus Judaeos?* A Christian Understanding of Judaism." *PS*, 12: 94–97.

1983a "The Convergences of Science and Religion: A Response." *PSTJ*, 36, 4: 15–20.

b "Myth." In *The Westminster Dictionary of Christian Theology*, ed. Alan Richardson and John Bowden. Philadelphia: Westminster Press: 389–91.

c "Pluralism." In *The Westminster Dictionary of Christian Theology:* 449–51.

1984a "Essentials of Process Philosophy." *Unitarian Universalist World*, 15 February: 5.

b "Process Theology and the Wesleyan Witness." *PSTJ*, 37, 3: 18–33.

c "On *Faith and Freedom:* A Response to Pixley's Review." *PS*, 13: 232–34.

d "Rudolf Bultmann and the Future of Revisionary Christology." In *Rudolf Bultmanns Werk und Wirkung*, ed. Bernd Jaspert. Darmstadt: Wissenschaftliche Buchgesellschaft, 155–73.

e "The Experience of God: Critical Reflections on Hartshorne's Theory of Analogy." In *Existence and Actuality: Conversations with Charles Hartshorne*, ed. John B. Cobb, Jr., and Franklin I. Gamwell. Chicago: University of Chicago Press, 16–37.

f Edition and translation: Rudolf Bultmann, *New Testament and Mythology and Other Basic Writings.* Philadelphia: Fortress Press.

1985a "Is the Gospel Message Liberating for Women?" *PSTJ,* 38, 3: 19–21.
b "Process Theology and the Wesleyan Witness." In *Wesleyan Theology Today: A Bicentennial Theological Consultation,* ed. Theodore Runyon. Nashville: Kingswood Books: 65–75.
c "The Metaphysics of Faith and Justice." *PS,* 14: 87–101.
d "Rudolf Bultmann and the Future of Revisionary Christology." In *Bultmann, Retrospect and Prospect: The Centenary Symposium at Wellesley,* ed. Edward C. Hobbs. Philadelphia: Fortress Press, 37–58.
e "Response to Gishin Tokiwa." *BCS,* 5: 131–38.
f Edition and translation: Rudolf Bultmann, *New Testament and Mythology and Other Basic Writings.* London: SCM Press.

1986a *On Theology.* San Francisco: Harper & Row.
b "The Service of Theology to the Servant Task of Pastoral Ministry." In *The Pastor as Servant,* ed. Earl E. Shelp and Ronald H. Sunderland. New York: Pilgrim Press, 81–101, 130.
c "On Teaching Theology." *Criterion,* 25, 1: 12–14.
d "Theological Perspectives on Punishment." *PSTJ,* 39, 3:20–24.
e "The Metaphysics of Faith and Justice." In *Gottes Zukunft—Zukunft der Welt, Festschrift für Jürgen Moltmann zum 60. Geburtstag,* ed. Hermann Deuser, Gerhard Marcel Martin, Konrad Stock, and Michael Welker. Munich: Christian Kaiser Verlag, 511–19.
f "Antwort an Josef Blank." In *Das neue Paradigma von Theologie, Strukturen und Dimensionen,* ed. Hans Küng and David Tracy. Zurich: Benziger Verlag, 57–65.

1987a "Rudolf Bultmann." In *The Encyclopedia of Religion,* ed. Mircea Eliade. New York: Macmillan, 2: 565–66.
b "The Nature and State of Theological Scholarship and Research." *Theological Education,* 24, 1: 120–31.
c "Concerning Belief in God." In *Faith and Creativity: Essays in Honor of Eugene H. Peters,* ed. George Nordgulen and George W. Shields. St. Louis: CBP Press, 81–94.

d   " 'For Freedom Christ Has Set Us Free': The Christian
      Understanding of Ultimate Transformation." *BCS*, 7: 47–
      58.

1988a   "The Problem of Normative Witness: A Response." *PSTJ*,
         41, 3: 22–26.
    b   "Problems in the Case for a Pluralistic Theology of Reli-
         gions," *JR*, 68: 493–507.

Contributors

Hans Dieter Betz is Professor of New Testament, Department of New Testament and Early Christian Literature, The Divinity School, University of Chicago.

John B. Cobb, Jr., is Ingraham Professor of Theology at the School of Theology at Claremont and Avery Professor in the Claremont Graduate School.

Philip E. Devenish is Coordinator of Ministry Studies and Assistant Professor of Practical Theology at The Divinity School, University of Chicago.

Victor Paul Furnish is University Distinguished Professor of New Testament, Perkins School of Theology, Southern Methodist University.

Franklin I. Gamwell is Dean and Professor of Ethics and Society, The Divinity School, University of Chicago.

Brian A. Gerrish is John Nuveen Professor and Professor of Historical Theology, The Divinity School, University of Chicago.

George L. Goodwin is Dean of Faculty and Associate Professor, Department of Religious Studies, College of St. Scholastica.

Charles Hartshorne is Professor Emeritus, Department of Philosophy, University of Texas, Austin.

Van A. Harvey is George Edwin Burnell Professor of Religious Studies, Stanford University.

Willi Marxsen is Professor Emeritus, University of Münster.

David Tracy is Andrew Thomas Greeley and Grace McNichols Greeley Distinguished Service Professor, The Divinity School, University of Chicago.

Maurice Wiles is Regius Professor of Divinity in the University of Oxford.